Gender, Equity, and Schooling

MISSOURI SYMPOSIUM ON RESEARCH AND EDUCATIONAL POLICY
VOLUME 2
GARLAND REFERENCE LIBRARY OF SOCIAL SCIENCE
VOLUME 1143

MISSOURI SYMPOSIUM ON RESEARCH AND EDUCATIONAL POLICY

BARBARA J. BANK, BRUCE J. BIDDLE, HARRIS COOPER, AND PETER M. HALL, *SERIES EDITORS*

RACE, ETHNICITY, AND MULTICULTURALISM
Policy and Practice
edited by Peter M. Hall

GENDER, EQUITY, AND SCHOOLING
Policy and Practice
edited by Barbara J. Bank and Peter M. Hall

Gender, Equity, and Schooling
Policy and Practice

Edited by
Barbara J. Bank
Peter M. Hall

Garland Publishing, Inc.
New York and London
1997

Library of Congress Cataloging-in-Publication Data

Gender, equity, and schooling : policy and practice / edited by Barbara J. Bank
and Peter M. Hall.
      p.   cm. — (Missouri Symposium on Research and Educational
Policy ; v. 2) (Garland reference library of social science ; v. 1143)
    Includes bibliographical references and indexes.
    ISBN 0-8153-2534-7 (hc. : alk. paper). — ISBN 0-8153-2535-5
(pbk. : alk. paper)
    1. Educational equalization—United States—Congresses. 2. Wom-
en—Education—United States—Congresses.   3. Sex discrimination in
education— United States—Congresses.   4. Education and state—United
States—Congresses.   I. Bank, Barbara J. II. Hall, Peter M.   III. Series.
IV. Series: Missouri Symposium on Research and Educational Policy.
Missouri Symposium on Research and Educational Policy ; v. 2.
LC213.2.G45   1997
370.19'345—dc20   96–40988
                                           CIP

Cover photograph by Tony Donovan, The Ivoryton Studio.
Paperback cover design by Robert Vankeirsbilck.

Printed on acid-free, 250-year-life paper
Manufactured in the United States of America

SERIES PREFACE

One of the abiding mysteries of American education concerns the uneasy relation between research, policy, and practices in our schools. On the one hand, Americans honor research, spend a good deal on research in the physical and biological sciences, think that research evidence *should* be used in social planning, and strongly encourage research in our classrooms and schools. On the other, appallingly little is now spent on educational research, the vast bulk of policy planning for education proceeds without benefit of research, and the actual practices of our classrooms and schools are often unknown or are at odds with (or harmed by) educational "reforms" touted by ideologues and politicians.

But despite all aridity, some talented researchers *do* manage to cobble together resources needed for insightful studies of American education, and then a second problem arises. Reports of the knowledge evolved in those studies normally appear in sources designed for peers: papers delivered at professional meetings, journal articles, technical reports, and (occasionally) books designed to be read by others in the research community. Unfortunately, such reports are *not* designed for educators, citizens, or political leaders interested in education, and so far our country has *not* evolved effective, national means for disseminating knowledge from educational research to users such as these. In addition, our country is massive, it generates a truly staggering amount of information, and even accessible reports of research knowledge concerned with education tend to get lost amidst the huge oversupply of competing messages.

Responding to this need, several years ago we made a proposal to our campus, the University of Missouri-Columbia, to sponsor a series of regular symposia on research and educational policy. Each symposium was to be held on our campus, focus on a topic of vital interest to educators and policymakers, bring researchers and potential users of educational research knowledge together, feature original contributions by major scholars who had conducted significant studies of the topic chosen, and generate a major volume of original research papers. Having established support for this proposal from administrators at our campus, we then asked whether Garland Publishing would produce the volumes that were generated from these symposia and received a warm welcome from Senior Editor, Marie Ellen Larcada.

Through this series, then, we hope to expand the influence of the Missouri Symposia beyond our campus, not only to provide sources of useful knowledge for educators and others vitally involved with American education, but also to stimulate further research and potential leadership from the research community on crucial educational issues. As of this writing, two volumes representing Missouri Symposia have now been completed, the first concerned with *Race, Ethnicity, and Multiculturalism*, the second focused on *Gender, Equity, and Schooling*. Both, indeed, take on crucial topics in education, both publish original papers that represent extensions of contributions that were first presented here on the Missouri campus, and both provide access to original and highly significant research contributions.

We hope that these two initial volumes will stimulate broad interest and will help to begin bridging the gulf between researchers and the education community. They will shortly be followed by others.

Bruce J. Biddle
Barbara J. Bank
Harris Cooper
Peter M. Hall

Columbia, MO

Contents

Preface

On March 30-31, 1995, the Second Missouri Symposium on Research and Educational Policy was held in Columbia. Like the first symposium, the second was designed to provide multidisciplinary perspectives and knowledge about research, policy, and practice organized around a theme of interest and importance to educators, academics, students, policy makers, and the general public. Whereas the first symposium had focused on race, ethnicity, and multiculturalism, the second focused on gender, equity, and schooling. Papers relevant to this theme were presented by Catherine Marshall, Donna Eder, and Michele Foster on the first day of the Symposium and by Cynthia Hudley, Valerie Lee, Marilyn Tallerico, and Nelly Stromquist on the second day.

Chapters 2-8 in this volume are based on the presented papers, but the book is not designed to be a report of the symposium proceedings. Instead, its purpose is to provide readers with an understanding of the gendered nature of schooling and educational policy at multiple levels. These levels include international agencies, national and state or provincial governments, local school administrations, teachers, and student peer groups. At all of these levels, actions are taken (or not taken) that affect the extent to which educational opportunities, treatment, and outcome are equitable not only by gender but also by race and class. The authors explain the nature of these actions, their interrelationships, their consequences, and the reasons why they often have unintended effects. In addition, the book examines the relationships among gender equity, academic achievement, and educational reform.

We are pleased that such a distinguished group of scholars agreed to participate in both the symposium and this volume. They bring considerable expertise to the topics they address in their chapters. In addition, they have been a pleasure to work with, and we thank them for their help and cooperation. We also thank Kathy Craighead and Pat Shanks for their good help in preparing the manuscript, Phyllis Korper of Garland Publishing for her fine editorial work, and Marie Ellen Larcada of Garland Publishing for her support.

The symposium and this volume would not have been possible without the financial support provided by a number of units of the University of Missouri at Columbia including the MU Lectures Committee, the Departments of Psychology and Sociology, the Women Studies Program, Extension Teaching, the College of Education, the College of Arts and Science, the Office of Research, and the Center for Research in Social Behavior. The Center also provided the administrative and clerical support needed for the symposium, and we thank Billye Adams for her valuable work in organizing those efforts.

GENDER, EQUITY, AND SCHOOLING

CHAPTER 1

Introduction: Some Paradoxes of Gender Equity in Schooling

Barbara J. Bank

During the 1960s when second-wave feminism[1] was emerging in the United States, the goal of gender equity in schooling seemed to be an unambiguous undertaking. What was necessary, it was said, was to eliminate unequal treatment of boys and girls in school. Tracking by gender should be eliminated, and the entire curriculum should be equally available to both sexes. Curricular materials that ignored or denigrated women should be replaced with materials that were free of gender stereotypes. Teachers should be made aware of their different behaviors toward boys and girls and should be required to treat students in an equitable manner. Schools that put resources into extracurricular activities for boys, such as athletic teams, should put equivalent resources into extracurricular activities for girls. Teachers and school counselors should make certain that their advice to students about academic matters, personal life, educational plans, and occupational goals was completely free of traditional assumptions about what is appropriately masculine and feminine.

Not only was it assumed that gender equity in schooling would result from a straightforward, determined effort to equalize opportunities and treatment across the sexes, but it was also assumed that gender equity in schooling would manifest itself, more or less automatically, in equal outcomes across the sexes. The outcomes that were stressed were those traditionally associated with schooling such as scores on national tests, access to and performance in institutions of higher education, and occupational aspirations and achievements. Thirty years ago, most of these outcomes favored boys over girls. More equal outcomes, it was assumed, would be the inevitable result of policies and programs designed to give girls and boys equal educational opportunities and equal treatment in school.

For both reasons of fairness and to provide equivalent role models for boys and girls, second-wave feminists and their allies also sought gender parity among teachers and school officials. In particular, it was argued that more women should be recruited into school administration and into teaching subjects, such as science and mathematics, in which male teachers predominated. Similarly, more men should be recruited into positions held largely by women such as elementary school teaching, particularly in the early grades. Like teachers, school administrators should be made aware of their different behaviors toward males and females and should be required to treat teachers of both sexes in an equitable manner, free of stereotypic assumptions about gender differences.

Although the steps necessary to achieve gender equity in the schools seemed unambiguous, they were not assumed to be easy. Some of the difficulties of changing school policies and practices were recognized by second-wave feminists and their allies as were the difficulties of abolishing traditional gender stereotypes. Some resistance was expected, and the need to provide legal and administrative frameworks for gender equity in schools was recognized. Nevertheless, it was assumed that most educators either already favored gender equity or could be persuaded to do so. Once these educators were given appropriate guidelines, training, and curricular materials, most were expected to join the effort to eliminate gender biases from the schools.

Thirty years later, the initial assumptions of second–wave feminists about gender equity in schooling seem overly optimistic and naive. Far from being an unambiguous goal, gender equity in schooling is now seen as a complex task full of contradictions. Some of these contradictions take the form of paradoxes that are structurally embedded in schools and in societal contexts for schooling. Four such paradoxes are discussed in this chapter. They were selected for three reasons. First, they fit my dictionary's definition of a paradox as "a statement seemingly absurd or contradictory, yet in fact true." Second, they express some of the tensions and problems that are dealt with in more detail by the authors of Chapters 2 through 8 in this volume. Third, they help us to understand some of the ambiguities, difficulties, and complexities educators and feminists encounter when they try to achieve gender equity in schools.

THE POLICY PARADOX: THE MORE THINGS CHANGE, THE MORE THEY REMAIN THE SAME

No one can read the contemporary literature concerned with gender and schooling without encountering evidence for extensive legal changes in the status of women and the relationship between the sexes. In the United States, these changes have taken a variety of forms. The Supreme Court has re-interpreted the Constitution; presidents have issued executive orders; legislators at federal and state levels have passed statutes; government agencies have issued regulations; and courts have interpreted and defined all of these governmental actions. As the following chapter by Nelly Stromquist makes clear, legal changes in the status of women have also been enacted in many other countries and by international agencies. In this chapter, however, I will keep the focus primarily on the United States where legal concepts of protection for women and reciprocal rights between the sexes have given way to legal practices based on equal opportunity and equal rights.

Gender policies at the level of the schools have been directly affected by two kinds of legal changes, those that deal with gender equity across contexts and those concerned specifically with gender and schooling. Included in the first category are the 1963 Equal Pay Act and Title VII of the 1964 Civil Rights Act. As its name implies, the Equal Pay Act mandates equal pay for equal work and outlaws gender discrimination in salaries and wages. Over the years, court interpretations of the act have determined that the work of men and women does not have to be identical, but it does have to be "substantially equal." The definition of "substantially equal" is fairly narrow, however, and both the judicial and executive branches of the federal government have resisted attempts to expand the Equal Pay Act to "comparable worth" situations in which women are paid less for jobs that require the same qualifications, skill levels, effort, and responsibility as jobs for which men are paid more. In addition, the Equal Pay Act permits differences in pay that are based on merit, seniority, productivity, and market circumstances, criteria that are often interpreted in ways that favor men over women.

Title VII forbids discrimination in employment not only on the basis of gender but also on the basis of race, color, religion, and national origin. The Equal Employment Opportunity Commission (EEOC) was created to enforce this law. Initially, the EEOC tended either to ignore gender discrimination (in favor of fighting racial discrimination) or to support certain kinds of gender discrimination, such as labor laws that "protected" women but not men from certain working conditions and demands. Under pressure from working women and from feminist organizations, the EEOC has developed more egalitarian guidelines for assessing gender discrimination. Congress has also expanded the coverage of Title VII in various ways since its initial passage. The Pregnancy Disability Act of 1978, for example, explicitly requires that pregnant women be treated like other women. The Courts have used such Congressional mandates as bases for a transition from gender discrimination and protective legislation to more equal employment opportunities for women.

Legal changes concerned specifically with gender and schooling did not appear at the federal level until the 1970s. Broadest in their goals and coverage are Title IX of the Educational Amendments of 1972, which prohibits sex discrimination in all federally aided education programs, and the Women's Educational Equity Act (WEEA) of 1977, which provides grants to design, implement, and evaluate educational programs and activities that will eliminate gender stereotyping and achieve equity. Narrower in scope but perhaps more influential was the Vocational Education Act of 1976, which required and funded sex-equity specialists in every state and charged them with the task of reviewing vocational education programs for sex stereotypes and bias. In addition, many states passed their own laws forbidding gender discrimination in primary and secondary education, with some states extending this prohibition to higher education as well.

So sweeping were these and other legal changes of the period that some writers have proclaimed that "a revolution in public policy toward women happened in the 1960s and 1970s" (Freeman 1995:365). Other writers are less convinced that legal changes have produced changes, let alone a revolution, in the processes of education. Morgan (1996:113), for example, argues that equal opportunity is a myth that "camouflage(s) a state of educational inequity that perpetuates the gender axis as an axis of privilege and oppression." It is simply *not* true, writes Morgan (1996:117), that "girls and boys, women and men, now experience equal opportunity in terms of access, response, privileges, and rewards in public educational settings." A succinct echo of Morgan's argument is offered by McCormick (1994:27): "Sexism in schools is still alive and well." Research reports supporting these arguments have been produced by the American Association of University Women (*The AAUW Report* 1992), Bell and Chase (1993), and Sadker and Sadker (1994).

What accounts for this paradox of numerous legal changes that favor gender equality and the contradictory finding that American schools (like those in other countries) continue to be rife with gender inequities? Most of the possible answers to this question can be grouped into four categories. These categories consist of answers based on the immutable nature of women and men, on the complexity of policy implementation, on the nature and scope of gender-relevant policies, and on power and resistance. Answers in the first category are rooted in the assumption that women and men are fundamentally different, that they have different interests, abilities, and aspirations, and that many of the behaviors and achievements they exhibit in school reflect their fundamental differences. Those who adopt this position argue that laws will have only limited effects on gender inequalities; they cannot change the basic—and different—dispositions of women and men that produce most of these inequalities. Consistent with this argument are claims that males do better in mathematics because they have greater spatial ability and are naturally more interested in numerical reasoning than girls, that girls get better grades in school because they are naturally more docile and cooperative than boys, that high school students have a natural tendency to choose courses that are gender appropriate, and that women teachers are less likely to become school administrators because they are naturally less ambitious and more family oriented than men.

Such arguments about what is "natural" for males and females have been attacked on a number of grounds. First, these claims often ignore cross-cultural evidence. Bank, Biddle, and Good (1980) and Baker and Jones (1992) review studies showing that, for both reading and mathematical achievement, females have been found to outperform males in some countries; males have been found to outperform females in others, and males and females have been found to achieve at equivalent levels in still others. Second, even within countries, the "natural" differences between the sexes are based on relatively small differences in average performance. In all cases, the differences among males and among females are larger than the average differences between gender groups. Third, the notion of "natural" differences ignores differences across situations and historical periods, both of which have been shown to have major effects on the definitions of what is "natural" behavior for males and females. Indeed, one of the tendencies of the legal system has been to base laws, presidential orders, and judicial opinions on situationally embedded assumptions about what is "natural" for the genders in a given historical period. As indicated above, these assumptions can and do change over time. Fourth, many of the "natural" differences between boys and girls are based on either subjective opinions of teachers or on standardized tests. The biases of the former are obvious and have been documented by many studies (reviewed in Bank et al. 1980), and the standardized tests are based on questionable and arbitrary suppositions (Gould 1981; Fischer et al. 1996). Finally, the assumption of "natural" gender differences is considered by many to be a sexist argument designed to resist change, justify the oppression of women, and preserve male power and privilege. As such, the assumption is more of a justification for gender inequality than it is an explanation of why inequality continues to exist in American schools. Given these compelling arguments against the notion of immutable differences between the genders, it is not surprising that none of the authors in this volume advocates this answer to the question of why legal changes have not done more to change educational practices.

More plausible answers that are mentioned by several authors are those centered on the complexity of policy implementation. A law, executive order, or court decision is *not* an unambiguous rule that everyone understands in the same way, that can, must, and will be supported and followed by everyone, and that has clear and anticipated consequences. The ambiguity of laws is nicely illustrated by the fact that Title IX, described above, was enacted into law in 1972, but it was not until 1976 that the Department of Health, Education, and Welfare (DHEW) disseminated the guidelines and regulations for implementing the law. Nor did these guidelines clarify Title IX for all times and all people. Court challenges (reviewed in Williams 1980) were subsequently raised to determine if the DHEW had correctly interpreted the law, if all programs in an educational institution were covered by the law or only those that received federal funds, if athletic programs for men and women could be "separate but equal," etc. Even if the judicial opinions that resulted from these challenges were totally unambiguous, which they weren't, there would still be problems with this method of defining laws. As Williams (1980:147) points out, decisions by most federal courts are limited to the jurisdiction of that court, and even Supreme Court decisions which affect the whole country are limited to situations that are similar to the one on which the Court based its judgement. The famous *Brown v. Board of Education of Topeka, Kansas* decision in 1954, for example, outlawed educational segregation by race but not by gender.

The policy process does not embrace only those in government whose job it is to enact, interpret, and enforce gender-equity laws for schooling. The process also involves school administrators, teachers, parents, and pupils, all of whom have their own interpretations of what gender is or should be, what gender equity means, what the intention of the law "really" is, how seriously they must take it, what effects it will or should have on school programs and practices. As Nelly Stromquist notes in Chapter 2, dissensus about these issues among the many actors involved is particularly likely to be high when the policy in question is controversial, as gender policies inevitably are.

While recognizing the ambiguities and complexities of the process of policy-making and implementation, Stromquist also notes that gender-relevant policies vary in their scope. By scope, she means the amount of social transformation the policy is intended to produce. To help us think about this variation and its implications, she presents a typology that divides gender-sensitive policies into three categories: coercive, supportive, and constructive. Her typology not only helps readers to think more clearly about gender policies at international and national levels but also calls our attention to the ways in which the narrow scope of a (coercive) policy, such as Title VII or Title IX, can contribute to the paradox in which laws to abolish gender inequities are enacted that fail to produce gender equity in the schools.

At the conclusion of her chapter, Stromquist discusses possible reasons why so many laws are too narrow in scope to produce the major social transformation that would be required to achieve gender equity not only in the United States but throughout the world. One of these reasons—favored by Stromquist—stresses the patriarchal, or male-dominated, nature of the state. Broad, constructive policies that would bring about gender equity in schools would also reduce male power, change basic social structures, eliminate the status quo, and produce equitable gender arrangements totally at odds with those that currently exist. In contrast, narrow, coercive policies give the impression of concern about women and gender equity without really changing existing power arrangements. Indeed, some of these policies, such as the Equal Pay Act, put the burden on women to show that they have been treated in an inequitable, discriminatory manner. Policies that call for governmental initiatives, such as Title VII, Title IX, and WEEA have either had their funding cut or have never been funded at the levels mandated in law. Symbolic action, Stromquist tells us, often substitutes for broad social change.

So impatient is Catherine Marshall with this protracted history of symbolic action—and with continuing inequities and sexism at all levels of schooling—that she devotes Chapter 3 to arguments in favor of "undomesticated" gender policy. Her wonderful title reminds us that the traditional roles of women have been both domestic and domesticated. Domestic refers to the emphasis women are expected to place upon home and family. Not only are they expected to put their own home and family ahead of employment and other public roles, but they are also expected to adopt domestic identities with regard to other groups and organizations of which they are a part (Weinbaum 1983). Attractive wife, dutiful daughter, supportive admirer, comforting mother, tidy housekeeper are only a few of the many domestic roles which girls and women have been expected to enact in school settings. It's not enough to play domestic roles, however, one must also perform them in a domesticated manner. Being the domineering wife or powerful mother is not acceptable. Instead, women should know their "place" in the power hierarchy and act accordingly. They should be tame, non-threatening, polite, and submissive.

Marshall rejects these prescriptions. Her call for undomesticated gender policy is not only a call for gender-equity policies that are broad in scope and content but also a call for "more revolutionary thinking and acting." She offers readers many suggestions about ways to challenge existing power arrangements and to shatter the policy paradox by preventing things from remaining the same.

THE ACHIEVEMENT PARADOX: GOOD GRADES DON'T MEAN YOU WIN

Although it is true that today's girls are still expected to be oriented toward marriage and mothering, it is also true that they are the targets of many of the same expectations that are directed at boys. Despite the gender differences that persist in education, "today girls, like boys, are educated to compete to get ahead, to believe in and strive for individual success—first in school and then in a competitive labor market—and to value persistent independence" (Hoffnung 1995:164). As far as schooling is concerned, there is considerable evidence to support the conclusion that girls not only have absorbed the message that they should achieve but also have been successful in doing so. In the United States, it has been true for many years that girls receive higher grades in elementary and secondary school and are more likely to graduate from high school than boys. More recently, it has also been true that women earn more than half of all the baccalaureate and master's degrees awarded annually in the United States (U.S. Department of Education 1993).

Despite their good grades and other educational achievements, girls and women have not been able to win the status and other rewards that are consistent with their educational credentials. In the work world, for example, women do not gain the same returns (salary, occupational prestige, promotions) on their education as men do (U.S. Department of Education 1993). Even in the schools, the emphasis may often be less on grades and academic achievement than on other standards of success. Certainly, one of the more common findings in studies of schools, especially junior and senior high schools, is the lack of attention that student peer groups give to anything associated with the academic life of the school. Everhart (1983:232), for example, concludes his study of peer cultures at a junior high school by noting that he rarely heard students discussing grades, assignments, or the subject matter that had been covered in class. Instead, students spent most of their time discussing after-school activities or the activities of their friends both in and out of school. Similar findings are reported by Cusick on the basis of his observations at a high school. After discussing the fact that a group of student athletes spent so little time discussing their teachers, Cusick (1973:97) observes:

> In the beginning of my study I thought that perhaps my presence was keeping the boys from revealing their true feelings about the teachers, but their behavior was consistent over the entire semester. While occasionally a teacher would be mentioned by one member, the topic never became general. Nor were related topics of marks, grades, academic work, or assignments ever made topics of general conversation.

Sometimes even high-achieving peer cultures ignore academic matters. Eder, Evans, and Parker (1995) note, with surprise, that a peer group at Woodview Middle School which included four boys who were in advance-track classes never discussed academic achievements or interests during lunch.

Although the occasional group of high school students has been found that values intellectual accomplishments and is accorded elite status in their school (Larkin 1979), the more common finding of a non-academic orientation within the student culture has led to an image of American schools as venues in which efforts by teachers and school administrators to create a climate of support and prestige for academic strivings are thwarted by peer pressures and the status systems students construct for themselves. Although this image may be an accurate portrait of some schools, it ignores research findings that question the extent to which some official school cultures actually do prize high academic standards and attainments. Cusick (1973:97) describes one of the teachers at Horatio Gates High School as someone who did little or no instructing. "He would begin (class) with some topic and almost immediately relate it to his war experiences, his home town, his school days, or his brother-in-law and would just ramble on meaninglessly all period." Although this teacher seems to be the worst of those whom Cusick observed, none of the others exhibited very high academic standards:

> It should be admitted that the school, on the whole, seemed to be very undemanding of students. One could easily see that those who were giving only bare compliance to the academic demands were not failing, nor were they being chastised by the teachers for non-achievement. They simply were not expected to do very much and just about anyone who gave at least a little effort could and did succeed (Cusick 1973:60-61).

Ten years later, Everhart (1983:84) made similar remarks about the low level of academic standards in the official school culture he observed:

> . . .the modal form of instruction at Harold Spencer (Junior High School) does not demand much of the student's time in school. Over all, only slightly more than half of the time a student spends in school is occupied by instructional activities. . . . Nor did instructional tasks, on the average, seem to demand much in the way of intellectual effort from students. It was relatively easy, for example, for John and Steve to discuss intramural football games while, almost subconsciously, working on a social studies assignment, a

practice indicative of the (low) intensity of intellectual work demanded of the students in the school.

Nor do low standards seem to have disappeared in the present decade. Like the students, the "(t)eachers (at Freeway High School) tend to adhere to the form rather than the substance of education," writes Weis (1990:81), with the result that "knowledge distributed through the classes has nothing to do with either thinking or challenging."

More research is needed to clarify the relationships between the academic values (or lack thereof) of an official school culture and the values and behaviors of the student peer cultures in that school. What is already clear from existing research is that many schools violate the popular image that they are places where an official culture that is focused on academic matters and is characterized by high achievement standards clashes with student peer cultures that have failed to accept the academic values of their schools. Instead, official school cultures often fail to develop themselves as contexts in which academic striving is expected, commonplace, and prized. Undoubtedly, there are many reasons for such failures (see, e.g., Powell, Farrar, and Cohen 1985), but their likelihood is probably increased by the heavy emphasis in the official cultures of many schools, especially in the United States, on extracurricular activities that contribute little to the academic mission of the school, and may even undermine it.

Among extracurricular organizations, particular emphasis tends to be given in most schools to boys' athletic teams particularly those, like football and basketball teams, that are highly visible to the student body (Eder, Evans, and Parker 1995). Coleman (1961) found that athletic success was the major source of prestige for young men in all ten of the high schools he studied, and similar findings have been reported for other high schools by Connell and his colleagues (1982; Kessler et al. 1985), Cusick (1973), Eckert (1989), and Wooden (1995).

Coleman (1961:172) explained the high prestige assigned to athletic success on the grounds that extracurricular activities, such as athletics, are seen by adolescents to be "activities of their 'own,' activities in which they can carry out positive actions on their own, in contrast to schoolwork, where they carry out 'assignments' from teachers." Coleman's explanation masks the extent to which extracurricular activities are part of the official school culture and the extent to which they can undermine the academic goals of the school. This latter problem is implicit in the comments of a high school teacher, interviewed by Cusick (1973:30),

who recalled with disgust the football rally at which, "The whole student body stood up and cheered the captain of the football team for *five minutes*! And I know that Kid! He can't Read! But that's the way this place is."

Although Cusick presents these comments to show the low regard in which students were held by teachers, the comments also reveal that the football rally was an official school function attended by everyone in the school.

At least in the United States, such rallies are commonplace. Schools that have only one convocation per year to present awards for academic excellence, artistic talent, and student leadership may have a football rally before every varsity game plus additional sports rallies during basketball and baseball seasons. Not only is school time devoted to sports rallies but considerable space in the school paper and yearbook is devoted to athletic contests. Rare is the American high school, or junior high school, that does not have a glass-fronted cabinet in the hallway displaying athletic trophies. Also common are banners, posters, and other forms of decoration that publicize forthcoming games and announce support for the school team. Unfortunately, as Donna Eder tells us in Chapter 4, the emphasis on athletic contests produces an emphasis on a tough, aggressive, competitive form of masculinity that characterizes not only sporting events but also the entire school culture.

What about females? Despite legislation in many countries, such as Title IX in the U.S., that prohibits gender discrimination in school programs, athletic programs for girls and women continue to lag behind those for boys and men. Even where inter-school competitions among girls' teams have been organized, they tend to attract less attention from students, school staff, and community members than boys' athletics. Nor are girls' athletics elaborated in the official school culture, but this may be changing, and there have traditionally been some exceptions. In rural and small town high schools in Iowa, girls' athletics have been an important, valued, and integral part of the extracurriculum. Perhaps this explains why Buhrmann and Jarvis (1971) found that girl athletes in Iowa received consistently higher status ratings from their male and female peers and teachers than non-athletes. Similarly, Buhrmann and Bratton (1977) report that girls who participated in interscholastic athletics in six rural and small town high schools in Alberta (Canada) were more popular with (i.e., better liked by) female and male peers than girls who are not athletes. The Canadian female athletes were also more likely than non-athletes to be nominated as members of the leading crowd in their school by both peers and teachers.

Despite such findings, girls are still more likely to gain popularity in a U.S. school by attaching themselves to male athletes than by playing on a girls' team (Eder and Kinney 1995). The most visible of these attachments is cheerleading, and many studies find a high-status student peer culture consisting of cheerleaders or of cheerleaders and some male athletes (Eder, Evans, and Parker 1995; Gordon 1957; Larkin 1979; Wooden 1995). Like athletes, cheerleaders compete for their positions, but the competition tends to be based not only on athletic skills but also on attractiveness and enthusiasm. Concerns about attractiveness are not unique to cheerleaders, but the existence of a cheerleading squad chosen for its physical appearance and energetic support of male athletes gives official school legitimation to a traditional form of femininity that has little, if anything, to do with academic and occupational achievements.

The emphasis on this traditional form of femininity also lends support to very traditional forms of male-female relations in which males are prized for their competitive superiority and women are prized for their looks and sexual appeal. Within this traditional context, it matters little if girls get good grades or complete more years of education than boys. These are not the criteria on which girls are likely to be judged by their peers or even by adults. Being pretty and popular and sexy—but not too sexy—makes a girl a winner; being a scholar does not. Unfortunately, as Eder shows us in Chapter 4, these traditional notions of femininity and of gender relations can become both ugly and dangerous.

THE STRUCTURAL PARADOX: SEPARATION MAY PRODUCE EQUALITY

Most Americans know that the 1954 decision of the Supreme Court in the case of *Brown v. Board of Education* outlawed educational segregation by race in the United States. In its written decision, the Court declared that separation of the races was inherently unequal. In doing so, the Court reversed the decision made in the *Plessy v. Ferguson* case of 1896. In that earlier case, the Supreme Court had ruled that separate facilities by race could be equal, a decision that legalized racial segregation in American public schools for over half a century. Both before and after the *Brown v. Board of Education* decision, the civil rights movement sought to eliminate racial segregation not only in schools but also in public facilities, in workplaces, and in all the other organizations and institutions of American society. To these ends, the decision that "separate is not equal" became a useful and popular slogan.

Among the groups who adopted this civil rights slogan were those that constituted the second wave of feminism or the women's liberation movement, as feminism was called in the 1960s. In their efforts to eliminate gender discrimination and to increase opportunities for women, second-wave feminists borrowed many ideas and tactics from the civil rights movement for racial equality, a movement in which many feminists had participated and had received their political educations. Thus, it was not surprising that feminists used the slogan "separate is not equal" to challenge the ideology of "separate spheres" which asserted men's legitimate control of the public arenas of economics, work, and politics, while assigning women to their place in the home. By using the "separate is not equal" slogan, feminists sought to make all women and men aware of the parallels between gender relations and race relations in America and to undermine romantic notions of the mother and homemaker on her pedestal protected from the rigors of public life.

Despite the similarities feminists saw between race relations and gender relations, the Supreme Court saw things differently. According to Freeman (1995:378), "(N)either the Court nor Congress has decided that schools segregated by sex hold quite the stigma as those segregated by race." As a result, Title IX does not prohibit single-sex schools at the elementary or secondary levels, except for vocational schools, but it does prohibit separate classrooms for different sexes, with only limited exceptions. Similar ambivalence characterizes court actions with regard to gender and schooling. Even though the Supreme Court has heard cases concerned with the constitutionality of single-sex public schools, it has either rendered no opinion (thereby affirming lower court decisions) or has made narrow decisions about these cases. To date, no sweeping decision about gender-segregated education in public schools comparable to *Brown v. Board of Education* has been rendered. Freeman (1995:378) suggests three reasons for these facts. First, "sex-segregated schools have never been part of a state policy to denigrate a particular group in the way that racial segregation was." Second, even when single sex schools were more common in the U.S. than they are today, there were still many coeducational schools available. Third, "(t)here is ambivalence also because of evidence that going to single-sex schools benefits at least some women."

Some males may also benefit, argue many advocates of single-sex schooling, and they suggest that the primary beneficiaries in the U.S. context may be African American male students. Such students are seen to be at great risk. Proportionately, they are more likely to be poor than their white male counterparts, and they are more likely to fail at school, to become involved in street gangs, to be arrested, and to be murdered than either their white male peers or African American females. A concern for their present and future welfare has prompted African American educators and parents to propose special educational environments for black males in the public schools. Although these environments are often called single-sex schools or classrooms, they usually are both single-sex (male) and single-race (African American).

The arguments favoring such environments (reviewed in Riordan 1994) vary across advocates, but four themes seem to emerge from the scholarly and journalistic writings that have focused on this subject. The first of these questions the benefits of racial desegregation. Forty years after *Brown v. Board of Education*, African American students in desegregated public schools continue to have lower grades and test scores and higher suspension and dropout rates than their white counterparts. Nor can these outcomes be attributed to innate shortcomings in the abilities or motivation of African Americans. Instead, a large literature (reviewed in Carter and Goodwin 1994) documents the facts that American teachers have lower expectations for African American than for white students, that they treat African American students, particularly males, in more negative ways than white students, and that they are more likely to punish African American students for the same offenses that white students can commit with few, if any, negative consequences. Clearly, mixed-race education does not mean equal education.

The second theme stressed by those who advocate single-sex education for African American males is the need these students are assumed to have for good role models of their same race and gender. This assumption is based on the belief that young black males often come from homes and neighborhoods in which there are either no adult males or adult males who are negative role models because they are unemployed, uneducated, or criminals. To counter these conditions, it is argued, young black males should be placed in classrooms taught by black male teachers with whom they can identify and who can understand and empathize with their experiences. Closely tied to this theme is a third, more pejorative argument that single-sex schools for young black males "will provide needed discipline" (Riordan 1994:179). Those who make this argument assume that discipline is not currently being imposed on young black males at home, in coeducational or integrated schools, or in the community. Further, it is assumed that discipline will keep young black males out of trouble, will keep them attending school, and will foster their educational achievement. Such assumptions are questionable and are considered by some to be racist. A less pejorative version of this discipline theme is suggested by Cynthia Hudley in Chapter 5 when she talks about the benefits for African American male students of a safe, orderly school environment.

The fourth argument that is frequently made by those who want single-race education for African Americans, both in single-sex and coeducational programs, stresses a culture-based education model. According to Leake and Faltz (1993:382), this model "encompass(es) concepts, content, themes, perspectives, and pedagogy reflective of African/American ontology." Classes based on this model attempt to overcome the Eurocentric biases of traditional American education and to develop curricula that are multicultural with particular emphasis on the heritage of Africans and African Americans. The goals of such educational programs, write Leake and Faltz (1993:383), are "to infuse the curriculum with specific content about Black people" and to develop and implement "instructional strategies that complement the culture and learning styles of Black children."

These arguments have had two opposing effects. On the one hand, they have aroused strong opposition from individuals and organizations. While not necessarily denying that single-sex, single-race education might benefit some African American male students, these opponents have argued that these programs violate the "separate is inherently unequal" doctrine that has been the law of the land since the *Brown v. Board of Education* decision was rendered in 1954. If such educational programs were to be widely established and condoned by the courts, they could be the harbingers of a new era of school segregation. Many of the organizations that espouse this position are recognized leaders in the fight for racial and gender equity in American society, such as the American Civil Liberties Union, the National Association for the Advancement of Colored People, and the National Organization for Women. Individuals who have led the fights for school integration, such as Kenneth Clark, whose research into the negative effects of segregation on black children helped justify the *Brown v. Board of Education* decision, have also opposed recent attempts at separate schooling. In an interview in *Ebony* magazine in 1991 (quoted in Riordan 1994:179), Clark opined that single-sex schools for African Americans would reassert the *Plessy v. Ferguson* doctrine that separate can be equal:

This is contrary to everything that we were fighting (for) and everything that research says about the benefits of learning (Black and White, male and female) together. Even military schools today are coeducational. So why are we talking about segregating and stigmatizing black males?

It is not single-sex classrooms that stigmatize black males, argue the proponents of these programs but rather the forces at work in the political economy of American society that have been described by Wilson (1987) and other analysts of poverty and disadvantage in the black community. If schools are going to help alleviate these problems, rather than adding to them, they must have the freedom to establish innovative programs including single-sex, single-race classrooms and schools for African American students. Leake and Faltz (1993:385) state the position forcefully:

Milwaukee has been criticized by education's bastions of integration for approving plans to develop two African-American Immersion Schools . . . . When critics warn that African-American students in general, Black males in particular, could be stigmatized by the separation of the Immersion School setting, we are compelled to challenge the notion that they are not already being stigmatized by the disproportionate share of the burden for busing that they bear. This pattern could very well send the message to the African-American child that if I don't sit next to a White person, I can't learn. There are also other factors that could have stigmatizing effects on African-American students such as their dismal academic achievement, suspension or expulsion records, or the nightly news that is a constant reminder that there are more Black males in prison in this country than in college.

But, do such schools and classrooms really have positive effects on students? Few systematic studies to answer this question exist. One exception is Riordan's (1990, 1994) analysis of data from a national study of Catholic school students. For the minority students enrolled in Catholic schools, Riordan (1994) provides evidence for the positive effects of single-sex schools in contrast to coeducational schools. These findings may not generalize to public school settings, however, where many attempts to establish single-race and single-sex programs have been the targets of political controversy and legal action. Also, as Valerie Lee tells us in Chapter 6, Catholic schools are substantially different educational environments, on average, than independent or public schools. Research into the effects of single-sex, single-race educational programs in the public schools is desperately needed. Fortunately, Cynthia Hudley (1995) has begun to examine the short-term outcomes of such educational programs. In Chapter 5, she describes her recent study of a segregated educational program for African American male students in a California middle school, and she discusses some of the research and policy questions about such programs that still need to be answered.

One of these questions concerns the kinds of programs that might best meet the educational needs of African American females. Although much has been written about single-sex schooling for girls and women, little attention has been given to racial and class differences among these students. Yet it seems likely that differences in their social backgrounds might produce differences in the reasons why students and parents might advocate single-sex schooling for girls. These reasons include the same four that have been given by advocates of single-sex, single-race schooling for African Americans. When applied to girls, however, two of these reasons have appeared in a traditional, conservative version that may do more to preserve the status quo of gender relations than to promote gender equity.

One of these two is a set of traditional arguments that stresses the essential differences between males and females and the different roles they are expected to play in life. Rooted in the nineteenth-century notion of "separate spheres," arguments favoring different roles are less popular today than they were when women were legally excluded from most of the occupations and professions available to men. In contrast, claims about essential differences between the sexes have reasserted themselves in the contemporary period, often in a feminist, non-traditional guise. Whereas older, conservative notions of essential differences tended to stress the limited energies and capacities of girls and women as reasons why they should not be exposed to the same rigorous educational experiences as males, contemporary versions of essentialism stress fundamental differences between the sexes that are not meant to derogate women. Instead, it is argued that girls and women are an oppressed group with many strengths. The proper education for them is one that builds upon their strengths, recognizes their "different voice" (Gilligan 1982), and incorporates "women's ways of knowing" (Belenky, Clinchy, Goldberger, and Tarule 1986) into teaching strategies and curricular materials. This proposal has obvious parallels to the culture-based education model that has been advocated for African American students. Unfortunately, as Valerie Lee points out in Chapter 6, this proposal can also become an excuse for giving girls a more nurturant, but less rigorous, education than their male counterparts.

A second traditional argument favoring single-sex schooling is one that stresses protection for girls and women. Tyack and Hansot (1990:90) cite an interesting example in their description of the reasons given by parents who opposed co-education in the public schools of Charlestown, Massachusetts, during the mid-nineteenth century:

> Above all, (the parents) feared what might happen if their daughters associated with low-life boys. Girls from eight to fourteen were at a "dangerous" time of life, during which they required "that watchful care, that attention to sexual differences, that jealous guarding of mental and physical purity, which, it is believed, cannot be had in a Mixed School." . . . by being exposed to a miscellaneous collection of the opposite sex during "a period when the mind receives its deepest impressions" and sexual impulses begin, youth might make the wrong choice of "worthy and suitable companions." The parents warned that "a mistake at this period, which care and prudence may prevent, often becomes a source of lasting misery."

The class-based opposition of the parents to co-educational schooling is obvious, as is their desire to "discipline" their daughters' sexuality and romantic impulses. Interestingly, these traditional concerns are echoed by the contemporary concerns about providing African American male students with discipline and protection.

Nor have such traditional reasons for choosing all-female schools disappeared in the contemporary period. In my current study of undergraduates at a non-elite women's college, I asked students why they chose this particular college. Several women told me that their parents chose the college (or supported their daughter's choice) because they thought it would provide a safe environment, and others commented on the social links between the sororities at their college and the fraternities at the nearby, more elite coeducational (formerly an all-men's) college. Similarly, Valerie Lee suggests in Chapter 6 that parents who send their daughters to elite all-girl secondary schools may do so for reasons of tradition and status preservation.

In contrast to these traditional reasons for choosing all-female schools are feminist and emancipatory arguments suggesting that single-sex schools provide females with educational equity in ways that coeducational schools do not and can not. Those who make such arguments usually begin with a review of the extensive research literature (e.g., The AAUW Report 1992; Sadker and Sadker 1994; Sandler 1987) that has documented the many ways in which girls and young women are disadvantaged in coeducational classrooms and schools. They get fewer opportunities than males to speak out in class, to develop leadership skills, to solve problems for themselves, to pursue courses regarded as "masculine," and to be exposed to female role models in prestigious, male-dominated fields such as educational administration or science. As a result of these limitations, it is said, women tend to lower their educational attainments and achievements. The solution to these problems—and the way to give women a more equitable education—is through single-sex classrooms and schools. Will this work? Yes, say those who have done research comparing state-funded single-sex and coeducational schools outside of the United States. According to Riordan's (1994) review of this research, most studies done in both developed and developing countries find that girls do better academically in the single-sex than in the coeducational schools. Even in the United States, where single-sex public schools are rare, studies of Catholic schools (Riordan 1990; Bryk, Lee, and Holland 1993) have produced the same finding.

Should all of us who believe in gender equity accept these feminist and emancipatory arguments for single-sex schooling? Should we all become advocates for single-sex schooling for girls and women? In Chapter 6, Valerie Lee presents a compelling case for a negative answer to this question. Single-sex schooling may solve some gender problems for female students, says Lee, but it may create others. Lee helps us deal with the structural paradox of separation and equality by presenting us with a theory of school organizational characteristics that enables us to predict when single-sex schooling will benefit students and when it won't.

THE POWER PARADOX: BEING A NUMERICAL MAJORITY DOESN'T MEAN YOU HAVE CONTROL

In her chapter concerned with professional women in the U.S., Kaufman (1995) refers to teaching as a "female-dominated profession." What she and others mean when they use this phrase is that the overwhelming majority of American teachers are women. What some writers also imply with this phrase is that the cultural images of teachers, particularly elementary-school teachers, are dominated by traditional, idealized assumptions about the nature of women and, especially, of mothers. Included among these assumptions are notions that women have maternal tendencies that attract them to infants and young children, that women are naturally more nuturant and caring than men, that women are more interested than men in building relationships with children, that women find mothering to be their primary source of self-fulfillment, and that mothers are willing to sacrifice for their children.

The notion that it is a natural, easy task for teachers to bring these womanly, motherly characteristics into the classroom probably accounts for the fact that teachers often feel that they are misunder-stood and unfairly criticized. Two such teachers are quoted by Biklen (1995:28). The first is a kindergarten teacher who says:

> How difficult it is to be a teacher. Teachers are underpaid and undervalued. How many people end the day after working nine to five at some corporation and go home and just sob because their work was so hard? Nobody understands what it's like to work around children all day—how hard it is and what it does to you.

The second, a first-grade teacher, also rejects the notion that working with children is natural and, therefore, easy for women:

> Teaching looks easy from the outside. I went into the bank the other day at a little after two (o'clock) and the teller said to me, "Ha, how do you like that—two o'clock and here you are out and my wife has to stay downtown and work until

five." I said, "Yeah, but you don't know what I do all day." That's what it looks like from the outside: the hours, the summer vacation—and people don't know what it's like to be responsible for thirty kids for six hours every day. It's very, very difficult.

Not only do "female-dominated" assumptions about what is natural and easy for women hide the hard and stressful work done by women teachers, but these assumptions also seem likely to affect the ways in which men teachers at the elementary level are perceived. One likely perception is that men who choose such jobs are making an unnatural, unmanly choice—unless, of course, they are using it as a stepping stone into educational administration. Another likely perception is that, because nurturing of young children is less natural for men than for women, men who teach in the primary grades must work harder to be as successful as their female counterparts. Unfortunately, research does not exist to tell us how common these perceptions are or what implications they have. Probably, one consequence is the well-documented shortage of male teachers at the primary levels. Another possibility is that male teachers get more credit for being nurturant, caring, and dedicated to their students than do their female colleagues whose equivalent behaviors are considered more natural and, therefore, less praiseworthy. It would be ironic to discover that the female imagery that dominates public perceptions of American teachers actually benefits men.

Despite their large numerical majority, women teachers in the United States have not been able to control either the images people have of their work or the conditions of the work itself. This is not to suggest that women teachers are simply passive victims of the circumstances in which they find themselves. Acker's (1995) review of the growing feminist literature concerned with teachers and teaching shows that by taking women's standpoints seriously, this literature has "invest(ed) women with the capacity to be creative social actors devising strategies within the constraints of their situations" (Acker 1995:142). Acker also warns us that "(t)heories that rest on observations about the extent to which teachers lack status, possess autonomy, or experience control also need to be more sensitive to national contexts" (Acker 1995:141). With these caveats in mind, it can be noted that recent analyses of American education (e.g., Berliner and Biddle 1995) have reported that (women) teachers are currently the targets of a virulent attack blaming them for many of the ills of American society and that this attack is probably energized by a substantial amount of misogyny.

As Michele Foster suggests in Chapter 7, it may also be energized by a considerable amount of racism. Many policies designed to reform American education have been aimed at the teaching profession, and some seem to be aimed against minority teachers. Foster describes these policies, their impact on recruitment and retention of minority teachers, and teachers' reactions to them. She ends her chapter with a call for educational policies and practices that take more account of teachers' opinions and experiences, especially those of women teachers of color who are so often silenced and ignored.

One reason why American women and minorities have had less to say about educational policies than their white male counterparts is that they are underrepresented in positions of authority in national, state, and local governments. Even within schools, for reasons Marilyn Tallerico discusses in Chapter 8, inequities in leadership positions persist, and women continue to be underrepresented among school administrators. Although it is true that teachers have some individual control over their classrooms and their pupils and that they have sometimes engaged in collective action to improve their working conditions (see Apple 1988), it is also true that their behaviors and outlook are crucially affected by the actions of administrators. Given current efforts on the part of many (male) school administrators to implement efforts by state agencies to control the day-to-day work of (women) teachers and to hold them "accountable" for student outcomes, it does not seem too farfetched to suggest that many schools are becoming battlegrounds for a war between the sexes.

Administrators can affect teachers' feelings and behaviors not only by efforts to control teachers but also by positive actions. In his research on teacher burnout, for example,

> Dworkin reported that the level of burnout and, in turn, the desire to quit teaching could be significantly reduced by the actions of the campus principal. Supportive principals—those who involve their teachers in campus decision making, seek their teachers' advice in curricular matters, and praise their teachers for work well done—are associated with significantly lower levels of teacher burnout than are unsupportive principals (LeCompte and Dworkin 1991:110).

Interestingly, sympathy and support from other teachers has not been found to be as effective as support from principals. "(T)he principal's behavior is paramount. Supportive coworkers, in the absence of a supportive principal, have no effect in lowering teacher burnout" (LeCompte and Dworkin 1991:111).

It is noteworthy in the present context that Dworkin defined supportive principals as those who had a collaborative style of leadership. In Chapter 8, Marilyn Tallerico cites research evidence showing that this style tends to be more common among female than male school administrators. This gender difference may be important not only because a supportive, collaborative style makes teachers feel better about themselves and their work, but also, as Valerie Lee suggests in Chapter 6, because this administrative style may actually increase the educational effectiveness of schools. Thus, it may matter less whether women teachers begin to use their large numbers to gain administrative control of schools than whether they (and male administrators) exercise this control in a manner that converts not only principal-teacher relationships but all relationships among school personnel and students into those that are more democratic and equitable.

Changes in administrators' gender, administrative style, and relationships among and between administrators, teachers, and students will not, by themselves, guarantee gender equity in American schools. But, perhaps efforts to achieve equity that are organized at the school level, such as the gender-responsible actions Marilyn Tallerico describes in Chapter 8, will have more success than top-down, often symbolic, efforts based on statutes, government regulations, and court orders. To say this is neither to say that top-down efforts should cease nor to encourage a return to the naive optimism with which many second-wave feminists approached the "unambiguous" goal of gender equity in schooling thirty years ago. As the chapters in this book make clear, we are still a long way from that goal, and the process of working for it is full of contradictions and conflicts.

NOTES
1.   In this chapter, I use the term second-wave feminism to refer to the women's liberation movement that emerged in the 1960s to challenge traditional sex roles and gender inequities. Although the challenge continues to the present, the term women's liberation movement is no longer popular. Instead, it is common to use the term feminism to refer to advocacy for women. Collective advocacy of this sort in the nineteenth and early twentieth centuries is now referred to as first-wave feminism. In the United States, this wave is said to have crested in 1920 when passage of the Nineteenth Amendment to the Constitution gave women the right to vote.

REFERENCES

The AAUW Report: How Schools Shortchange Girls. 1992. Washington, DC: The American Association of University Women Educational Foundation.

Acker, Sandra. 1995. "Gender and Teachers' Work." *Review of Research in Education* 21:99-162.

Apple, Michael. 1988. *Teachers and Texts*. New York: Routledge.

Baker, David P., and Deborah Perkins Jones. 1992. "Opportunity and Performance: A Sociological Explanation for Gender Differences in Academic Mathematics." Pp. 193-203 in *Education and Gender Equality*, edited by J. Wrigley. London: The Falmer Press.

Bank, Barbara J., Bruce J. Biddle, and Thomas L. Good. 1980. "Sex Roles, Classroom Instruction, and Reading Achievement." *Journal of Educational Psychology*, 72:119-132.

Belenky, Mary Field, Blythe McVicker Clinchy, Nancy Rule Goldberger, and Jill Mattuck Tarule. 1986. *Women's Ways of Knowing: The Development of Self, Voice, and Mind*. New York: Basic Books.

Bell, Colleen, and Susan Chase. 1993. "The Underrepresentation of Women in School Leadership." Pp. 141-154 in *The New Politics of Race and Gender*, edited by C. Marshall. Washington, DC: The Falmer Press.

Berliner, David C., and Bruce J. Biddle. 1995. *The Manufactured Crisis: Myths, Fraud, and the Attack on America's Public Schools*. Reading, MA: Addison-Wesley Publishing Co.

Biklen, Sari Knopp. 1995. *School Work: Gender and the Cultural Construction of Teaching*. New York: Teachers College Press.

Bryk, Anthony S., Valerie E. Lee, and Peter B. Holland. 1993. *Catholic Schools and the Common Good*. Cambridge, MA: Harvard University Press.

Buhrmann, Hans G., and Robert D. Bratton. 1977. "Athletic Participation and Status of Alberta High School Girls." *International Review of Sport Sociology* 12:57-67.

Buhrmann, Hans G., and M. S. Jarvis. 1971. "Athletics and Status: An Examination of the Relationship Between Athletic Participation and Various Status Measures of High School Girls." *Canadian Association of Health, Physical Education, and Recreation Journal* 37:14-17.

Carter, Robert T., and Lin Goodwin. 1994. "Racial Identity and Education." *Review of Research in Education* 20:291-336.

Coleman, James S. 1961. *The Adolescent Society: The Social Life of the Teenager and Its Impact on Education*. New York: The Free Press of Glencoe.

Connell, R. W., D. J. Ashenden, S. Kessler, and G. W. Dowsett. 1982. *Making the Difference: Schools, Families and Social Division*. Sydney, Australia: George Allen & Unwin.

Cusick, Phillip A. 1973. *Inside High School: The Student's World*. New York: Holt, Rinehart and Winston, Inc.

Eckert, Penelope. 1989. *Jocks & Burnouts: Social Categories and Identity in the High School*. New York; Teachers College Press.

Eder, Donna, with Catherine Colleen Evans, and Stephen Parker. 1995. *School Talk: Gender and Adolescent Culture*. New Brunswick, NJ: Rutgers University Press.

Eder, Donna, and David A. Kinney. 1995. "The Effects of Middle School Extracurricular Activities on Adolescents' Popularity and Peer Status. *Youth & Society* 26:298-324.

Everhart, Robert B. 1983. *Reading, Writing and Resistance: Adolescence and Labor in a Junior High School*. Boston: Routledge & Kegan Paul.

Fischer, Claude S., Michael Hout, Martin Sanchez Jankowski, Samuel R. Lucas, Ann Swidler, and Kim Voss. 1996. *Inequality by Design: Cracking the Bell Curve Myth*. Princeton, N.J.: Princeton University Press.

Freeman, Jo. 1995. "The Revolution for Women in Law and Public Policy." Pp. 365-404 in *Women: A Feminist Perspective* (5th edition), edited by J. Freeman. Mountain View, CA: Mayfield Publishing Co.

Gilligan, Carol. 1982. *In a Different Voice: Psychological Theory and Women's Development*. Cambridge, MA: Harvard University Press.

Gordon, C. Wayne. 1957. *The Social System of the High School: A Study in the Sociology of Adolescence*. Glencoe, IL: The Free Press.

Gould, Stephen Jay. 1981. *The Mismeasure of Man*. New York: W. W. Norton.

Hoffnung, Michele. 1995. "Motherhood: Contemporary Conflict for Women." Pp. 162-181 in *Women: A Feminist Perspective* (5th edition), edited by J. Freeman. Mountain View, CA: Mayfield Publishing Co.

Hudley, Cynthia. 1995. "Assessing the Impact of Separate Schooling for African-American Male Adolescents." *Journal of Early Adolescence* 15:38-57.

Kaufman, Debra Renee. 1995. "Professional Women: How Real Are the Recent Gains?" Pp. 287-305 in *Women: A Feminist Perspective* (5th edition), edited by J. Freeman. Mountain View, CA: Mayfield Publishing Co.

Kessler, S., D. J. Ashenden, R. W. Connell, and G. W. Dowsett. 1985. "Gender Relations in Secondary Schooling." *Sociology of Education* 58:34-48.

Larkin, Ralph W. 1979. *Suburban Youth in Cultural Crisis*. New York: Oxford University Press.

Leake, Donald O., and Christine J. Faltz. 1993. "Do We Need to Desegregate All of Our Black Schools?" *Educational Policy* 7:370-387.

LeCompte, Margaret Diane, and Anthony Gary Dworkin. 1991. *Giving Up on School: Student Dropouts and Teacher Burnouts*. Newbury Park, CA: Corwin Press Inc.

McCormick, Theresa Mickey. 1994. *Creating the Nonsexist Classroom: A Multicultural Approach*. New York: Teachers College Press.

Morgan, Kathryn Pauly. 1996. "Describing the Emperor's New Clothes: Three Myths of Educational (In-)Equity." Pp. 105-122 in *The Gender Question in Education: Theory, Pedagogy, & Politics*, edited by A. Diller, B. Houston, K. P. Morgan, and M. Ayim. Boulder, CO: Westview Press.

Powell, Arthur G., Eleanor Farrar, and David K. Cohen. 1985. *The Shopping Mall High School: Winners and Losers in the Educational Marketplace*. Boston: Houghton Mifflin.

Riordan, Cornelius. 1990. *Girls and Boys in School: Together or Separate?* New York: Teachers College Press.

Riordan, Cornelius. 1994. "Single-Gender Schools: Outcomes for African and Hispanic Americans." *Research in Sociology of Education and Socialization* 10:177-205.

Sadker, Myra, and David Sadker. 1994. *How America's Schools Cheat Girls*. New York: Charles Scribner.

Sandler, Bernice Resnick. 1987. "The Classroom Climate: Still a Chilly One for Women." Pp. 113-123 in *Educating Men and Women Together*, edited by C. Lasser. Urbana, IL: University of Illinois Press.

Tyack, David, and Elisabeth Hansot. 1990. *Learning Together: A History of Coeducation in American Public Schools*. New Haven, CT: Yale University Press.

U.S. Department of Education, National Center for Educational Statistics. 1993. *Digest of Educational Statistics*. Washington, DC: U.S. Government Printing Office.

Weinbaum, Batya. 1983. *Pictures of Patriarchy*. Boston: South End Press.

Weis, Lois. 1990. *Working Class Without Work: High School Students in a De-industrializing Economy*. New York: Routledge.

Williams, Peg. 1980. "Laws Prohibiting Sex Discrimination in the Schools." Pp. 143-164 in *Sex Equity in Education*, edited by J. Stockard, P. A. Schmuck, K. Kempner, P. Williams, S. K. Edson, and M. A. Smith. New York: Academic Press.

Wilson, William Julius. 1987. *The Truly Disadvantaged: The Inner City, the Underclass, and Public Policy*. Chicago: University of Chicago Press.

Wooden, Wayne S. 1995. *Renegade Kids, Suburban Outlaws: From Youth Culture to Delinquency*. Belmont, CA: Wadsworth Publishing Co.

CHAPTER 2

State Policies and Gender Equity: Comparative Perspectives

Nelly P. Stromquist

UNDERSTANDING POLICY

The term policy is an elusive concept. In fact, it has been asserted that no term in the social sciences has suffered more ambiguity and abuse in recent decades (Leichter 1979). In principle, it refers to official statements of intention to act on certain problems. But in actual practice, policies can take multiple forms: legislation, official recommendations in reports by governmental agencies or departments, and results from commissions appointed by governments. Increasingly, policies are being established by international bodies through international conferences which, though not conventions that carry legal obligation, commit countries morally to follow specific recommendations. In developing countries another form of policy creation occurs through projects carried out by countries with external support.

In the form of public declarations, educational policies follow, at a minimum, a four-stage process, beginning with problem identification, and moving into policy formulation and authorization (laws passed), implementation, and termination or change (Harman 1984). Since these phases activate different actors, often there is a disjuncture between these phases, and occasionally good policies in design are poorly implemented in the field. Students of public policy, however, are also aware that policies are not "a concrete constant object or text that is transmitted from place to place." Instead, policies are produced by individuals acting within contexts that offer constraints and opportunities (Hall in progress). A recognition of the complexity of policy should make us realize that there are multiple elements at work, such as intentionality, agency, interaction, power, and temporality that condition social contexts (Hall 1995). One definition of policy, according to Oszlak (1984:5), is that it is "a set of successive decision making vis-à-vis issues socially problematized." This insightful conceptualization helps to recognize that policies are intended to be solutions to perceived problems, that these solutions must have a minimum level of societal support, and that problem definition moves through various waves of decisionmaking. In other words, contrary to the view that posits a linear sequence in the formulation of policy, we are beginning to recognize that as several actors deal with the policies—from politicians to bureaucrats to school staff—they introduce some modifications to policy through these persons' interpretation of the policies and extent to which they comply with it.

The presence of contingency factors in the formulation and implementation of public policies, however, should not be interpreted to suggest that all policies are unpredictable. Deviations from intention and objectives over time are particularly true in the case of controversial or non-consensual policies, as gender policies are. There are strong elements of surprise and contingency surrounding policies, particularly their implementation. But, to the extent that these policies remain contested terrains between opposing forces, it is sometimes possible to forecast victories by the stronger parties. This paper does not discard the possibility of contingency factors in the processes of policy setting and implementation. We wish to describe the character and objectives of educational gender policies and to explain the extent to which these policies have sought to promote significant changes within the educational system. Our interest, therefore, is on capturing the similarity behind apparently distinct gender policies on education. This paper seeks to provide a comparative review of gender policies in education, both domestic and foreign, documenting the range of meaning and scope that have characterized gender policies on educational equity and offering explanations for the achievements of these policies.

GENDER POLICIES
The generation of public policy, and thus direct demands upon the state, have been sought by many feminists. Issues involved in these demands have been equal status for women, the removal of sexual discrimination, the introduction of anti-sexual harassment regula-

tions, and the introduction of quotas to ensure women's representation.

There is no consensus, however, within the feminist movement regarding the role of the state in gender relations. The group generally characterized as "liberal feminists" considers that the state is neutral and that it will correct gender inequalities when provided with the pertinent information about disparities. Another group, comprising feminists endorsing either "radical" or "socialist" perspectives, is more inclined to see the state as a patriarchal institution that reflects gender divisions as well as produces them. In the latter perspective, women are generally excluded from access to state resources directly by their absence from state offices and indirectly by the "gendered" political forces brought to bear on the state (Connell 1987; Pateman 1988). Indeed, according to the *Human Development Report 1993*, women constitute just over 10 percent of the world's parliamentary representatives and consistently less than 4 percent of cabinet ministers or holders of similar positions of executive authority.[1]

The state shapes gender relations through rules on divorce, marriage, abortion, contraception, wage discrimination, sexuality, prostitution, pornography, rape, and wife battering (Walby 1990). The patriarchal nature of the state, however, is not considered static. It is asserted that dominant forces have modernized gender by enabling the full participation of women in the labor force. But, at the same time, the state has neutralized feminist demands through various concessions that, while improving the situation, do not eliminate fundamental obstacles to women's equality. One of the state responses in the domain of education is to recognize the principle of equal opportunity, rather than the need for anti-sexist education (Yates 1993; Kelly 1988).

Over time, the feminist position of distancing itself from the state has moved toward the utilization of a double strategy: working with the state by putting pressure on it and conducting independent work through women's groups, particularly nongovernmental organizations (NGOs). This new posture has come following the recognition that women have better chances of gaining influence through the political process (alliances with supportive men, lobbying for women's interests) than through the market or through NGOs, which tend to be small and fragmented (Young 1988).

In looking at the behavior of states, feminist thinkers have also observed that state policies are not always in the direction of the status quo. While states see women and families as an inseparable dyad, in which the problems of one become the problems of the other, often the state assumes contradictory policies toward women. On the one hand, the need to count on women as mothers and housewives leads the state to formulate very conventional projects along gender lines. On the other hand, the need to rely on women as labor—even if that labor is easily exploitable, cheap, and manipulable—creates opportunities for women to join the labor market, gain some measure of financial autonomy, and eventually question their conditions of subordination. Likewise, global trends in favor of democratic norms make it necessary for states to extend equal rights to all citizens. These contradictions create windows of opportunity for transformative possibilities and organized action.

The economic, social, and political inequalities of women throughout the world continue despite 20 years of active work by the women's movement. One of the most accepted indicators of socioeconomic well-being is the Human Development Index (HDI), presented in the annual *Human Development Reports* produced by United Nations Development Program (UNDP). This index summarizes the conditions of the population in a country in terms of life expectancy at birth, educational attainment, and adjusted real gross domestic product per capita. UNDP has also developed a gender-sensitive HDI, built on the basis of the standing of women relative to men in terms of life expectancy, adult literacy, wage rates, and mean years of schooling. The *Human Development Report* for 1993 found that the average women's HDI is only 60 percent that of males[2] (UNDP 1993:26). Terming women "the world's largest excluded group," the same report also noted that women have serious disadvantages compared to men in employment, higher education, legal rights, financial assets, and political representation. This report provides clear evidence that industrialization is not concomitant with women's equality, the most notable example being Japan, whose HDI ranks first in the world but, when adjusted for gender disparity, takes 17th place. As with gender, ethnicity is another variable of importance in producing socioeconomic inequality: if the population of the U.S. were divided into ethnic groups, the HDI for the white population would rank 1st among nations while the black population would rank 31st and the Hispanic population "even lower" (UNDP 1993:26).

While there is no agreement among feminist thinkers regarding the role of gender under capitalism, it is increasingly accepted that women are one of the important elements in the process of accumulation (through their *re*productive domestic work) which supersedes class boundaries and which is also supported by extraeconomic relations of domination (Feijoo 1993). Women, however, do not represent a homogeneous group nor do they all see themselves in the same circumstances. Middle-class women's issues focus on improved access to higher education, rights of married women, improvement in labor legislation. These interests are not shared by poor women because few poor women attend university, enter into official marriages, and work in the formal sector of the economy. The problems of poor women concentrate instead on housing, debt problems, health, and unemployment (Fisher 1993). The emergence of issues that cut across social classes such as the women's right to control their bodies (including abortion) and the prevalence of wife battering creates greater unity among women.

GENDER POLICIES IN EDUCATION

As stated earlier, the UNDP's *Human Development Report 1993* notes the substantial disadvantage of women. Yet, it does not address causes or actors/institutions accounting for this situation. This position is common to many government and international agency declarations. There is a clear preference for designing projects to address inequalities for women in access to schooling and the labor force; much less emphasis is spent in identifying social, economic, and ideological forces underlying the subordination and domination of women.

To understand the intention of policymakers (as well as to help them in the design of effective policies), scholars have focused on the examination of policy instruments—"the mechanisms that translate substantive policy goals into concrete actions" (McDonnell and Elmore 1987:133).[3] To analyze gender policies I am proposing a classification based on the level of social transformation intended by the legislation. Three such types can be identified: *coercive* laws—those enacted to prevent sexual discrimination from taking place or continuing to take place (the "stick" aspect of the law); *supportive* laws—those which create bodies to promote or monitor the implementation of new practices (e.g., creation of women's commissions, women's units, ministries in charge of women's affairs, etc.); and *constructive* laws—those that provide incentives or new practices in educational institutions concerning program and course development, teacher training, more scholarships for women, etc. (the "carrot" aspect of the law). Table 1 presents a classification of generic and gender-focused policies, comparing the typology offered by McDonnell and Elmore (1987) with mine.

If gender differences in society are intimately connected to the management of ideology and discourse, feminist theory would argue that policies are needed to modify the practices by which schools create gender and prepare male as well as female students for parenting and domestic life. Policies would also be needed to develop alternatives to the conventional sexual division of labor in the nuclear family and the economy (Deem forthcoming). To assist with this twin set of objectives, research should be promoted, particularly qualitative studies of schooling, so that the "sexual underworld of schooling" through sexually and racially abusive language and harassment, patronizing behavior toward female students, and race-laden notions of femininity and masculinity becomes transparent (Arnot 1993). In other words, constructive policies are a must.

Gender policies can be of three kinds in terms of their scope: general policies against discrimination (covering all areas, not just education), policies specific to education but addressing women by implication only, and policies specific to women's education. General policies against discrimination are, obviously, coercive in nature. Policies specific to education or to women's education can be coercive, supportive, or constructive.

Gender Policies in Education at the National Level
Several empirical studies of state educational policies related to gender are emerging. This research covers mostly policies in advanced industrial countries such as Sweden, Australia, Denmark, Germany, the U.K., the U.S., France, Italy, Spain, Canada, and Hungary. But less developed countries are also being studied, and these include Argentina, Burkina Faso, Sri Lanka, Uruguay, South Korea, and Zimbabwe.[4]

In the view of most governments, the key problem regarding women's education is essentially one of access—i.e., "ensuring equal opportunity of women at all levels of education." They also recognize the need to ensure for women adequate access to training, science, and technology. When educational content is considered, they will, without great reluctance, call for the elimination of sexual

Table 1. Comparison of Generic and Gender-Related Policies

Generic Policies		
Type	Desired Effect	Enforcement
Mandate	Eliminate discrimination, waste, damage, etc.	Punishment to encourage compliance
System Changing	Devolution of authority, creation of new agencies	State's goodwill; funds to create new institutions
Capacity Building	New capacities in individuals and institutions	Money for training and institutional improvements
Inducements	Provision of new services and administration of new services	Money for provision of services

Gender-Sensitive Policies		
Type	Desired Effect	Enforcement
Coercive	Eliminate discrimination	Withdrawal of contracts or fines to encourage compliance
Supportive	Institutions/units to promote gender issues and monitor coercive and constructive gender legislation	Funds to create new institutions/units
Constructive	New Behaviors, knowledge, and attitudes regarding women and men in society	Funds to enable curriculum changes, teacher training and retraining, and research

stereotypes from textbooks and other educational materials. The emphasis on women's access to the knowledge and skills provided through schooling carries the assumption that schools are "neutral institutions which will impart knowledge to women on an equal basis as they do to men and that the knowledge which schools impart will be of the same value to women as to men" (Kelly 1988:12).

There is a constant avoidance, whether conscious or unconscious, of more complex curricular issues such as modifying the types of knowledge transmitted and including new visions of a more gender-egalitarian society. This occurs not only in lower levels of schooling but also at the university level. As a result, knowledge gained in these institutions leaves untouched the ideological messages and educational practices that reproduce male and female identities. For instance, economic textbooks at the college level invoke the occupational "crowding" model or the statistical discrimination models in explaining the relatively lower income of women but fail to explain why women or minorities continue to acquire the traditional skills that lead to occupational crowding and explain occupational choices as the result of maximizing behaviors by people on the basis of exogenously-given preferences such as technologies, endowments, and institutions (Feiner and Roberts 1990). When policies are developed to increase the number of girls in math and sciences, the problem is constructed as women's poor representation in non-traditional careers. This naturalizes the problem as being the result of individual choices and achievement and takes attention away from the service sector, which is the major area of employment for women (Yates 1993).

The area of educational content—or curriculum—should be of utmost importance in developing gender policies. As Connell remarks, the "how much and the who [i.e., access] cannot be separated from the what." In his words:

> Each particular way of constructing the curriculum (i.e., organizing the field of knowledge and defining how it is to be taught and learned) carries social effects. Curriculum empowers and disempowers, authorizes and de-authorizes, recognizes and misrecognizes different social groups and their knowledge and their identities. For instance, curriculum developed from academic institutions controlled by men has, in a variety of ways, authorized the practices and experiences

of men and marginalized those of women" (Connell 1994:14).

Despite the importance of content, curriculum reform—in the few cases when it is attempted—relies on strategies of assimilation. Examining the report of the Schools Commission of 1987, which presented the *National Policy for the Education of Girls in Australian Schools*, Yates finds that the report talks of the need to broaden students' perspective, enhance girls' participation and achievement, meet the needs of girls, increase girls' confidence in mathematics, and ensure inclusive content, practices, process and environments (1993:174), but it avoids entering into any politics of contested meaning.

Regardless of levels of economic development and political philosophy (the latter generally moving toward uniformity, namely the democratic state with a market economy), all countries present strong similarities in the condition of women's and men's education. Among the similarities are the following: (a) their educational systems are undergoing a process of continuous expansion; (b) with steadily increasing enrollment, girls also tend to increase their schooling participation; (c) in most countries textbooks continue to present sexual stereotypes; (d) teachers tend to have low expectations of girls and treat them differently from boys—to the girls' disadvantage; (e) while many women are teachers, few are administrators; (f) there are few women in university faculty positions; (g) there is still a large concentration of women in traditionally feminine fields of study, and a low representation in fields important to national development such as agriculture and science and technology, with the consequence that the occupational segregation and income differentials among men and women continue; and (h) almost universally, women exhibit higher rates of illiteracy.

States engage in very limited work to increase the feminist consciousness of adult women. There is a strong parallel between treatment of girls in school and women in adult educational programs: both are apolitical, extending and promoting conventional definitions of masculinity and femininity. In general terms, many governmental policies continue to see women as passive recipients of welfare; therefore, policies are addressed mainly to low-income urban, rural, or indigenous women so that these women may improve their abilities in sewing, nutrition, health, family planning, and handicrafts, and so that their children may have better life chances. These policies reflect the state's willingness to provide welfare to the most needy women but not to grant autonomy to them nor to women as a whole group. With very few exceptions—cases in which feminist educators position themselves in the state bureaucracy, as in India and Argentina, the only groups working on the raising of gender awareness among adult women are the women's nongovernmental organizations (NGOs).

Educational Gender Policies in Developed Countries. To give concreteness to the assertions made above, I present the educational policies in three industrialized nations in greater detail. These countries—the United Kingdom, Canada, and the United States—have been selected because they have predominantly Anglo-Saxon cultures and have total gender parity at the primary and secondary levels of schooling, thus permitting examination of educational policies beyond a focus on basic access.

The United Kingdom has three separate educational systems, which set their own policies: England and Wales, Scotland, and Northern Ireland. At the national level there is one general gender policy, the Sex Discrimination Act of 1975, which prohibits direct and indirect gender discrimination (the latter including setting up conditions not needed for a job but tending to be more difficult to satisfy for women than for men, such as years of experience abroad). Part III of this act provides for equal access to schooling, facilities, and courses for women. The act also establishes an Equal Opportunity Commission to work toward the elimination of discrimination, promote equality between men and women, and monitor the implementation of the act. The Commission can carry out investigations, assist people to avoid discrimination, and undertake research. The budget of the Commission is small and has been cut in real terms in recent years (Sutherland 1994).

In 1977 the three U.K. governments expressed commitment to equality of opportunity and provision in education by enacting the 1977 *Green Paper on Education in the Schools.* A subsequent document, *The School Curriculum,* sought to provide equal treatment of men and women in the curriculum. Reportedly, both policies have not been supported by concomitant teacher training (Tomes 1985). Feminists in the U.K. have demanded more "gender-inclusive" curricula to give greater coverage to the achievements of women in several domains and to remove exam questions that are generally sexist. They have also required the development of several strategies and initiatives to overcome the problems of sexism in education, including self-assessment for teachers (*Genderwatch*, a handbook for teacher self-assessment). These demands remain unfulfilled (Deem forthcoming).

Canada is of considerable interest because it is generally considered one of the most advanced in the treatment of gender issues. The national government passed a general law on Equal Rights (including education) in 1977, which prohibits discrimination along gender lines. Since education is a provincial responsibility, there is considerable variability at this level. All provinces have anti-discrimination laws in education, but only one, Ontario, mandates programs to promote equality of educational access. Two provinces (Quebec and Nova Scotia) have designed comprehensive educational laws. Three provinces have policies for teacher training on anti-sexism, but the training is voluntary. Data on policy achievements indicate that very few provinces have addressed school program changes. Most of the progress has taken place in terms of making industrial and home economics courses open to boys and girls, and removing sexual stereotypes from textbooks; Quebec Province is now considered the leader in the francophone world in removing sexism from language. Six provinces have modified their higher education programs to enable women to re-enter studies through distance education and part-time university programs or by earning credit for relevant experience. Only two provinces have provided financial aid for some categories of women. In education, a number of provinces have issued directives to eliminate sexual stereotypes, and the majority of provinces offer childcare services in post-secondary institutions. The available studies on Canadian gender policies in education make no reference to resources, but it seems clear that allocations have taken place, at least for the teacher training courses and financial aid for women (Baudoux 1994).

The United States has passed gender-related policies at the federal and state levels. As in the case of Canada, the U.S. presents considerable variation at the state level, with 13 states having laws prohibiting discrimination at all levels of education and 31 prohibiting discrimination in primary and secondary education programs. Here, I will focus attention only on policies at the federal level. The federal government passed in 1972 a comprehensive act on gender equity in education. Title IX prohibits sex discrimination of students in a number of areas: admissions, recruitment, wages, scholarships, housing facilities, access to courses, financial assistance, and athletics; Title IX also prohibits discrimination of school personnel such as teachers, administrators, and counselors. The federal government also passed the Women's Educational Equity Act (WEEA) in 1974. It funds state governments, research centers and individual researchers to develop, evaluate, and disseminate curricula, textbooks, provide pre- and in-service teacher training, improve career guidance, and promote quality of education for women. Another legislation of importance, the Vocational Education Act[5], addresses vocational and technical education and funds efforts to eliminate sex bias and discrimination as well as to provide counseling programs to foster women's participation in nontraditional female occupations.

The Vocational Education Act, which serves students in secondary and post-secondary vocational education, has received substantial allocations for its gender-related programs. In contrast, Title IX and WEEA—serving the bulk of students—have received very limited funds for their implementation. During the Reagan and Bush administrations, courts redefined the intention of the legislation concerning Title IX and reduced it considerably by interpreting its mandate to apply only to *programs*, not to the entire institution or university receiving federal funds. WEEA was supposed to receive $49 million per year. At its highest point, it received $10 million and after that point decreased a million per year until it reached a mere $500,000 in 1993 (Stromquist 1993a). Under Reagan, the state became mobilized directly and indirectly against feminism and other progressive interests, so feminists had to use the state not to promote new interests but to defend those previously achieved (Nelson and Johnson 1994). In 1994, during the more socially sensitive Clinton administration, WEEA was reauthorized at $5 million per year. This, to cover a country with 15,000 local school districts, 3,500 colleges and universities, and 9,000 institutions of post-secondary education, amounts to an investment of $181 per institution.

The character of the gender policies enacted in the three developed countries discussed above produce the following picture: In the U.K. the educational gender policies are mostly coercive and to a lesser extent constructive and supportive. In Canada the gender policies cover the entire gamut: coercive, supportive, and constructive; however, only a few provinces have engaged in any of these efforts. The U.S. has engaged in coercive and to a much lesser degree in constructive policies. Except for the Vocational Education Act, which enables the appointment of district-level officials to monitor and promote implementation of this legislation, the U.S. has not enacted supportive policies.

It should be noted that none of these three countries nor others for which gender policy studies are available (Sutherland and Baudoux 1994) engage in *positive discrimination*, a policy which gives preference to members of a group for education, jobs, or promotion over people with equal or better qualifications; at most, states have engaged in *positive action* or *affirmative action*, i.e., the obligation by employers to promote equal opportunity for women and ethnic minorities (Carter 1988).

Educational Gender Policies in Developing Countries. Developing countries present serious problems in the participation of women in school, even at basic levels of education. Access of girls and women to education in Latin America is reaching parity in terms of gross enrollment ratios, but disparities in primary schooling between girls and boys reach about 33 percentage points in Africa and 18 percentage points in Asia. At the secondary school level they reach a difference of 37 and 26 percentage points for Africa and Asia, respectively (UN 1991:50-53). The educational policies of Sri Lanka and Argentina are of interest because these countries are some of the most educationally advanced in the Third World.

Sri Lanka has evinced an enrollment in primary and secondary education very close to gender parity since the early 1960s. Guided by this parity, the government has concluded that gender specific policies to ensure the access of girls and women to education are not necessary and considers that it is implementing gender-neutral policies. The state acknowledges difficulties in the access of girls to primary schooling in Muslim populations in the Eastern Province and among tea plantation workers of South Indian origin. It notices that more boys than girls drop out, particularly at the secondary level, so presumably the boys are more disadvantaged than girls. Textbooks have not been modified although research has detected sexual stereotypes in them. The Sri Lankan government also acknowledges that women can enter only one of the three agricultural colleges in the country and that in the one college where they are admitted, women can represent only 20 percent of the total intake. It also notes that 75 percent of women in technical colleges are enrolled in commercial courses and that women in vocational courses are enrolled in secretarial and sewing classes. Since the state pursues a gender-neutral policy, there is no allocation of funds to address gender issues (Jayaweera 1994). Incidentally, the case of Sri Lanka is very similar to that of Hungary in its socialist days. Women there, by virtue of having parity in primary and secondary schooling, were declared to face no obstacles in education.

As part of the return to democracy in Argentina, the government was very responsive to demands made by civil society. In 1991, it created a National Program for the Promotion of Equal Opportunity for Women in the Educational Area (PRIOM), established through an agreement between the Ministry of Education and Culture and the National Women's Council. This program identified and implemented a comprehensive agenda: raising gender awareness and providing training for teachers, students, and administrative staff; providing special programs at all levels and types to improve the educational potential of women; providing vocational, professional, and educational advice to improve the participation and performance of women in political, professional, and social life; introducing women's issues in textbooks to describe not only women's role in the family but also in history, economics, politics, and society; conducting research projects to attain a wide, systematic, and permanent knowledge of women's conditions in education, and creating a data bank on problems facing women in the educational sphere (Ministerio de Cultura y Educacion 1992). PRIOM implemented its program in 20 provinces. It also linked with Women's Units in provincial governments, universities, and women's NGOs. In 1995, just as PRIOM was moving into integrating the new gender curriculum into the ongoing efforts to improve the national curricula in other aspects, the Catholic Church of Argentina attacked its work, accusing PRIOM's coordinator of trying to destroy the family and introduce homosexuality in the schools. One of the main reasons for the Church's opposition—to which the government responded by dismantling the program—was that PRIOM was committed to work on the questions of sex education and women's control over their bodies.

Gender Policies in Education at the International Level

Educational policies affecting women are shaped through a variety of international efforts: the institutional priorities by bilateral and multilateral agencies, international conferences dealing with development issues (in which education usually appears as an important feature), and the various international conferences on women (of which there have been four so far and in which education has been a persistent sub-theme).

International Funding from Bilateral and Multilateral Agencies. When discussing educational policies in developing countries (and increasingly policies for other social services), it is necessary to refer to external assistance. In these days of economic contraction in many developing countries, international development assistance provides a crucial means to engage in efforts other than the regular supply of education. In the poorest countries, international assistance is needed even for the expansion of schools. Providing external assistance, there are two main sets of actors, the bilateral and the multilateral organizations—the latter essentially those belonging to the UN system.

Bilateral development agencies represent their own donor state. Multinational development agencies—essentially the organizations of the UN family—reflect also their member states.[6] The mediating role of staff members within these agencies can bring greater definition to the nature of problems within the educational sector and result in greater or lesser support for gender projects and programs. The leverage of these agencies in introducing gender-sensitive efforts is related to the size of their contributions and other forms of political support given to the recipient countries.

At present, there is much interest among developing countries in expanding the access of girls to primary schools. To this effect, a number of countries are—with external assistance—engaging in efforts such as building schools closer to the students' homes, eliminating or reducing school fees for girls, eliminating the need for uniforms (which acts against poor families), building more residential schools for adolescent girls, and hiring more women as facilitators and teachers to encourage parents to enroll their daughters (whose sexuality will thus not be in danger). Only in a handful of cases have textbooks been reviewed for sexual stereotypes and corrected accordingly. Anti-sexist content in books and in attitudes of teachers has seldom been promoted (Stromquist

1994). Overall, these efforts make accommodations to patriarchy rather than challenge it. These efforts, it must be said, have not been codified as national policies although they represent the closest measure to actually having a policy. In fact, because these projects are often the only ones addressing gender issues, some observers confuse discrete projects with national policy (see, for instance, the recent work by King and Hill 1993).

There are several instances—certainly not many—of projects promoting the empowerment or autonomy of adult women. These projects, with very few exceptions, are being conducted by women NGOs (Stromquist 1994).

International Conferences. Through the holding of international conferences, important forms of support for work on gender issues are created. Further, these conferences affect both developed and developing countries. The various UN world conferences on women (Mexico 1975; Copenhagen 1980; Nairobi 1985; Beijing 1995) have served to sharpen the nature and range of problems affecting women and have promoted the construction of gender-sensitive policies and programs. During these worldwide conferences on women, which were attended by state officials, women in NGOs held parallel conferences or what they called "counter-meetings" in the same cities and presented their deliberations and recommendations to their state representatives, often with considerable success in terms of having their viewpoints incorporated in the final official documents. Historian Francisca Miller considers the most important legacy of the UN Decade for Women to have been that political parties and governments seeking legitimacy now find it advantageous to address women's issues (1991:188).

One of the most powerful UN documents, the Convention on the Elimination of All Forms of Discrimination Against Women (CEDAW), in force since 1981 and ratified by 148 states as of November 1995, is a legally-binding agreement and represents the strongest indictment against patriarchal rule as it attacks wife battering, early marriages, and sexual discrimination in education and work. Although many countries have expressed reservations about a number of articles in this Convention, there is increasing world pressure to implement it. The Human Rights Conference in Vienna (1993) acted as a major prod for the renewed impetus for CEDAW and succeeded in having women's rights included among the human rights. Recent worldwide conferences, such as those on the Environment and Development (Rio 1992), Population and Development (Cairo 1994), Social Development (Copenhagen 1995), and the Fourth Conference on Women (Beijing 1995)[7] have been of particular importance in keeping the gender issue alive in governmental agendas as well as in developing ties of solidarity across nation states. One such common issue is the identification of domestic violence as a widespread social problem affecting women.

Since the International Women's Year in 1975, governments have made commitments to ensure equality of access to all types and levels of education and to reformulate the content and practices of education to make them more gender sensitive. Gains have been discernable in access to schooling, but it is not clear to what extent these are simply the product of the educational system's propensity to grow over time. Many of the educational recommendations (a form of policy) in the various women's world conferences remain unheeded, but these issues are increasingly defined in more precise and clear terms as well as discussed by larger groups of stakeholders.

While there has always been social contagion among countries, this has been accelerated by virtue of the formal creation of economic blocs. The European Economic Commission mandated in 1982 the formation of a Council for Women's and Men's Parity at national levels. This policy caused Italy and Spain to set up such a body. The European Court of Justice created to enforce the Treaty of Rome makes decisions binding on member states; its dealing with issues such as equal pay, pensions, and retirement has had repercussions in the legislation of other European countries. The European Court of Human Rights in Strasbourg has been addressing questions of sexual and racial discriminations of immigrants. The decisions of these supranational bodies have (and will have) indirect effects on gender equity in education.

The Nairobi conference in 1985 closed the UN Decade for Women with a document, *Forward Looking Strategies* (*FLS*), which identified areas of action in specific sectors such as employment, education, health, agriculture, and industry to be conducted by national governments and international agencies. Specifically in the area of education, *FLS* made many recommendations on access, textbooks, teacher training, literacy programs for women, vocational education, and career counseling. This rich set of recommendations to be implemented by the nations of the world shows weak implementation ten years later. Most reports produced to evaluate country performance on the *FLS* concentrate on enrollment figures at all three levels of education. Enrollments have certainly gone up although gender concentration in certain fields of study continues. It is not clear to what extent the enrollment growth is simply a manifestation of the inexorable expansion of schooling: as parents get more education, they want more education for their children. The Beijing conference in 1995 reiterated the *FLS* recommendations in a new document, the *Platform for Action*. This document presented a more complete and cohesive set of recommendations and tightened the enforcing and monitoring mechanisms. While it identified units within the UN and governments to serve as monitoring mechanisms, it did not succeed in establishing financial minimums to ensure implementation.

Nonetheless, international conferences have immense value as public forums with much participation and exchange of views. International forums promote attention to women and bring to the public arena a highly visible focus on the work of states. Usually these meetings end in recommendations—whether consensual or deeply fought. Although recommendations agreed upon at international *conferences*—as opposed to those signed in international *conventions*—possess no legal validity, these official declarations can be used as leverage.

Reasons for Differences Between National and International Policies

Supranational policies emerging from economic blocs involve mostly coercive and to a lesser degree supportive legislation. Recommendations accepted at international meetings propose all three types of state legislation, ranging from coercive to constructivist efforts. National policies tend to concentrate on coercive policies or what has been called "gender-neutral policies."

David (1981) notes that, from a feminist perspective, policy prescriptions cannot be identified "without understanding the reason for the contours of the phenomena involving the creation and maintenance of gender" (p. 116). She argues that analysis based on a political economy approach can be effective in producing explanations of state policies. Within this framework, it could be asked, "why are the gender policies suggested at the international levels comprehensive and thus more focused on social system change than are national policies?" Perhaps the explanation lies in the lack of legal obligation these international declarations carry. By endorsing the various policies that are recommended, the states appear responsive and gender sensitive. In the club of nations, they earn status by being progressive; among their respective citizens, they are perceived as democratic and just. Endorsing declarations of international conferences does not oblige countries in regard to implementation and thus serves the role of legitimation rather than a corrective role.

Domestically, states are more cautious. While they are increasingly responding to feminist pressure by issuing gender-equity legislation, the evidence suggests some common features about these laws. The legislation often presents narrow parameters, concentrating on prohibition of undesirable behaviors rather than on the development of attitudes and knowledge designed to construct an alternative social order. The few legislative measures aimed at constructive objectives tend to offer limited funds, certainly disproportionate to the total need. There have been several efforts to engage in supportive legislation via the creation of women's units or similar bureaus. More studies are needed about the funds and authority provided by these laws; existing evidence reveals that such units have been generally poorly endowed in terms of personnel, resources, and overall influence. The exceptions are few; among them Canada, which established a federal Minister Responsible for the Status of Women[8] and various women's units operating at the provincial level, and the counterpart units in Scandinavian countries.

Why are there more coercive than constructive laws at the national level? Several reasons emerge. Coercive laws are considerably less expensive than the other two. They may or may not be followed up by enforcing mechanisms; if the enforcement units have limited authority, the implementation of these laws can be severely weakened. The laws may also be designed so that action is limited. As Meehan and Sevenhuijsen (1991) have observed regarding the gender equity acts passed in the U.K. and the U.S., these laws individualize equal opportunities so that there must be endless one-woman struggles for even limited kinds of changes to occur.

Supportive laws are more threatening because they establish governmental agencies that demand regular state allocations and which could eventually challenge some other state institutions' access to resources. Reviewing gender legislation in the Nordic countries, Eduards et al. (1985) notice that most of the gender laws enacted in the region are gender-neutral, passive forms of legislation which give both sexes the same opportunities in society but avoid conflict. Gelb and Palley's (1982) review of five gender-related initiatives in the U.S. came to the conclusion that laws are successful when women abide by the "political rules of the game." They identify four rules: (1) being perceived as legitimate, (2) focusing on incremental issues, (3) providing information and concentrating on mobilizing allies, and (4) defining the situation by manipulating symbols favorable to their cause.

These authors found that the least successful gender-legislation in the U.S.—Title IX—even though it was merely coercive, ran into problems when the opposition felt that access of girls to sports could result in role change policies, "which appear to produce change in the dependent female role of wife, mother, and homemakers, holding the potential for greater sexual freedom and independence in a variety of contexts" (1982:6). A similar point is made by Nelson (1984), who studied the issue of child abuse in the U.S. She observed that while some features of child abuse law were non-threatening to the status quo, such as "abuse reporting laws," others such as those mandating "protective custody provisions" had all kinds of implications and connections to greater problems such as poverty, racism, and patriarchy. In consequence, the child abuse legislation that was eventually enacted had strong limits. Nelson (1984:137) attributed these outcomes to the existence of a liberal state, which is willing to support incremental, not radical, changes. She also raised a challenge for feminists, stating,

> They can support incremental change, retaining some hope of success but knowing their efforts are not adequate to the problem. Or they can support more comprehensive change whose time may never come. In the liberal state, the "good" usually triumphs over the "best," at least for a while.

Constructivist laws in education call for teacher training and retraining along gender lines[9], curriculum development and design of curricular materials, new or supplemental textbooks, dissemination of the new educational materials, and research to either identify new problems related to the experience of gender in schools and society or to assess the impact of the existing legislation. Clearly, constructivist legislation requires considerable financial resources. In contrast, through coercive legislation the state not only appears sympathetic, modern, and responsive but can obtain these perceptible benefits through very small investment.

PROMOTERS OF GENDER POLICIES
Carter (1988:65) observes that:

> Individual attempts to use the law without adequate organizational backing and in an unfavorable political and economic context can at best only result in limited successes. But the law can be a valuable instrument of change if well framed and enforced, if it is backed by political pressure and supplemented by positive action and general economic and social policies strengthening women's position.

A variety of social actors has emerged in support of gender issues in society in general and in education in particular. They include coalitions of NGOs (domestic and international) but also individual agents strategically located in state institutions (ministries and other agencies), bilateral and multilateral agencies, and universities. Also important sources of support have been sympathetic males in leading positions in international development agencies.

Feminists and NGOs
To introduce educational changes feminists have used two channels: (1) pressure on the state to bring about improvements in public, formal education, and (2) establishment and expansion of independent NGOs operated by women. Each channel offers different possibilities: the state is one of the most massive institutions in society and thus capable of affecting a large number of people, but it is reluctant to engage in substantially transformative action. Women NGOs tend to be much more transformative, but their work is conducted at the micropolitical level and is limited in geographical and numerical scope.

UNDP (1993:96) has noted that,

> Until the early 1980s, most NGO interventions were gender-blind, like those of other development agencies. Although there was always a small number of projects and programs assisting grassroots women's groups, the specific needs of women in general antipoverty programs were often ignored.

But in terms of gender-related transformative actions, it is widely accepted that women-run NGOs function as key agencies for any feminist social transformation (Deere and Leon 1987). Some observers of the actions carried out by women's groups coincide in assessing their work as conscious efforts to redefine and reconstitute boundaries between public and private and between political and personal spheres.

Among the women NGOs special mention must be made of groups of professional women with high levels of access to state decisionmaking. One such group is the Forum for African Women Educationalists (FAWE), a membership organization which brings together African women ministers of education, women vice chancellors of universities, and other senior women policy makers in education. Funded in 1992 as a nonprofit international NGO, FAWE seeks to promote investment in education in general and in girls' education in particular.

It is important to highlight some social class differences among women's groups. Most women NGOs tend to be run by middle-class women; on the other hand, there is significant action being carried out by low-income women in poor urban communities. These latter groups, involved in neighborhood movements, have struggled to obtain economic services such as housing, food, jobs, and education for their children. These efforts emerge from the women's collective interests and needs and address basically "practical needs" (Molyneux 1985; Radcliffe and Westwood 1993; Moulin and Pereira 1994). While these poor women have not rejected their domestic role, they have used it as a pivot to gain strength and legitimacy for their demands upon the state. There is evidence that in several cases these women have moved their domestic concerns into the public arena, redefining the meanings associated with domesticity to include participation and struggle (Safa 1990; Stromquist 1993b; Radcliffe and Westwood 1993; Schild 1994).

The Women's Environment and Development Organization (WEDO), a coalition of activists and academics in the feminist movement, held a special meeting in December 1994 attended by 148 women from 50 countries. As a result of the deliberations, WEDO initiated a 180-day "women's global campaign" designed to bring attention to gender issues and to develop a list of objectives, strategies, and actions. In its preamble, the document drafted at the meeting, stated:

In the closing years of the twentieth century, the international women's movement is bigger, more active, more inclusive and far reaching, more diverse across cultural, class, color, ethnic, age, sexual orientation, economic, ideological, religious, and geographic lines than ever before in history. It is also more creative, more analytic, more grounded in struggle, more knowledgeable about women's history and accomplishments, more politically experienced, more skilled and successful in organizing and more visionary about the kind of future we want for women and girls, men and boys, children and our living planet in the next century (WEDO 1994:1).

The demands expressed by WEDO are among the strongest and clearest in the international arena. WEDO targeted for change the UN Secretariat and the entire UN system. It sought to expand the mandate of the Commission on the Status of Women from the so-called "gender issues" to the large role of applying gender perspectives to all items on the UN agenda. WEDO also petitioned for an annual budget of $300-400 million for the United Development Fund for Women (UNIFEM) and the Institute for Research and Training for Women (INSTRAW), (which together were operating at about $16 million during 1995) by encouraging the reallocation of resources (WEDO 1994:9) and demanding more academics and NGO specialists to work with the UN Division for the Advancement of Women. Members of WEDO are convinced that changes along gender lines will require "continuing and greater access to the human and financial resources that the World Bank and UNDP possess to assure that gender equity is achieved and maintained" (WEDO 1994:9).

Examining the WEDO report, it is evident that there is a high level of political awareness among the participants in the women's movement. One indication of this awareness is the members' reluctance to endorse a "focus on specific areas of needs such as education of girls or employment." They fear this will result in "isolating such needs from the cluster of rights that will establish women's entitlements to services and programs. The indivisibility of rights is critical to the advancement and empowerment of women" (WEDO 1994:11).

Academic feminists (including men) have also played a significant role. Academics in the U.K., particularly, have conducted careful examinations of governmental policy as it relates to gender. Their analysis has been incisive, and they have argued that failure to intervene in sexual or racial conflict of schooling constitutes a "significant political act in favor of the current gender order" (Arnot 1993). In universities throughout the world but primarily in industrialized nations, women's studies have emerged, providing a richer and more diverse conception of culture and knowledge. In the U.S., it is estimated that over 600 women's studies programs exist. While it cannot be affirmed that these programs have influenced the rest of the curriculum, they have succeeded in attracting a good number of students to engage in more critical views of gender in society. It can only be surmised that the new generations will promote policies that are different from those in the past.

Men Leaders in International Development Organizations
Staudt (1985) maintains that gender policies are redistributive because they ultimately seek to reallocate resources between women and men. Gender policies imply altering deeply held values and ideologies, not only among recipients but within donor agency personnel. Over the past 10 years, international development agencies have grown more sensitive to women's concerns, created women's units in their organizations, funded important research, and designed better and more gender-sensitive projects (Stromquist 1994). Despite this significant progress, the majority of professionals in a sizable number of bilateral and international agencies are not eager to promote projects that will specifically benefit women. Given these conditions, the advocacy by the agencies' organizational leaders (who are primarily men) has been an important source for agency change.

Several men in leading positions in international organizations have expressed positions that have been highly supportive of gender issues. These people include Lawrence Summers who, while a chief economist at the World Bank, produced a much-quoted and influential paper entitled *Investing in All the People* (1992). Another man who has supported the cause of women is Jan Pronk, who, in September 1990, while serving as Dutch Minister for Foreign Affairs, presented to the Netherlands Parliament a white paper entitled *A World of Difference*. This document endorses autonomy as a central concept in the improvement of women's conditions in developing countries (The Netherlands Ministry of Foreign Affairs 1991)[10]. The status of these two individuals plus the fact that they were men themselves contributed substantial legitimacy to the notion of gender issues.

Women in International Development Agencies and Academia
Women's organizations have challenged not only the agenda of traditional politics but also the traditional *ways of doing politics*. These organizations have brought up the importance of daily life (Fisher 1993) and promoted training and education as a priority to help women with their lack of political experience. Although women have been making their demands for transformative action from outside the state (via their participation in NGOs), important changes have also taken place within. Bilateral and multilateral agencies have more gender specialists than 10 years ago and, in most cases, they have set up Women's Units (Stromquist 1994). The role of these women has been crucial in helping shape the gender policies of these agencies, though their contributions have not yet been the subjects of research studies.

Ironically, although schools and classrooms are widely accepted today as sites where culture and ideology are transmitted, imposed, and produced, feminist interventions to affect the content and experience of schooling have not been as strong or successful as needed. Anti-sexist knowledge, which not only attacks sexism and racism but also seeks to foster the creation of an alternative social order with modified conceptions of femininity and masculinity, difference, and power, has yet to be demanded in more systematic and massive ways. Many observers today consider that education is "a contested terrain between those who seek to use state supported schools as a means to discipline, control and exclude subordinate groups, and those who see education as a means to engaged democracy" (Weiler 1993:223). Yet this realization has been much more pronounced among progressive feminists in education than among feminists in other disciplines. As a whole, feminists still do not pay sufficient attention to the ideological role of the state and tend to concentrate on work-related issues (public and private) and other tangible problems such as childcare, health, and domestic violence.

CONCLUSIONS
Prevailing government policies—in education and other social domains—do not promote a process to alter power structures. Coercive policies facilitate distribution more than redistribution of

social goods because while they increase the representation of oppressed groups, they do not foster in them new social understandings and visions.

Three alternative hypotheses can be offered for the pattern of state behaviors that have been documented in this paper: One hypothesis builds on theories regarding the adoption and implementation of innovations and treats gender policies as an instance of significant organizational innovation. On the basis of a persuasive synthesis of research on the implementation of innovations, Fullan (1994) affirms that if the features of an innovation are unclear or the governments have a large number of incompetent bureaucrats who do not have the skills to implement the innovation in their system or do not have the technical knowledge to estimate the costs of the new practice, the attempted innovation will fail to be implemented (see also, Deble 1988; McDonnell and Elmore 1987). In reviewing the various gender policies, it appears that some clarity regarding the nature of the innovations may be in order, but the states' willingness to function mostly with coercive policies and to assign few resources for all types of gender policies suggests that this hypothesis does not fit reality.

A second hypothesis, using and extending the concepts of pluralism and interest group politics proposed by Dahl (1967), argues that states might not implement innovations if they do not face enough pressure to do so. From this perspective, it could be said that gender policies have emerged through the pressure of women's and feminist movements, but, though these actors have been able to exert pressure for the adoption of legislation, their subsequent leverage on questions of allocation of funds and monitoring of policy implementation has been weak. A social segment that could have served as a powerful promoter of gender policies in education—the teacher unions—has been absent in the efforts to create a gender-sensitive education via the policy arena. The few feminists in governments and those within the feminist movement have exhausted their energy at the policy enactment phase. This hypothesis does find support in the national cases we have reviewed.

A third hypothesis draws on feminist theories regarding the construction of the state as a male and patriarchal entity (Pateman 1988; Connell 1987) and the concept of legitimacy proposed by Habermas (1975). According to this hypothesis, the state does not consider gender issues a priority because they threaten both the status quo and its own hegemony. States seek to satisfy first the needs of the economy and then those derived from patriarchal ideology. However, because there is a contemporary crisis of legitimacy—with states in both industrialized and developing countries becoming increasingly contested and criticized—states must engage in democratic but relatively innocuous and symbolic action to show their responsiveness to all citizens (see also Edelman 1971). Since most gender policies do not question relations between women and men but treat gender as an "additive category" (Agarwal 1994), the basic social structures are retained. Contrary to the position taken by Gelb and Palley (1982) that states change slowly because they are liberal and prefer to engage in incremental change, it could be argued that states—liberal or not—change slowly because they are patriarchal and do not wish to alter a status quo beneficial to their interests. Nonetheless, several gender policies may be formulated, but there will be a clearly symbolic emphasis in their passage. As a result, implementation of policies is weakened by allocating limited funds and reducing these resources over time, by redefining legal intentions, or by claiming that the gender "problem" has been resolved.

This hypothesis is strongly validated by the analyses presented above. Education offers substantial symbolic returns to the state. By its very nature, education holds the promise of inclusion and distributive justice. As Weiler observes, education affords compensatory legitimation because it plays up the powerful symbols of legality, rationality, and democracy (1983). In the most advanced industrial states, there has been specific legislation on the condition of women's education; the main gender aspects, however, have been circumscribed to the low representation of women in nontraditional careers. But, as Yates (1993) incisively remarks, most women work in the service sector, a pattern that continues to operate uninterrupted. In developing countries the political agenda has been defined in terms of access to schooling, thus deferring more crucial objectives of social transformation. With few exceptions—mostly in countries with considerable female participation in the labor force—legislation on gender equity in education has been accompanied by minimal amounts of financial resources. The efforts carried out by women, however, have been crucial in introducing a new social agenda and in holding the state publicly responsible for responding to gender concerns. The symbolic terrain is a terrain where both state and feminists operate.

A corollary of this hypothesis is that controversial or weakly-supported policies will be less susceptive to contingency conditions than other policies. The reason for this relatively predictable trajectory is that policies that are controversial are those which tend to affect ingrained values and norms in society. Therefore opposition to them will be more widespread and likely to emerge at many points; in addition, the social regulatory aspects of state behaviors make these policies predictable. As Harding observes, in societies marked by race, ethnicity, class, gender, sexuality, and other markers, those in control "both organize and set limits on what persons who perform such activities can understand about themselves and the world around them" (Harding 1993:54). While the form and timing of this opposition may vary, the constant will be a tendency to defeat the intervention.

To conclude, it should be underscored that feminists must learn to see schools as part of the state rather than civil society. Schools represent much more the organized power of society than the perceptions and desires of groups at large. This position is crucial. From this vantage point, it must be asked, under what circumstance will state policy encourage the organization of women into autonomous organizations? This may not occur in the near future, but it should not stop initiatives by feminists. On the other hand, feminists should be wary of policies that by accommodating women to the status quo serve to reinforce patriarchal relations and the sexual division of labor.

NOTES

1. The available data do not permit clear comparisons. However, it could be argued that women have a lower level of representation in formal politics than in the formal economy sector, for there are 35 countries in which women represent more than 25 percent of those in administrative and managerial positions (1990 data) but only 28 countries in which women constitute more than 15 percent of the ministers and subministers and 25 countries where they represent at least 20 percent of parliamentary representatives (both 1994 data) (UN 1995:151-155).

2. It could be suggested that the fact that such data exist for only 33 countries in 1991, of which 22 were industrial countries (UNDP 1993:101), is indicative of the limited importance given to women in developing countries.

3. In examining various types of policy, McDonnell and Elmore (1987) propose a classification for state policies in general. This generic classification cannot be readily applied to gender equity policies, most of which should aim necessarily at systemic social change.

4. For a comparative study of educational policies in 13 industrialized and developing countries, see Sutherland and Baudoux (1994). For this study, I rely on primary data for all references to the U.S. (Stromquist 1993a) and on secondary data for the other countries. These countries offer a high degree of variability in the issues they cover, and, as a result, data are missing for several aspects.

5. The acts on vocational education were passed three times. Initially known as the Vocational Educational Act, the current version is called the Carl Perkins Vocational and Applied Technology Act of 1990.

6. Philosopher Stephen Toulmin calls the UN a "cartel of state governments" (1995:4), a powerful description that highlights the fact that certain states influence policy not only domestic but foreign despite rhetorical efforts to minimize "intervention" in other countries.

7. The various international efforts along gender lines have always been initiated by women's groups, generally in development (WID) networks within NGOs (Maguire 1984). The Convention for the Elimination of All Forms of Discrimination Against Women received strong support following the 1975 meeting in Mexico for the International Women's Year. The ideas contained in the convention had their origin in efforts by the Women's Commission in the Organization of American States in existence since the 1920s. The Fourth World Conference of Women (Beijing 1995) included, for the first time, delegations of young women, thus facilitating the creation of new generations of feminists.

8. The federal minister is supported by a department called the Status of Women Canada (SWC), which reports directly to her. Interestingly, this ministerial position has existed since 1971 and SWC since 1976.

9. Few teachers consider it their task to alter gender divisions. This should not be surprising in that teachers, as is true for the rest of the population, have been socialized along traditional conceptions of femininity and masculinity. Moreover, it has been found that male students present opposition to gender equality in the classroom. Studies about primary and secondary schooling show that boys demand more teacher time than girls (Carter 1988; AAUW 1992).

10. The positions by both Summers and Pronk borrowed from feminist contributions from their staff (in the case of the World Bank) and academics (in the case of the Netherlands).

REFERENCES

Agarwal, Bina. 1994. "Gender and Command over Property. A Critical Gap in Economic Analysis and Policy in South Asia." *World Development* 22:1455-1478.

American Association of University Women. 1992. *How Schools Shortchange Girls.* Washington, D.C.: American Association of University Women.

Arnot, Madeleine. 1993. "A Crisis in Patriarchy? British Feminist Educational Politics and State Regulation of Gender." Pp. 186-209 in *Feminism and Social Justice in Education: International Perspectives*, edited by M. Arnot and K. Weiler. London: The Falmer Press.

Baudoux, Claudine. 1994. "Politiques educatives et droits des femmes au Canada." Pp. 95-138 in *Femmes et education: Politiques nationales et variations internationales*, edited by M. Sutherland and C. Baudoux. Les Cahiers du LABRAPS, vol 13. Quebec: University of Laval.

Carter, April. 1988. *The Politics of Women's Rights.* London: Longman.

Connell, Robert. 1987. *Gender and Power.* Stanford, CA: Stanford University Press.

Connell, Robert. 1994. "The State, Gender, and Sexual Politics: Theory and Appraisal." Pp. 136-173 in *Power/Gender. Social Relations in Theory and Practice*, edited by H. L. Radtke and H. Stam. London: Sage Publications.

Dahl, Robert. 1967. *Pluralist Democracy in the United States: Conflict and Consent.* Chicago: Rand McNally.

David, Miriam. 1981. "Social Policy and Education: Towards a Political Economy of Schooling and Sexual Divisions." *British Journal of Sociology of Education* 2:115-127.

Deble, Isabelle. 1988. "Reflections on a Methodology for Integrating Women's Concerns Into Development Activities." Pp. 209-224 in *Women and Economic Development*, edited by K. Young. Paris: UNESCO and Berg Publishers Ltd.

Deem, Rosemary. Forthcoming. "Feminist Interventions in Schooling 1975-1990." In *Radical Education*, edited by D. Reader and A. Raffarsi. London: Lawrence and Wishat.

Deere, Diana, and Magdalena Leon (Eds.). 1987. *Rural Women and State Policy: Feminist Perspectives in Latin American Agricultural Development.* Boulder: Westview Press.

Edelman, Murray. 1971. *The Symbolic Uses of Politics.* Urbana: University of Illinois Press.

Eduards, Maud, Beatrice Halsaa, and Hege Skjeie. 1985. "Equality: How Equal Are Public Equity Policies in the Nordic Countries?" Pp. 134-159 in *Unfinished Democracy. Women in Nordic Politics*, edited by E. Haavio-Mannila et al. Oxford: Pergamon Press.

Feijoo, Maria del Carmen (Ed.). 1993. *Tiempo & espacio: Las luchas de las mujeres Latinoamericanas.* Buenos Aires: Comision Latinoamericana de Ciencias Sociales.

Feiner, Susan, and Bruce Roberts. 1990. "Hidden by the Invisible Hand: Neoclassical Economic Theory and the Textbook Treatment of Race and Gender," *Gender and Society* 4:159-181.

Fisher, Jo. 1993. *Out of the Shadows. Women, Resistance, and Politics in South America.* London: Latin American Bureau.

Fullan, Michael. 1994. "Implementation of Innovations." Pp. 2839-2847 in *The International Encyclopedia of Education* (2nd. Ed.), edited by T. Husen and T. N. Postlethwaite. Kidlington, Oxford: Elsevier Science Ltd.

Gelb, Joyce, and Marian Palley. 1982. *Women and Public Policies.* Princeton: Princeton University Press.

Habermas, Jurgen. 1975. *Legitimation Crisis.* Boston: Beacon Press.

Hall, Peter. 1995. "The Consequences of Qualitative Analysis for Sociological Theory: Beyond the Microlevel." *The Sociological Quarterly* 36:397-423.

Hall, Peter. In progress. "The Social Organization of the Policy Process: Linking Intentions, Actions, and Levels." Columbia, MO: University of Missouri.

Harding, Sandra. 1993. "Rethinking Standpoint Epistemology: What Is Strong Objectivity?" Pp. 49-82 in *Feminist Epistemologies,* edited by L. Alcoff and E. Potter. New York: Routledge.

Harman, Grant. 1984. "Conceptual and Theoretical Issues." Pp. 13-27 in *Educational Policy. An International Survey*, edited by J. H. Hough. London: Croom Helm.

Jayaweera, Swarna. 1994. National Policies for the Education of Girls and Women in Sri Lanka." Pp. 299-325 in *Femmes et education: Politiques nationales et variations internationales*, edited by M. Sutherland and C. Baudoux. Les Cahiers du LABRAPS, vol 13. Quebec: University of Laval.

Kelly, Gail. 1988. "Liberating Women's Education from Development. A Critique of the Women in Development Literature." Buffalo: State University of New York at Buffalo, mimeo.

King, Elizabeth, and Anne Hill (Eds.). 1993. *Women's Education in Developing Countries. Barriers, Benefits, and Policies*. Published for the World Bank. Baltimore and London: The Johns Hopkins University Press.

Leichter, Howard. 1979. *A Comparative Approach to Policy Analysis*. Cambridge: Cambridge University Press.

Maguire, Patricia. 1984. *Women in Development*. Amherst, Massachusetts: School of Education, University of Massachusetts.

McDonnell, Lorraine, and Richard Elmore. 1987. "Getting the Job Done: Alternative Policy Instruments." *Educational Evaluation and Policy Analysis* 9:133-153.

Meehan, Elizabeth, and Selma Sevenhuijsen. 1991. *Equality Politics and Gender*. London: Sage.

Miller, Francisca. 1991. *Latin American Women and the Search for Social Justice*. Hanover and London: University Press of New England.

Ministerio de Cultura y Educacion. 1992. *Programa nacional de promocion de la igualdad de oportunidades para la mujer en la area educativa*. Buenos Aires: Ministerio de Cultura y Educacion.

Molyneux, Maxine. 1985. "Mobilization without Emancipation? Women's Interests, State, and Revolution in Nicaragua." *Feminist Studies* 11:227-254.

Moulin, Nelly, and Isabel Pereira. 1994. "Neighborhood Associations and the Fight for Public Schooling in Rio de Janeiro State." Pp. 151-168 in *Education in Urban Areas. Cross-National Dimensions*, edited by N. P. Stromquist. Westport, CT: Praeger.

Nelson, Barbara. 1984. *Making an Issue of Child Abuse. Political Agenda Setting for Social Problems*. Chicago: The University of Chicago Press.

Nelson, Barbara, and Nancy Johnson. April, 1994. Agendas Politicas Feministas en los 90, *Mujeres en accion*, ISIS International, pp. 29-40.

Oszlak, Oscar. 1984. *Politicas publicas y regimenes politicos. Reflexiones a partir de algunas experiencias Latinoamericanas*. Buenos Aires: Estudios CEDES.

Pateman, Carole. 1988. *The Sexual Contract*. Stanford, CA: Stanford University Press.

Pronk, Jan. (1991). *A World of Difference*. The Hague: The Netherlands Ministry of Foreign Affairs.

Radcliffe, Sarah, and Sallie Westwood (Eds.). 1993. *Viva. Women and Popular Protest in Latin America*. New York: Routledge.

Safa, Helen. 1990. "Women's Social Movements in Latin America." *Gender and Society* 4:354-369.

Schild, Veronica. 1994. "Recasting 'Popular' Movements. Gender and Political Learning in Neighborhood Organizations in Chile." *Latin American Perspectives* 21:59-80.

Staudt, Kathleen. 1985. *Women, Foreign Assistance, and Advocacy Administration*. New York: Praeger.

Stromquist, Nelly. 1994. *Gender and Basic Education in International Development Cooperation*. New York: UNICEF.

Stromquist, Nelly. 1993a. "Sex-Equity Legislation in Education: The State as Promoter of Women's Rights." *Review of Educational Research* 63:379-407.

Stromquist, Nelly. 1993b. "The Political Experience of Women: Linking Micro- and Macro-Democracies," *La Educacion*, year 37, no. 116, III, pp. 341-559.

Summers, Lawrence. May 1992. *Investing in All the People*. Washington, D.C.: The World Bank.

Sutherland, Margaret. 1994. "National Policies for the Education of Girls and Women: The Situation in the United Kingdom." Pp. 397-430 in *Femmes et education: Politiques nationales et variations internationales*, edited by M. Sutherland and C. Baudoux. Les Cahiers du LABRAPS, vol 13. Quebec: University of Laval.

Sutherland, Margaret, and Claudine Baudoux (Eds.). 1994. *Femmes et education: Politiques nationales et variations internationales*. Les Cahiers du LABRAPS, vol. 13. Quebec: University of Laval.

Tomes, Hilary. 1985. "Women and Education." Pp. 73-83 in *The Invisible Decade. UK Women and the UN Decade 1976-1985*, edited by G. Ashworth and L. Bonnerjea. Aldershot, U.K.: Gower.

Toulmin, Stephen. 1995. "Wither the Nation-State?" *CMTS Newsletter*, vol. 1, no. 1.

United Nations. 1985. *The Nairobi Forward-Looking Strategies for the Advancement of Women*. New York: United Nations.

United Nations. 1991. *The World's Women 1970-1990. Trends and Statistics*. New York: United Nations.

United Nations. 1995. *The World's Women 1995. Trends and Statistics*. New York: United Nations.

United Nations Development Program. 1993. *Human Development Report 1993*. New York: United National Development Program.

Walby, Sylvia. 1990. *Theorizing Patriarchy*. Oxford: Basil Blackwell.

WEDO. December, 1994. "Women's Global Strategies Meeting." New York: Women's Environment and Development Organization, mimeo.

Weiler, Hans N. 1983. "West Germany: Educational Policy as Compensatory Legitimation." Pp. 33-54 in *Politics and Education: Cases from Eleven Nations*, edited by R. M. Thomas. Oxford: Pergamon Press, 1983.

Weiler, Kathleen. 1993. "Feminism and the Struggle for a Democratic Education: A View from the United States." Pp. 210-225 in *Feminism and Social Justice in Education: International Perspectives*, edited by M. Arnot and K. Weiler. London: The Falmer Press.

Yates, Lyn. 1993. "Feminism and Australian State Policy. Some Questions for the 1990s." Pp. 167-185 in *Feminism and Social Justice in Education: International Perspectives*, edited by M. Arnot and K. Weiler. London: The Falmer Press.

Young, Kate. 1988. "Introduction." Pp. 1-30 in *Women and Economic Development*, edited by K. Young. Paris: UNESCO and Berg Publishers Ltd.

CHAPTER 3

Undomesticated Gender Policy

Catherine Marshall

AIN'T I A WOMAN?[1]
That man over there say
a woman needs to be helped into carriages
Nobody ever helped me into carriages
or over mud puddles
or gives me the best place. . .
And ain't I a woman?
I have borne 13 children
and seen most all sold into slavery
That little man in black over there say
a woman can't have as much rights as a man
If the first woman God ever made
was strong enough to turn the world
upside down, all alone
Together women ought to be able to turn it
right side up again.

Sojourner Truth, 1797-1883

Sojourner Truth was misbehaving, defying the definitions of
propriety in her time, responding to the abolitionist preacher who
was telling the audience that the men had to assume leadership in
the movement. Such strong stands and challenges are necessary
when progress for reform is too constrained. In this chapter, I will
present a challenge to be like Sojourner, unladylike, anti-
organization, and even anti-professional, because to rethink policy
for gender equity in education is to defy dominant values and to
challenge organizational and professional assumptions that

support inequities. To be effective, the thinking and action for gender equity must include new coalitions and a range of actions, including some that are seemingly impractical, unnatural, mean, and outrageous--in the nature of political revolutions. For, as Audre Lorde (1984:112) said: "The master's tools will never dismantle the master's house." We need to be outrageous because of the intractability and invisibility of the problem of gender inequity and the constrained conceptualization of that problem.

THE DOMESTICATED NATURE OF GENDER POLICY

The dictionary says domesticated means "of or in the household (of animals), brought into subjection to or dependence on man. . .kept by man, household servant." We educators have been domesticated by having learned in schools how ladies behave and how good citizens work in a representative democracy. We have also learned in our professional socialization to accept the dominant view—the wisdom and advice of those in top positions in professional associations, bureaucracies, and politics—of what is fair and practical in policy and political action. So, proposals for tough, funded, and enforced policy to re-create schools to effect gender equity sound unreasonable, unable to get political support, not practical. Propose spending huge budgets for gender equity or passing enforceable mandates for gender equity training for school superintendents, and U.S. citizens and policymakers would say: "We can't do that."

The Policies, Programs, and Outcomes We (Don't) Want

If we wanted to create something that convened youth to help them develop, what would we create? Would we want to create competition, separation by gender? Would we establish formal and informal curricula telling boys and girls that white males are and should be center stage and that the public sphere (e.g. government and the marketplace) should be kept separate from the private concerns of family, emotion, values, and community? Would we want girls exposed to an unwritten curriculum of white male privilege? Would we set up schools with employment models and patterns of interactions that demonstrate that females should have lower pay and authority or that sexual harassment occurs just because "boys will be boys"? Would we support gender displays (Weis 1995:15) such as the adoration of the male body (sports) with the cutest females cheering on this adoration? Would 94 percent of the top leaders be men? Would we allow adults with low expectations for girls *near* this place?

Policy Efforts for Gender Equity
The women's movement and researchers concerned with sexism in schooling *have* supported some policy activity against gender inequities in the last third of the twentieth century. But their approaches—research, federal policies, and activism—have been constrained and had limited results (Stromquist 1993; Stromquist in this volume).

Research. Research has identified a range of problems connected to gender inequities and schooling. The simplest research described demographics and outcomes, such as the numbers of girls enrolled in advanced math. More complex research looked at interacting variables that contributed to these outcomes, documenting the problems and their glaring problematic outcomes: few women pursue careers in science or administration; girls' low self-esteem is connected to teen-age pregnancy; a chilly climate for women exists in higher education; there is a gender gap in incomes of male and female high school graduates; and so on.

Federal Policies. The central thrust of federal policies for gender equity was opening access to white male domains—a limited liberal agenda. Title IX *sounds* impressive but we still have only 6 percent of superintendents female, still have sexual harassment in schools, still have disproportionately high expenditures for football programs for boys, and unequal extracurricular programs in which girls can participate.

Importantly, Title IX was constrained by the 1984 Supreme Court decision in the case of *Grove City v. Bell*. The court ruled that Title IX regulations applied only to those school programs and activities directly funded by the federal government. If a particular program (e.g., student housing) was found to discriminate, only that program, not the institution, could be punished. In large part, this decision resulted from huge protests by those who were afraid of the possible horrors of unisex bathrooms or of actually having to fund athletics for girls at levels that matched boys' football and basketball—an "outrageous" idea!

Title IX has been ineffective because of its limited conceptualization and its lack of incentive, training, or enforcement mechanisms (e.g., ideas like quotas for achieving parity for women administrators were squashed; the idea of monitoring textbooks to eliminate sex stereotyping was met with an outcry for First Amendment freedom of expression). Policymakers eschewed any enforcement mechanism that forced states to implement gender equity, and states eschewed any mechanism that forced locals to do so. (U.S. education policy efforts often respect worshippers of the religion of localism, the assumption that local communities must not be dictated to by state or federal governments; see Wirt and Kirst 1992).

Twenty-five years after the enactment of Title IX, girls are still unable to gain attention for their sports achievements.[2] It took 20 years and a privately initiated lawsuit before schools were told that Title IX does oblige them to intervene to stop sexual harassment. More generally, in this 1992 case, *Franklin v. Gwinnett County Public Schools*, the Supreme Court ruled that districts could be held liable for monetary damages for Title IX violations. Prior to this decision, Title IX had no "teeth."

The Women's Educational Equity Act (WEEA) of 1974 left it to the initiative of states and localities to apply and compete for the assistance provided—grants and contracts to promote research; to develop and evaluate curricula, textbooks, other educational materials, and pre- and in-service programs for education personnel; and to support increased opportunities and guidance programs for adult women in vocational and physical education and educational administration. Its highest funding, for the entire U.S. educational system, was $10 million in 1981, but funding was down to $500,000 in 1992, a sum which covered only the WEEA Publishing Center. Its director was fired during the Reagan-Bush era. In addition, Klein (1988) reports that all federal funding for sex equity research declined from $28 million in 1980 to less than $13 million in 1987.

The Vocational Education Act (VEA) of 1976 required and funded a sex-equity coordinator in each state who reviewed vocational education programs for sex stereotypes and bias. The Carl Perkins Vocational Education Act of 1984 provided money to be set aside for programs to eliminate sex bias, with special attention to single parents and homemakers, to the tune of $27 million in 1987 and $60 million in 1988. Stromquist (1993:383) called it "the largest allocation of federal dollars specifically for the vocational training of girls and women in U.S. history."

Desegregation Assistance Centers and such have been in existence for a long time with limited effect (Stromquist 1993). Other national initiatives, such as the Office for Civil Rights, Affirmative Action, required individual complainants to file, wait—often years, meanwhile to be labelled as troublemakers—and to have their case managed by an understaffed agency which spent more time on race equity and which, at one point, was managed by the likes of Clarence Thomas.

Activism. Finally, women's professional, volunteer, and political activism supported gender equity: special caucuses of the American Association of School Administrators (AASA) with Effie Jones collecting data on women's status, Task Forces and Commissions for Women, American Association of University Women (AAUW)[3] publications and scholarships, and lobbying by the Women's Political Caucus, League of Women Voters, National Women's Law Center, etc. Among these lobbying groups, however, educational equity was not given as high a priority as, for example, child care, feminization of poverty, and freedom of choice. Safety and minimal quality-of-life issues were considered first, before education. One exception is the 1992 AAUW report *How Schools Shortchange Girls*, perhaps the most comprehensive review, partisan analysis, and advocacy document for gender equity in schooling that has yet appeared.

Policy Contexts

The gender policies of the 1970s were enacted in a national policy culture that *was* taking initiative for equity, especially for minorities. However, Congress initially resisted the idea of adding a ban on sex discrimination to the 1964 Civil Rights bill. In their analysis of this resistance, Fishel and Pottker (1977:137) point out that "the most striking aspect of congressional behavior concerning women in education has been the superficiality of the interest expressed." The Equal Rights Amendment (ERA) was not ratified by the states so there is no constitutional basis for protecting women. Courts' interpretations in sex discrimination cases do not apply strict scrutiny. This means that plaintiffs who claim sex discrimination or unfair barriers on account of sex must find their own funding and find ways to prove the existence of discrimination and the intent to discriminate. The burden falls on the victim who also risks backlash and being labelled as a troublemaker, ruining her future access and setting her up for retribution. Class action lawsuits have been a partial answer.

Sports—the aggressive male domain—got lots of attention in debates about Title IX. The American dream/myth has been that underprivileged boys can rise out of the ghetto to be superstars (like Mike Tyson and O. J. Simpson), and football and basketball are great money-makers. So, the thought of disrupting this system for girls' equity through Title IX has drawn great resistance. Still, there's been a 600 percent rise in access to sports for female athletes (though not commensurate scholarships). In 1973 women got 1 percent of sports-scholarship money; in 1981, 22 percent. Unfortunately, when more money became available for coaching female sports, men got the jobs (Stromquist 1993).

The national policy culture of the 1980s focused on education but not on equity (Clark and Astuto 1986). The wave-making educational reform documents of the 80s commanded that national and state attention be paid to improving schools' performance. The National Commission on Excellence in Education (1983) did not mention girls at risk in *A Nation at Risk,* and except for a few scholars and non-mainstream (malestream) researchers and policy bureaucrats (such as Glazer 1991; Klein 1988; Sadker, Sadker, and Steindam 1989; Tetrault and Schmuck 1985), *nobody noticed.* Sadker and her colleagues (1989) surveyed educators and found that when asked whether or not the reform movement had increased female equity, many did not know. More than half said "no" when asked if the reform movement had increased female academic achievement, interest in math and science, entrance into educational administration, participation in sports, and retention in school.

Finally, the conceptualization of gender issues was constrained by a focus on letting girls into male domains. The policy culture did not countenance interventions to alter the patterns in schooling that reproduce inequitable gender relations. Nor did the policy culture countenance interventions that reconceptualized gender constructions, redefined family life, or revalued women's work. Gender and power relations in the workplace and personal relationships—the deeper assumptions undergirding gender issues—were not on the policy agenda.

Outcomes and Evaluations
Evaluations and research on the efficacy of gender equity policies over the last 20 years are scarce. Stromquist (1993) reports mixed results concerning degree programs: The percentages of females in higher education have risen (although completion rates for advanced degrees are still lower for females than for males). The rise in women's completion rates, compared to men's, is especially dramatic at the Ph.D. level, going from 16 percent to 36 percent. Women are now more than 50 percent of the masters' and doctoral students in educational administration. Feminist and women's studies programs offer about 30,000 courses in U.S. universities. Although these programs have been ghettoized on some campuses, they have also gained strength because of the growing emphasis on cultural diversity.

Title IX and VEA helped to reduce career stereotypes by eliminating the practice among medical and engineering schools of limiting admissions of females to 10 percent of total admissions. After Title IX, schools couldn't expel pregnant girls or force them into special programs. But only a few schools have done anything more than to stop the formal exclusion, such as creating constructive programs. AAUW found girls were still victims of discriminatory treatment. VEA's efficacy has been highly dependent on the ability and resourcefulness of the state sex equity coordinator and the state's interest in the law. Finally, curricula were not reorganized to incorporate realities of women's lives as they are affected by their fertility and childrearing.

The AAUW (1992) called gender issues "the evaded curriculum" in their review of pre- and in-service education training for teachers (Stromquist 1993). The few training programs that exist have been mostly volunteer efforts with no federal support. Contributions of women educators were not mentioned; most educational administration students never hear about Mary Parker Follett or Ella Flagg-Young, important figures influencing theory and policy for administration. There's still plentiful evidence of classroom practices that are unfair to girls in terms of attention, remediation, acceptance, praise, and criticism. An AAUW (1992:62) review of research concluded that "although sexism has decreased in some elementary texts, the problems persist, especially at the secondary level, in terms of what is considered important enough to study."

The feminist movement and Title IX inspired some local textbook review committees, and some big textbook publishers created sex equity guidelines—primarily in response to market forces (state adoption practices), not to policy. Title IX addressed curriculum indirectly and refrained from dictating a suitable curriculum content. So, changes have been voluntary and spotty. Meager WEEA funding helped, and it has funded 700 projects, but as Stromquist (1993:388) said, "in a universe of 50 state educational agencies, 15,500 public school districts, and 10,000 postsecondary institutions, this is no more than a drop of water."[4]

New Initiatives

Federal policy-making in 1994-95 demonstrates some effort to make gender equity real. Even though many programs were subsumed under block grants—giving states leeway in how, or whether, they address gender equity—strong efforts were made to earmark a percentage of the vocational education block grant for sex equity and displaced homemaker programs and to make vocational programs accountable for meeting the needs of girls and women (AAUW 1995). Many of these efforts failed. Furthermore, during passage of the reauthorization of the Elementary and Secondary Education Act (ESEA), some "musts" were turned into "mays"; so Congress is allowing, not mandating, gender equity. In their memorandum reporting on federal funding for educational equity, the National Coalition for Women and Girls in Education (NCWGE) report that "the equity provisions *don't* mandate specific activities in states and schools. In most cases, they *allow*, but do not require, ESEA-funded programs to have components to advance equity" (NCWGE 1995:1). Thus, 1994-95 was a year of good news and bad news.[5]

Personal Reflections on Gender Policy

A few vignettes from my own experiences from the 1960s to the present as teacher, university student, and professor provide historical illustrations of the limitations of gender equity policies:

- In 1975, as a teacher, I tried to champion a girl for the baseball team, using Title IX, but a) there were no Title IX guidelines (which took years to develop); and b) the girl's mother stopped it because she did not want to cause problems for her family due to Title IX requirements that the victim must do the enforcement and, therefore, fears reprisals.

- In graduate school, there were full-support scholarships for Chicanos but none for women, so, the various inequities had different weights.

- In my twenty-one years as an education professional I have always been employed in workplaces with an employment model whose informal curriculum lesson taught that men lead and women support. Whether as a teacher in South Kingstown, RI, a graduate and postdoctoral student at the University of California, Santa Barbara, and UCLA, respectively, or a professor at the University of Pennsylvania, Vanderbilt, or UNC-Chapel Hill, I have never had a female "boss." I have a store of memories of micropolitical interactions that enforced the assumption that men are in charge and this is as it should be.

- In applying for WEEA funds in 1982 to support women in education administration, I encountered guidelines demanding that any grant proposal demonstrate how the program would equally benefit men.

- I served as a consultant in a class action suit against Los Angeles schools that resulted in a consent decree, in 1980, mandating quotas, but the decree was not enforced.

- I served as an expert witness when an individual sued her employer, the Connecticut teacher union. She lost because she was unable to prove that her lobbying abilities and advanced degrees made her better qualified than the man who got the promotion *and* that there was discriminatory intent.

- I watched as Assistant Secretary for Education Diane Ravitch declared in 1993, in response to the AAUW report on sex equity in education, that there is no longer an issue—it's been taken care of.

● I was sexually harassed by someone in authority over me in my first year as an assistant professor. Like Anita Hill, who was protecting her career by not blowing the whistle (sexual harassment had not even been defined), I had to reshape my self-esteem and survival strategies. Both Anita and I knew that naming it as harassment, articulating how it violated our sense of self and made us small, and naming our perpetrator would hurt our careers, and we would not be saved by federal policies.

● When a young woman was gang-raped at a University of Pennsylvania fraternity, the men involved were given community service as a punishment. The woman had to deal with people saying it's her fault because she went to that party and was drinking. The men, presumably, got their Ivy League degrees; the woman dropped out of school. The president and provost of the university who managed this outcome have gone on to top positions in foundations and government. In the same year, I was told by well-intended senior professors in my field that I was hurting my career by talking so openly about gender issues.

● I was told, in a conference about research agenda with a 1992 National Association of Secondary School Principals (NASSP) Task Force on Assistant Principals: "Our board can't grapple with gender equity yet--race, urban issues, yes, but not gender." I found that of the millions of tax dollars spent compiling statistics on education, the federal government does not even collect statistics on the number of female administrators.

● I learned that the law did not protect me against my department chair yelling and threatening me, taking away my research assistants, and giving credit for my work to male colleagues—this would not stand up in court as sex discrimination. Additionally, if I fought it, I would spend a lot of money and time and get next to nothing in damages, and I would have to endure a barrage of accusations mounted by a well-funded university defense.

So, over the years, I watched how schools' laws, rules, and practices reinforced men's opportunities and set women's as a low priority. If female educators did similar reviews of their personal experiences with gender equity, they might abandon their ladylike domestication.

EXPLAINING THE DOMESTICATION OF GENDER POLICY
Several themes that provide explanations for policy developments in the U.S. are discussed in this section of the chapter.

Legitimated Silencing
Apple (1994:353) says, "It is . . . crucial to locate the 'silences'—the 'absent presences'—in all school messages." Females' silences, falterings, and exclusions are treated as non-events—sort of the way things are, and certainly not something that overburdened educators can be expected to stop. Our assumptions have been constructed in such a way that we do not even *notice* certain silenced "marginal" issues, and those assumptions handicap and limit our policy. We barely notice when teachers say things like "take it like a man" or "Ms. Green, if you became principal, do you really think you could handle those crowds at the basketball games?" or when a social studies teacher says: "Let's skip the section on women's rights, they have too many rights already" (Weis 1995:11).

We treat these scenes as non-events or non-issues. The often-invisible ways in which social interaction is structured, power wielded, and privileged interests protected are "social constructions (that) are so tightly legitimated that certain questions are unaskable and certain phenomena remain unobservable making persistent dilemmas of schools' part in racism, classism, sexism, poverty perpetuation into non-issues and non-events" (Anderson 1990:42). School administrators' legitimacy depends upon their promotion of social constructions, myths, and unexamined assumptions supportive of social Darwinism, meritocracy, Anglo-uniformity, and scientific management. Blackmore and Kenway (1993:9) assert that schools "have, over time, developed certain knowledges, policies and practices, rules and regulations, and ultimately certain patterns of power which have systematically structured unequal relationships," and this has become a "gender order," a gender regime that is so naturalized and institutionalized that it is not to be questioned or challenged. The dominant paradigm in administrative theory assumes that conflict is bad and must be repressed and controlled, but women's perspectives, needs, and rights are conflict-producing; they *do* challenge the dominant group, and they *do* cause trouble.

Lack of Intent

"Equity" policies give only the *perception* that schools are doing something, but these policies are flawed in fundamental ways: (1) they rely on the current system for enforcement, a system primarily run by and for the benefit of an elite of privileged white males; (2) they are translated, blunted, opportunistically adopted, and coopted by street-level bureaucrats (Weatherly and Lipsky 1977) in loosely coupled systems (Weick 1976) according to their values, with little to no accountability or evaluation; (3) they fail to take account of the existence of class stratification and racial inequities and the ways that these inequities are intricately tied to gender structuring.

No policies are countenanced if they might threaten the privileges and comforts of the dominants. Furthermore, research dissemination, and utilization of research findings depend upon funding and support of political institutions. Policies and programs depend upon the good will of white males such as those in Congress or in the superintendency. We cannot assume that the social and political institutions constructed with male assumptions and male power can be tools for creating equity. When gender equity policies conflict with and challenge a sacred institution or "constitutional" assumptions (both in the literal sense of the American Constitution and in Sarason's (1982) definition of practices that are so embedded as to become unquestionable), those gender policies are readily compromised. Minogue (1983:73) said, "Nothing gets done which is unacceptable to dominant or influential political groups, which may be defined to include the 'bureaucratic leadership group'." There has been a serious problem with weak enforcement of all federal civil rights laws, including Title IX; these laws have never worked well for women in education (Council of Chief State School Officers, Resource Center on Educational Equity 1993).

If the mention of elite, privileged white males running our institutions seems extreme, recall the outcomes of the Anita Hill/Clarence Thomas[6] and Tailhook[7] incidents. The chilling messages are that the Senate will manage the interpretation of sexual harassment (Anita Hill) and the Armed Forces will try to repress women's voices (Tailhook).

Limited Theories and Facts Used in Policy Formulations

The dominant paradigm provides legitimacy for only liberal feminist agenda, constrains the policy options, and allows only domesticated, controlled policies. Curricular assumptions are not challenged. Nowhere in the curriculum are students exposed to gendered issues related to the home. When the domestic/private sphere is discussed, as in the social sciences, the perspective is androcentric, and "the private sphere is simply a place for men to go back to" (Weis 1995:13) after political and military events. With the continuation of the structure whereby teachers (women) are controlled and monitored by administrators (men), "there is no valorization of an active female voice" (Weis 1995:16); so, when women speak, or take leadership, it is only with the sponsorship of males (Marshall 1992; Marshall 1995; Ortiz and Marshall 1988). Research in Australia, England, and the U.S. (see Eder in this volume) reveals that boys label girls as "sluts, period bags, big tits, dogs, AIDS"; that boys' sex talk involves attacking girls and "(g)etting what they want and then throwing her away" (Weis 1995:17); and that "good girls" are passive. Despite such findings, research and policy for the elimination of sexual harassment is *not* a major issue on education reform agenda.

Gender policies have gained legitimacy and support only when couched in liberal feminism which recognizes inequities and aims to fix them by promoting equal access to men's spheres and by small fixes of the system. U.S. policies have not countenanced other feminisms that acknowledge "women's ways" or the political and power issues.

"Women's ways" or cultural feminism recognizes that women are different from men and that the dominant and valued ways of being, doing, acting, choosing, valuing, talking have been male oriented. So, separate, special programs for women should be supported; assumptions about gender should be questioned; and women's ways of knowing, talking, and so forth should be re-valued (Dietz 1992).

Power-and-politics feminisms would do away with current structures and policies because, as MacKinnon (1989:170) said: "Male power is systemic, coercive, legitimized and epistemic; it is the regime." Revolution and new ways of conceptualizing rights, government, and organizational life must be constructed because male power is so built into the existing regime. And, as Kathy Ferguson (1984:174) said, "Those who own the means of enunciation are in a position to appropriate the dominant truth claims for their own purposes."[8] The reins of power and control are imbedded with assumptions about the cultural value of men, that "men's ways" are the more valuable. As shown by Faludi (1991) and Steinem (1994), feminist challengers are undermined by backlash and manipulation by conservatives, religion, the media, and the cigarette, beer, make-up, and fashion industries. For those pioneers who seek to challenge and redefine assumptions while working within the system, the reward is expulsion. Witness Joycelyn Elders[9] with her frank talk about sex education.

So, limited thinking and sexist assumptions go unquestioned and are built into policies. Our solutions to 14-year-old mothers living on welfare and having more babies are policies to punish the girls. Is it not interesting that, in the midst of all the rhetoric, we fail to define policies that would focus on the males involved? Is it not interesting that the Department of Education has not bothered to collect statistics on the percentages of women in educational administration (Bell and Chase 1993)? This is limited thinking.

TOWARD MORE REVOLUTIONARY THINKING AND ACTION

What if critical and feminist scholars are correct in saying that schools do more than just reflect society; that schools "contribute actively to inequalities by gender" (Weis 1995:4); that they play an important function in reinforcing and reifying sexism; and that they do nothing to interrupt patriarchy. What if Weis (1995) is correct in saying that the gendered patriarchy of schools encourages the production of the following societal outcomes: 1) Spousal and child abuse (most of the victims are female), which is not seen as a problem, like math scores, to be addressed by our schools; 2) Women's disadvantaged work in the paid labor force which is at lower pay and in less favorable conditions (less autonomy and fewer benefits) than men's; 3) The feminization of poverty resulting from the combination of single parenting, women's inequality in the job market, and lack of child care; and 4) Women's working of a "double day" by performing paid work in the public sphere and then performing unpaid domestic work in the private sphere?[10]

We know that the problems produced by patriarchy have not been solved. Not in my experience. Not in the experience of women who hit the glass ceiling nor of those who exercise leadership in other than male-normed ways. And, not in the experiences of girls who learn better in work groups than in competition. What do we do? How do we get out of this fundamentally flawed policy activity? How do we get beyond preaching to the choir? The fact of male hegemony—the political/power systems embedded in the culture and the exclusion of women—*has to be included as a visible part* of all discussions of change in practice and in theory, not just in footnotes and not just in three-day conferences for the deficient! It cannot remain an area of silence.

The last sections of this chapter focus on the political problem and, given the limits of current thinking, the need for political revolution. Thomas Kuhn (1970:93) said, "Political revolutions aim to change political institutions in ways that those institutions themselves prohibit." To get action requires a new kind of thinking about the issue: a re-framing. The current way of thinking still allows people to be blind to the facts, to blame the victim (deficit model), to exclude and use excuses like, "well, male faculty just won't listen to a woman." New *collective* activity by a critical mass of activist educators must challenge masculinist assumptions. We have to do more than research and develop new learning technologies—strategies that are mostly liberal and thus safe and domesticated. We have to devise better strategies than those that leave all the work on women's shoulders and that keep gender equity as a marginal non-issue, not worthy of pulling away important people to pay attention, take time, and invest in change.

Recall the theme from Audre Lorde's (1984:112) provocative quote: The master's tools will never dismantle the master's house." First, we have to look at how the master's tools are designed to work best for the master. One of the tools is defining and controlling what makes an idea unreasonable, impractical, or irrational. Remember, "Those who own the means of enunciation are in a position to appropriate the dominant truth claims for their own purposes" (Ferguson 1984:174). Our knowledge is controlled and managed, and if we slip out of the dominant paradigm and veer from the preferred and legitimated truths about what's good, practical, useful, feasible policy, we are labeled as crazy, incompetent, non-tenurable, and so forth. Remember that the reins of power and control—the political institutions from the U.S. Senate, to the local school, to the unstated rules about who has the right to initiate policy action, to articulate values, to speak assertively or authoritatively[11]—were set up with imbedded assumptions about the cultural value of men's ways, which were assumed to be correct and legitimate. The power to enunciate the truths about women's needs, women's values, and the worth of women's ways of thinking, learning, caring, relating, talking were appropriated by those in power, *and those institutions have not changed.*

New Theoretical Tools
Promising and emerging theory and analysis can radically alter thinking about schools, leadership, values, and women.

Insights from Power-and-Politics Feminisms. Feminist theory holds promise for new thinking about the problem and the deeper, more fundamental changes needed to eliminate gender inequities. The exclusion of women's voices and values (Ferguson 1984) fosters policy and practices that clear out emotion, connection, allowance for special needs and, concurrently, separate the private and public spheres of people's lives. MacKinnon (1989) shows how white, propertied males as the formulators, the managers, and the beneficiaries of the political and the legal system prevent governments from reconceptualizing child support enforcement, sexual harassment, and gun control. MacKinnon (1989:242) posits that any meaningful approach to sex equality must grasp "women's reality from the inside, developing its specificities, facing the intractability and pervasiveness of male power."

Power-and-politics feminisms show that liberal policy has recognized that our institutions have treated women and men differently but has failed to notice the power, dominance, and oppression that aligns with the gender difference. The problem is not just that girls have not had equal access to science careers; the problem is also a complex system whereby schools support boys for careers that get them power and money. The problem is not just that girls learn passivity and their lower place in the societal strata by seeing female educators being controlled by men; the problem is also how that gender identity supports sex abusers whose victims are mostly women. Apple (1994:350) said it well: "We must always think political when we think educational." Power-and-politics feminisms provide that needed political insight and calls for a feminist theory of the State, a fundamental re-thinking by laying "demands on the state that may be difficult to dodge without putting legitimacy at risk" (Connell 1990:533). Franzway (quoted in Connell 1990:531) has shown how the involvement of the state is unavoidable, saying "the question is not whether feminism will deal with the state but how, on what terms, with what tactics, toward what goals." Such theoretical development must account for the fact that "the state is simultaneously classed, gendered, and raced" (Apple 1994:357) but will provide a basis for jumping over the theoretical and political dead ends in gender equity.

Insights from Women's Ways Feminisms. "Women's ways" feminisms suggest revaluing for educational policy, goals, structures, and leaders. Schools should be conceived of as collaborative, non-competitive places that teach teamwork and community building and that emphasize the responsibilities kids should experience for everyone's development, not just for their own. The insights of Noddings (1984) and Gilligan (1982) imply that the incorporation of women's voices, philosophies, and personal and professional perspectives in the formulation of missions, policy goals, practice, and theory in education would demand an ethic of care that emphasizes alternative and inclusive models of leadership that build relationships and connections among leaders, teachers, families, and communities. Gilligan's (1982) important challenge posits that women's moral decision-making is attuned to community, relationship maintenance, and nurturance—seeking ways to make sure everyone is okay—whereas men's moral decision-making is more attuned to issues of competing rights and to principles of justice. Noddings (1984, 1992) challenges us to structure educational organizations to be places where the dominant value is caring, where caring relationships are facilitated, where everyone understands that the nurturance of young children and adults is the main mission, and where showing concern and connectedness is more important than efficiency and, yes, even SAT scores.[12] She makes her case easily when citing statistics on violence, adolescent drug use, suicide. She posits that women have been doing the nurturance and connecting work of families and organizations all along *in spite of* organizational goals and leadership models.

The three C's of care, concern, and connection spoken of by Jane Roland Martin (1994) as values basic to moral leadership for schools and the critical humanist leader (Foster 1986) are reconceptualizations of leadership theory to incorporate feminist leadership. Regan (1990) asserted that the vertical structure of education organizations demands a competitive mode which allows some to attain high positions of command, control, and status. But a whole different world exists "inhabited primarily by women, people of color, and low-status white males. Its organization is horizontal and collaborative . . . . This is where caring, nurturing, relationship, and community building happen" (Regan 1990:568). Further, "womanism"—a form of feminism that recognizes the ways race, class, and gender are interwoven and are all reinforced by schools' acceptance of a patriarchy that excludes and devalues the private sphere and reifies class, race, and gender separations (Robinson 1995)—joins together minorities and majority women in reconceptualizing school values.

Feminist Critical Policy Analysis. Making connections among feminist analysis, policy analysis, and critical theory provides a new kind of analysis: feminist critical policy analysis (see Marshall and Anderson 1995; Marshall 1997). In brief, it starts with the critical theorists' determination to ferret out how our institutions are set up to benefit an elite and keep non-elites domesticated and useful to them, adds the radical feminist notion that our institutions are set up in ways that use sex as a key classification and privilege white males while oppressing females, and adds the focus of critical policy analysis on the micro- and macropolitical processes at work with their intended and unintended consequences.

Theorizing Government Responsibility. Finally, a theoretical leap, indeed a paradigm shift, is needed to generate effective moves for gender equity through schooling. The tragedies, injustices, and wasteful consequences of sexism justify forceful government policy statements, such as the National Policy for Gender Equity in

Australia, which can be used as a strong framework buttressing court, professional, and personal action. In the U.S., the federal government and courts have a major role to play in establishing equity policies (and the push to end racial segregation in education is an example—albeit an imperfect one—of the use of federal and court tools). To do so means putting aside states' rights, religions of localism, sacred traditions that benefitted dominants, and redistributing power, benefits, and costs. Such shifts would support policies and programs that are openly anti-sexist, that promote government intervention and positive discrimination to correct systemic inequities. Getting the tragic and wasteful consequences of gender inequities on the national agenda is a challenge, however, in a nation still worrying about whether Hillary Clinton likes to bake cookies, a nation where the analyses of "at-risk" children do not include mention of gender issues.

This section has discussed some theoretical bases for very different policies and programs for gender equity. The next sections describe some possible actions, from moderate to radical, that may make a difference and contribute to this needed leap.

Policy Proposals and Political Actions: The Safe and Domesticated Ones

Without being deceived that this will solve the fundamental structural and institutional issues, educators can focus on identifying what works, in small ways, in the current systems. The proposals in this section are a collection of ideas compiled from past, present and possible actions, programs, and policies. They are based mostly on the author's knowledge of gender equity initiatives in the U.S. and Australia but also rely on her imagination.

1. Identify and collaborate with pro-feminist men, giving credit and helping to make good intentions become concrete actions (see Marshall, Koch, Pearce, and Baroni 1996).

2. Develop in-depth programs for pre- and in-service teacher training focusing on feminist pedagogy, collaborative learning, gender-responsible leadership. One class, one book chapter, or one two-hour workshop will not do. Use existing programs like Gender/Ethnic Expectations and Student Achievement (GESA) that provide the kind of training for teachers in math and science that helps them learn modes of instruction that are sensitive to the needs

of historically underrepresented students and that make math and science accessible to all students.[13]

3. Use the Women's Educational Equity Act Publishing Center[14] with its 20 years of gender-equity publications on such topics as the education of women in Native America, female dropouts, creating sex-fair family day care, and sex equity in sports leadership.

4. Piggyback on popular, "legitimate" policy issues and mechanisms. For example, in Queensland, Australia, feminist policymakers have used policymakers' desire to stop domestic abuse and violence against women to legitimate the development by the state education department of an anti-sexism curriculum for grades K-3. In the same Australian state, the strong thrust in the state education department to create a "Quality Assurance" process is being used as a mechanism to get schools to inspect gender equity, along with literacy and numeracy achievements.

5. Use the "Barbara Jordan strategy": get into the system and use the system to beat the system. Even when one of her colleagues always referred to her as "the nigger mammy washerwoman," she used her rhetorical skills, equivalent to those of James Earl Jones, to state her faith in the Con-sti-tu-tion, ignoring that it originally would not have given her, as a black and/or as a woman, the vote, ignoring that she was called "the white folks' black woman" (Ivins 1994).

6. Borrow ideas from the Australian femocrats, the feminists who got themselves in positions in bureaus and government agencies so they could shape the rules, regulations and resources for programs that affect women. Part of the strength of gender policy in Australian schools comes from its emergence in alliances among women educators, the teachers unions, and parent groups. U.S. policy would be strengthened by alliances between women educators and other women's rights groups, ranging from AAUW to the National Organization for Women, that focus on political pressure for gender equity in schools.

7. Use Ferguson's (1984:119) strategy of "confrontation from within." Ferguson's characterization is very different from Kanter's (1977) "office wife." Ferguson (1984:118) uses the term "mad dogs" in the blue collar world for the workers who oppose management. Those who confront from within are seen as rebels or misfits, fighters, wild persons, or perhaps as intellectuals. Such persons often

have some outside source of income, and they scorn "bullshit conferences" where management calls in the workers to "talk out problems" in an encounter group setting.

8. Establish an Institute for Retraining the Professorate for all education professors, funded by foundations and professional associations (Marshall and Rusch 1995). Push our professional associations, to which we pay dues, and foundations to create and fund new processes and structures, such as women's training and support programs (like Bridges[15] and Bryn Mawr College/HERS Mid-America Summer Institute for Women in Higher Education Administration[16]). Create an annual national conference of practitioners, researchers, and policymakers to expand the thinking on schooling and women's opportunities for personal, political, and economic success and to make gender equity happen in schools. (In Australia, such a conference was funded by the national government and seen as a critical support for networking, policy strategy, and shared insights.)

9. Use approaches that "add women and stir," such as Emily's List, a systematic effort to collect funds to support women candidates for political office. Get women to contribute to women's campaigns and leadership candidacy, so we'll have more women in politics and bureaucratic and administrative leadership. Create a movement to encourage women to write wills leaving their wealth to school programs that focus attention on female achievements, rights, and leadership.

10. Nurture female strength and leadership by creating charter schools, private schools like the one in Toronto that openly states a feminist agenda in its charter, or publicly funded girls-only feminist schools like two in South Australia. (According to one Australian femocrat, the feminist vision and pedagogy in one of these schools was so successful at fostering freedom of expression and self-worth that the girls were "out of control"! Undomesticated indeed!) Or, create consciousness-raising experiences for girls and women in schools to get beyond the systemic silencing surrounding gender inequities. Or, create and fund programs for girls that confer rewards, attractiveness, leadership, teamwork and collaborative experiences just as sports do for boys.

11. In curriculum changes, "add and stir women" into history books but include many kinds of women and also integrate the private and public. Clearly identify the Susan B. Anthonys, Eleanor

Roosevelts, Gloria Steinems, and Sandra Day O'Connors as women who had educational, class, and racial advantages and used them to make a difference in the current system. But then demonstrate how private, domestic, emotional roles affect women's appearance in the male-dominated public spheres. Then add the *more rebellious* women, the Margaret Sangers and Rosa Parkses who defied the American system and its laws; the *leaders* who brought gender issues into the political arena and redefined those issues, as did Sojourner Truth, Jane Addams, and Mary Lyons, who founded Mt. Holyoke College as an institution especially for women; and the *rebel rabblerousers*, such as Angela Davis, Carrie Chapman Catt, Rosa Luxembourg, and Emma Goldman. Young women should be exposed to the possibility that Goldman's anarchism could be an appropriate response to an oppressive capitalist system; that a Mt. Holyoke symbolizes the possibility that women's intellect and leadership can be best nurtured when men are absent.[17]

12. Find ways to expand the gender equity agenda to incorporate political, social, economic, labor market, family, personal safety, emotional and life choice issues. For example, literature and history curricula should integrate the "private sphere," including the herstory of the unnoticed pioneers who, by bearing children and making the homelife, became the foremothers of our country—an area totally neglected when knowledge is defined as the male and public sphere. Schoolchildren should learn that the pioneer women took risks far greater than women and girls do now; so, when they are afraid to look weird by speaking out or by enjoying math or "men's work" or by wanting to start a school for feminists, they will have actual role models. Similarly, they should know that women's literature is not just sheltered Emily Dickinson writing poems but also *Women Who Run with the Wolves*, a recapturing of legends of strong, terrible, wild, witchy women who give girls rowdy role models and an understanding of the ways in which history and literature have been contorted to focus on men's values and accomplishments. Girls should also be exposed to novels such as *The Color Purple* so that they learn that race, class, and gender issues are not just about the right to vote but also about the right to be safe, to have independence and pride, and to own your own body.

13. Create safe places in schools for females: playground times, clubs, and sports free of harassment and judgments of males. Create

women-only forums for consciousness-raising, coping with sexism and barriers to opportunity, and political strategizing.

More Outrageous Policy Action

Some strategies and policies may sound outrageous, wasteful, radical and downright mean. But these can garner needed attention.

1. Start vigilante networking, like the Magic Marker Terrorists, Brown University female students who disseminated lists of males who sexually harass women. Such action starts a shared conversation with graffiti on bathroom stalls *naming* men who assault or otherwise mistreat women when Brown's punishment of such men was to send them home for a few weeks for psychiatric examination.

2. Make certification, valuation, and promotion of teachers and administrators dependent on their ability to intensely monitor gender inequities and their willingness to punish boy students with suspension, loss of driver's license, expulsion from the football team for bad behavior toward girls. To those who say, "You can't do that," use this rationale: If school officials can figure out the intricate rules of football and can hire and put into uniforms the squads of highly motivated referees needed to make sure football players obey the rules on the field, then school officials can also figure out ways to monitor sexist, discriminatory, harassing behavior. All that is required is the desire to do it.

3. Include among requirements for all professional, university, and state certification, hiring, staff development, and promotion that educators demonstrate—by portfolio, assessment center, and so forth—their knowledge of and behavior for gender equity *and* their results. Put bans or probation on new educators who cannot *do* gender equity.

4. Impose fines on individuals in top positions in school districts and university programs who do not show gender equity *outcomes*, that is, results among professional staff and students.

5. Declare invalid any school boards or state departments of education without 50 percent or more women, thus *forcing* gender equity where education policy and regulations are made. *Or* require, for every election for political and professional policy positions in education, that there be a position which must be filled by a woman (similar to the platform of the fledgling Women's Party in Australia).

6. Move quickly to create an employment model in schooling in which women hold at least 50 percent of leadership positions. Freeze hiring of males until the proportion of women among school leaders parallels the proportion of women in the teaching pool. Label school districts with male-dominated hierarchies "deficient" or "delinquent."

Making Fun of the Gender Order

Educators can gather momentum and solidarity while having fun through more radical but safe kinds of rebellion such as the following small ways of upsetting the gender order.

1. Feminist fun and subtle rebellion: Collect stories of safe and camaraderie-building strength and rebellion. Just as slaves used to sing melodious songs to make the overseer think they were happy in their work even though they were singing songs of escape and rebellion, so too women, by quiet and funny and subtle acts, can convey a sense that, while they are not in charge, they have good intentions of putting something over on those who keep control. Let your eyes meet across the table at a meeting; use nicknames such as "little Napoleon" and "the boy dean," to cite the more temperate examples.

2. Ridicule: Deny respect to and point out the illogic of sexist rules and of people who presume male superiority and oppress women. For example, when the sports commission told the former chair of the Oklahoma City School Board that girls' half-court basketball helped girls because it gave more girls access to the team, she recommended that boys have that same chance at half-court rules (knowing full well that such rules ruin any chance at the "big-time" in boys *or* girls basketball).

3. Use silly toys that upset the traditions and norms of bureaucracy, professionalism, and deference. Keep on your desk the fighting nun puppet or carry squirt guns to meetings as symbolic threats against sexist assumptions.

Going Feral: Being Unladylike, Disrupting, Unprofessional, Unreasonable, Outrageous

History demonstrates that change of deep-seated cultural assumptions may require radical action. Upsetting the gender regime may require something more action oriented than just rethinking and new theory, new curricula, and more policy. Recall Sojourner Truth, who saw through the myths sustained by patriarchy that require "good behavior," and glean inspiration from the radical feminist methods of our foremothers. Emmaline Pankhurst went farther, and a British newspaper (quoted in MacKenzie 1975) described the tactics of the radical suffragist:

> A series of attacks on golf links was instituted . . . with the direct and very practical object of reminding the full and self-satisfied English public that when the liberties of English women were being stolen from them was not the time to think of sports. The women selected country clubs where prominent Liberal politicians were wont to take their weekend pleasures, and with acids they burned great patches of turf, rendering the golf greens useless for the time being. They burned the words: "Votes for women."

Our feminist foremothers knew that such political activity required risk and getting your hands dirty. Here are a few quotes on risk-taking and its difficulties taken from MacKenzie (1975) and *Quotable Women* (1989):

> "You must do the thing you think you cannot do."--Eleanor Roosevelt
> "It is hard to fight an enemy who has outposts in your head."--Sally Kempton
> "And the trouble is, if you don't risk anything you risk even more."--Erica Jong

NOTES

1. There is no exact copy of this speech that was given at the Women's Rights Convention in Akron, Ohio, in 1852. The speech has been adapted to poetic format by Erlene Stetson from the copy found in Fauset (1938). These passages are selected excerpts from Stetson's original adaptation.

2. The University of North Carolina (UNC) women's basketball team won the national championship in 1994 with far less fanfare than when the men's team won in 1993. The virtually unnoticed UNC women's soccer team has won 11 of the past 12 national championships.

3. For information, contact the American Association of University Women at 1111 16th Street N.W., Washington, DC, 20036-4873; (202) 785-7700.

4. WEEA did produce some 130 products—videotapes, curriculum guides, training modules, etc.--but only three of its publications have sold more than 5,000 copies.

5. Recent new legislative moves worth watching, according to AAUW (1994) and Klein and Ortman (1994), include (1) the Gender Equity in Education Act (H.R. 1793) and Improving America's School Act (HR 6); (2) the evaluation of gender equity policies that will be conducted by the Office of Women's Equity in the Department of Education; (3) the Reauthorization of the Elementary and Secondary Education Act in 1994 which included the following provisions: the Women's Educational Equity Act Program is authorized to expend $3.9 million for model programs, research, and promotion of gender equity; the Department of Education will have a Special Assistant for Gender Equity; Title I and Title II funds for professional development must include strategies for meeting underrepresented, diverse, and minority student needs, which could include females in math and science; absence of sexual harassment is included as an element in the definition of "safe schools" grants; dropout prevention funds may be spent for pregnant and parenting teens; and school data that are collected must be disaggregated by sex.

6. In 1991, law school professor Anita Hill testified before the Senate Judiciary Committee at confirmation hearings for Clarence Thomas's appointment as a Supreme Court Justice. She reported that he sexually harassed her while they were co-workers at the Equal Employment Opportunity Commission (EEOC). In spite of Hill's testimony, Thomas was subsequently appointed to serve on the United States Supreme Court.

7. In October 1991, women navy personnel, many of them officers, reported being groped and grabbed as they were pushed along a gauntlet of intoxicated pilots in the hallway of a Las Vegas hotel at the annual Tailhook conference. High-ranking naval officers unsuccessfully attempted to cover up the women's reports of sexual harassment.

8. Think of how policy for higher education could be influenced by "expertise": In 1873, Harvard professor Edward Clark warned that medical theories proved that higher education would cause women's uteruses to atrophy. G. Stanley Hall, reviewing thirty years of medical testimonies, went a step further to claim education would cause women to lose their mammary functions. R.R. Coleman, a medical doctor, unleashed his opprobrium (quoted in Ehrenreich and English 1978:115): "Women beware. You are on the brink of destruction . . . you are attempting to cultivate your mind . . . Beware! Science pronounces that the woman who studies is lost."

9. Dr. Elders was fired as Surgeon General by the Clinton administration in December 1994 for suggesting at an international health conference that masturbation should be discussed in sex education classes as part of an effort to prevent teen-age pregnancies and the spread of AIDS and other sexually transmitted diseases.

10. Women's "double day" is enforced by women's inability to break through "the domestic code," the assumption that the private sphere—from child rearing, laundry, cooking, and cleaning to family emotional support—is women's work.

11. See Marshall, Mitchell, and Wirt (1989) and Marshall and Mitchell (1991) for discussions about assumptive worlds in macro- and micropolitical policymaking.

12. Marshall, Rogers, Steele, and Patterson (1996) posit that this caring dimension in administration is not uniquely female but it is filtered out as administrators climb up the administrative career ladder.

13. GESA is funded by a grant awarded to the University of North Carolina at Greensboro (UNC-G) by the National Science Foundation through the UNC Math and Science Network. Project Directors are Dr. George Bright and Dr. Brenda Woodruff who may be contacted at the School of Education, UNC-G, Greensboro, NC 27412.

14. For information, contact the Women's Educational Equity Act Publishing Center, Educational Developmental Center, 55 Chapel Street, Suite 200, Newton, MA 02158; (800) 225-3088.

15. For information, contact Rachel M. Davies, Program Coordinator, The University of North Carolina at Chapel Hill, Division of Continuing Education, Campus Box 1020, The Friday Center, Chapel Hill, NC 27599-1020; (919) 962-3000.

16. For information, contact Dr. Cynthia Secor, Director, HERS Mid-America, University of Denver, Colorado Women's College Campus, Denver, CO 80220; (303) 871-6832.

17. A good resource for recapturing this history is the Wellesley Center for Research on Women, 106 Central Street, Wellesley, MA 02181; (617) 283-2503.

REFERENCES

American Association of University Women (AAUW). 1994. *Elementary and Secondary Education Act: Summary of Gender Equity Provisions.* Washington, DC : Author.

American Association of University Women (AAUW). 1995. "Title IX Enforcement Hearing." *Action Alert* 15(6):3.

Anderson, Gary L. 1990. "Toward a Critical Constructivist Approach to School Administration: Invisibility, Legitimation, and the Study of Non-Events." *Educational Administration Quarterly* 26(1):38-59.

Apple, Michael. 1994. "Text and Context: The State and Gender in Educational Policy." *Curriculum Inquiry* 24(3):349-359.

Bell, Colleen, and Susan Chase. 1993. "The Underrepresentation of Women in School Leadership." Pp. 141-154 in *The New Politics of Race and Gender,* edited by C. Marshall. London: Falmer Press.

Blackmore, Jill, and Jane Kenway (Eds.). 1993. *Gender Matters in Educational Administration and Policy.* London: Falmer.

Clark, David L., and Terry A. Astuto. 1986. "The Significance and Permanence of Changes in Federal Education Policy." *Educational Researcher* 15(8):4-13.

Connell, Robert W. 1990. "The State, Gender, and Sexual Politics." *Theory and Society* 19:507-544.

Council of Chief State School Officers, Resource Center on Educational Equity. 1993. "The Continuing Struggle for Female Leadership in Education: Partial Analysis and Recommendations." *Concerns,* November, 1993:1-8.

Dietz, Mary. 1992. "Context Is All: Feminism and Theories of Citizenship." Pp. 63-85 in *Dimensions of Radical Democracy: Pluralism, Citizenship, Community,* edited by C. Mouffe. London: Verso.

Ehrenreich, Barbara, and Diedre English. 1978. *For Her Own Good: 150 Years of Experts' Advice.* Garden City, NY: Anchor Press.

Faludi, Susan. 1991. *Backlash: The Undeclared War Against American Women.* New York: Crown Press.

Fauset, Arthus Huff. 1938. *Sojourner, God's Faithful Pilgrim.* Chapel Hill: University of North Carolina Press.

Ferguson, Kathy E. 1984. *The Feminist Case against Bureaucracy.* Philadelphia: Temple University Press.

Fishel, Andrew, and Janice Pottker. 1977. *National Politics and Sex Discrimination in Education.* Lexington, MA: D.C. Heath.

Foster, William. 1986. *Paradigms and Promises: New Approaches to Educational Administration*. Buffalo, NY: Prometheus Books.

Gilligan, Carol. 1982. *In a Different Voice: Psychological Theory and Women's Development*. Cambridge, Mass: Harvard University Press.

Glazer, Judith S. 1991. "Feminism and Professionalism in Teaching and Educational Administration." *Educational Administration Quarterly* 27(3):321-342.

Ivins, Molly. 1994. "'First-and-Only' Follow Barbara Jordan." *Raleigh News and Observer*, August 11, 1994:15.

Kanter, Rosabeth Moss. 1977. *Men and Women of the Corporation*. New York: Basic Books.

Klein, Susan. 1988. "Using Sex Equity Research to Improve Educational Policies." *Theory into Practice* 2(2):152-160.

Klein, Susan, and Patricia E. Ortman. 1994. "Continuing the Journey Toward Gender Equity." *Educational Researcher* 23(8):13-21.

Kuhn, Thomas S. 1970. *The Structure of Scientific Revolutions*. 2nd ed. Chicago: University of Chicago Press.

Lorde, Audre. 1984. *Sister Outsider*. Freedom, GA: Crossing Press.

MacKenzie, Midge. 1975. *Shoulder to Shoulder*. New York: Knopf.

MacKinnon, Catherine A. 1989. *Toward a Feminist Theory of the State*. Cambridge, MA: Harvard University Press.

Marshall, Catherine. 1992. "School Administrators' Values: A Focus on Atypicals." *Educational Administration Quarterly* 28(3):368-386.

Marshall, Catherine. 1995. "Imagining Leadership." *Educational Administration Quarterly* 31(3):484-492.

Marshall, Catherine (Ed.). 1997. *Dismantling the Master's House: Feminist Critical Policy Analysis*. London: Falmer Press.

Marshall, Catherine, and Gary L. Anderson. 1995. "Rethinking the Private and Public Spheres: Feminist and Cultural Studies Perspectives on the Politics of Education." Pp. 169-182 in *The Study of Educational Politics*, edited by J. Scribner and D. Layton. London: Falmer Press.

Marshall, Catherine, Megan Koch, Kim Pearce, and Jill Baroni. 1996. *Will Men Help? Pro-Feminist Men in Universities*. Chapel Hill: University of North Carolina. Unpublished.

Marshall, Catherine, and Barbara A. Mitchell. 1991. "The Assumptive Worlds of Fledgling Administrators." *Education and Urban Society* 23(4):396-415.

Marshall, Catherine, Douglas Mitchell, and Frederick Wirt. 1989. *Culture and Education Policy in the American States*. London: Falmer Press.

Marshall, Catherine, Dwight Rogers, Jean Steele, and Jean Patterson. 1996. "Caring as Career: An Alternative Perspective for Educational Administration." *Educational Administration Quarterly* 32(2):271-294.

Marshall, Catherine, and Edith Rusch. 1995. "Gender Filters." Pp. 79-94 in *Gender and Changing Educational Management*, edited by B. Limerick and R. Lingard. Rylamere, NSW, Australia: Hodder Education Press.

Martin, Jane Roland. 1994. *Changing the Educational Landscape: Philosophy, Women and Curriculum*. New York: Routledge.

Minogue, Martin. 1983. "Theory and Practice in Public Policy and Administration." *Policy and Politics* 11(1):63-85.

National Coalition for Women and Girls in Education (NCWGE). 1995. *Memorandum: Federal Funding Available for Educational Equity Efforts.* Washington, D.C.: Author.

National Commission on Excellence in Education. 1983. *A Nation At Risk: The Imperatives for Educational Reform.* Washington, DC: U.S. Department of Education.

Noddings, Nel. 1984. *Caring.* New York: Teachers College Press.

Noddings, Nel. 1992. *The Challenge to Care in Schools: An Alternative Approach to Education.* New York: Teachers College Press.

Ortiz, Flora Ida, and Catherine Marshall. 1988. "Women in Educational Administration." Pp. 123-141 in *Handbook of Research on Educational Administration,* edited by N. J. Boyan. New York: Longman.

Quotable Women: A Collection of Shared Thoughts. 1989. Philadelphia: The Running Press.

Regan, Helen B. 1990. "Not for Women Only: School Administration as a Feminist Activity." *Teachers College Record* 91(4):565-577.

Robinson, Lori S. 1995. "A Feminist Vision." *Emerge,* March, 1995:20-23.

Sadker, Myra, David Sadker, and Sharon Steindam. 1989. "Gender Equity and Educational Reform." *Educational Leadership* 46(6):44-47.

Sarason, Seymour B. 1982. *The Culture of the School and the Problem of Change.* 2nd ed. Boston: Allyn & Bacon.

Steinem, Gloria. 1994. *Moving Beyond Words.* New York: Simon & Schuster.

Stromquist, Nelly P. 1993. "Sex-Equity Legislation in Education: The State as Promoter of Women's Rights." *Review of Educational Research* 63(4):379-407.

Tetrault, Mary Kay, and Patricia Schmuck. 1985. "Equity, Educational Reform and Gender." *Issues in Education* 3(1):45-67.

Weatherly, Richard, and Michael Lipsky. 1977. "Street-Level Bureaucrats and Institutional Innovation: Implementing Special-Education Reform." *Harvard Educational Review* 47(2):171-197.

Weick, Karl E. 1976. "Educational Organizations as Loosely Coupled Systems." *Administrative Science Quarterly* 21:1-18.

Weis, Lois. 1995. "Gender and the Reports: The Case of the Missing Piece." Pp. 173-192 in *Commission Reports, Reforms, and Educational Policy,* edited by M. Ginsberg and M. Plank. Greenwood, CT: Praeger Publishers.

Wirt, Frederick M., and Michael W. Kirst. 1992. *Schools in Conflict.* 3rd ed. Berkeley, CA: McCutchan.

CHAPTER 4

Sexual Aggression within the School Culture

Donna Eder[1]

We have an increasingly serious problem within our schools—the problem of sexual aggression. It is not an entirely new problem but one that is escalating in terms of frequency and intensity. Many more girls today report being the victims of some form of sexual aggression by male peers, and recent studies of sexual harassment in public schools indicate that this is a growing problem in all regions of the country and in many different types of communities.

In this chapter I will examine some of the sources of sexual aggression within the school culture. This does not mean that there aren't additional sources outside of this culture. MTV, video games, and current movies also have been found to convey themes of sexual aggression. But since schools are supported by public funds and attendance is mandatory, it is critical that we examine those sources that are within the school culture.

This essay is part of a larger study of gender and adolescent school culture (Eder, Evans, and Parker 1995). One of the goals of that project was to move beyond the study of gender differences to a focus on gendered practices, a concept first promoted by Connell and his colleagues (Kessler, Ashenden, Connell, and Dowsett 1985; Connell, Ashenden, Kessler, and Dowsett 1982; Connell 1987.) While studies of gender differences often imply more similarity within gender groups than actually exists, a focus on gendered practices helps us better understand the systematic processes through which both girls and boys are socialized to have distinct concerns, values, and styles of acting.

The work by Connell and his colleagues in Australian secondary schools was some of the first to show that masculinity as well as femininity is socially constructed through athletics and other routine practices. While masculinity and femininity often took on multiple forms within a single school, one form was most predominant and valued. Even in upper-class schools, the most predominant form of masculinity focused on aggressiveness and stemmed largely from participation in athletics. Football in particular was intended to develop masculinity by using physical strength to demonstrate and test one's superiority over others.

More recently, researchers have begun to investigate the formation and perpetuation of gender inequality within the school peer culture. Thorne (1993) found that as early as elementary school, boys use sexual insults and approach relations with girls in a daring, aggressive manner. In high school, Lees (1993) shows how girls are controlled by a double standard, defining active male sexuality as normal and active female sexuality as deviant. This control often occurs through negative labels such as "slut" and "whore," which define girls primarily by their sexual reputation.

The widespread nature of sexual harassment by peers has been identified by other researchers. Larkin (1994) studied girls in four Canadian high schools and found that sexual harassment was so pervasive that most girls had come to accept it as a natural part of school life. The girls in her study initially had some difficulty recalling specific incidents because they were so routine but gradually came to realize that these negative experiences were part of a widespread problem that included verbal and visual forms of harassment as well as physical forms such as having their buttocks and chests grabbed or touched. The verbal forms consisted largely of labels implying that females are inferior to males ("baby," "chick," "fucking broad," "bitch," and "bimbo"), while the visual forms included being shown pornography, having to witness crude sexual behaviors, and intrusive gaze.

In a larger study of American girls, Stein (1993) found that sexual harassment is a frequent occurrence in elementary and secondary schools across the country, in small towns and large cities alike. It included having clothing lifted up or pulled down, personalized graffiti, sexualized taunts and skits, as well as physical contact, including sexual assaults and rape. Most girls in her study reported having few effective strategies for dealing with this harassment. Also, because of the lack of response from adults, many girls had become resigned to sexual harassment as part of school life.

The most systematic study of sexual harassment in the United States is a nationwide survey conducted by the AAUW. In a later analysis of these data, Lee and her colleagues (Lee, Croninger, Linn, and Chen 1995) found that girls were more likely than boys to have experienced some type of sexual harassment in school which bothered or upset them (83 percent versus 60 percent) and were more likely than boys to have experienced more severe forms of harassment. Almost all of the students who were harassed (96 percent) identified peers as one of the sources of this harassment. Sexual harassment was defined as unwanted sexual behaviors which interfered with their lives and included sexual comments, spreading sexual rumors, gay and lesbian labels, being touched in a sexual way, having clothing pulled off or down, and being forced to kiss or perform other sexual acts.

In this study we attempted to understand the formation and perpetuation of gender inequality in schools by focusing on two types of gendered activities, extracurricular activities such as athletics and common speech routines. The latter focus was influenced by Goffman (1974), Corsaro (1992), and Lees (1993) who have identified the importance of routine speech activities such as insulting and story-telling as essential components of the socialization process. Since these routines occur on almost a daily basis they tend to be taken-for-granted practices which are seldom reflected upon. Instead, the gender messages conveyed through some of these routines lead many to think that these are natural aspects of being male or female.

Language routines are also worth studying because they involve opportunities for modifying and producing new aspects of peer culture (Corsaro and Eder 1990; 1994.) Corsaro (1988; 1992) has shown this to be true for children as young as three and four, who have their own distinct peer cultures, with their own interpretations and embellishments. While boys are not using speech routines to challenge gender messages as often as girls, both girls and boys could be encouraged to make wider use of the creative potential in informal talk (Eder, Evans, and Parker 1995).

This essay is based on a larger study in which we attempted to understand the structure and uses of the most common forms of informal talk in a middle school, including gossip and teasing as well as insulting and story-telling (Eder 1990; Eder 1991; Eder and

Enke 1991). We also attempted to understand both male and female peer cultures from their own perspectives before taking on the more difficult subject of gender inequality (Eder 1985; Eder and Parker 1987; Parker 1991; Eder, Evans, and Parker 1995). While some aspects of this inequality were evident in our field notes from the beginning, we felt that it was essential to first understand the nature of aggression and toughness in boys' interactions with each other before trying to understand the nature of sexual aggression in interactions with girls.

A TEAM ETHNOGRAPHY APPROACH TO SCHOOL CULTURE

A middle school was chosen as the setting for this study since this is a crucial age for both gender socialization and the development of orientations toward male-female relations. In selecting a school for this study I wanted to find a school that would be typical of other schools in the Midwest and that had a range of social class backgrounds, including working- and lower-class students. While the students at the school were predominantly Euro-American, they came from rural homes as well as urban ones. The school itself offered a limited number of extracurricular activities for students during and after school. Both girls and boys could choose up to four different athletic activities and participate in a range of instrumental and choral activities. In addition, girls had an option to try out for the cheerleading squad. This range of extra-curricular activities is typical of middle and junior high schools in the Midwest.

Since it was also essential to study groups that represented the full range of social statuses and social class backgrounds in the school, our approach became one of a team ethnography with three female researchers and one male. Initially our goal was to balance the greater amount of research already done on adolescent boys by studying a wide range of female groups. Then we discovered the importance of studying males as well as females if we were to adequately examine gendered practices within the school. One of the researchers, Stephanie Sanford, left the study after the first year, while Steve Parker and Catherine Evans both continued on to help analyze the data. This paper draws heavily on data collected by Steve in all male peer groups.

We were never asked to assume roles of authority in the setting and joined groups as any new student would have to without relying on introductions from adults. Instead, we relied on our associations with students through extracurricular activities, clubs outside of school, and contacts through students to gain entry into various peer groups. This meant that some of our first days in the field were painful as we sought entry into informal groups. I couldn't gain immediate entry into an eighth grade group given the tight cliques at that level and even put in my field notes that they were stuck up. But on my second attempt several weeks later, a girl I knew from volleyball approached me and said, "What are you doing sitting by yourself; come sit with me."

When we met students, we introduced ourselves by telling them we were from Indiana University or simply "from IU" and that we were interested in doing a study to find out what they liked to talk about and what their interests were. I told them that I would be coming to lunch on a regular basis for the entire year and that someday I might write a book about what I found out. Most students were somewhat flattered that we had chosen their school to study, and many were excited by the idea of a book. However, some students never quite understood why we were so interested in their lives. Halfway through the year one eighth grader turned to me and said, "I still don't understand why you come to eat lunch with us when you could be eating lunch with college boys."

Altogether we ended up studying 15 groups during the three years that we were in the field—nine female groups, five male groups, and one mixed-gender group. All four researchers observed lunch time interaction at least twice weekly for periods of time ranging from five to twelve months. We adopted roles of quiet group members and never took notes openly in the setting. Instead we recorded them immediately upon leaving the setting and, later in the study, we brought audio-tape recorders and eventually a video-recorder to record some of the lunchtime conversations.

During the data collection period, our research team met regularly to share information about what we were observing as well as to compare interpretations of key events and activities. It was particularly important to have both "insider" and "outsider" perspectives on gender-related behavior. For example, Steve was not at all surprised by the coaches' behavior during practices or by the boys' aggressive style at lunch, believing that he was finding "nothing new." However, all of the females on the project were surprised by the high degree of aggressiveness promoted by both the coaches and adolescent males, viewing it as a strong contrast to our own experiences as adolescent females as well as a contrast to most of the girls in the study. At the same time, Steve was not only able to develop a strong rapport with the male students, but he also provided important interpretations of ritual insulting from his perspective as a male. (For more information on methodology see Eder, Evans, and Parker 1995).

THE DEVELOPMENT OF AGGRESSIVE MASCULINITY

In this school, learning how to be male was closely tied with learning how to be more aggressive. It was evident from Steve's field notes, that certain school-sponsored activities placed a strong emphasis on the value of being aggressive. The message promoted in all of the male sports, and especially in wrestling and football, was one of winning at all costs. This included the importance of being aggressive, tough, and willing to physically hurt one's opponent. Particularly aggressive acts such as throwing someone down on the concrete or humiliating an opponent during a wrestling match met with coach and team member approval. The promotion of aggressive behavior was often explicitly tied to players' sense of being masculine in traditional ways as in this example:

> During the drills Coach Adams emphasized being meaner than they had been before. He said that he wanted animals but that he had a bunch of "nice boys." When he said "nice boys," he paused and softened his voice. [Steve's notes]

Homosexual labels and feminine labels were also applied by both the coaches and fellow players to boys who weren't viewed as being tough enough. For example, several boys agreed that one of their team mates was "turning into a fag" because he didn't want to get hit in practice anymore. Another boy was called a "big pussy" because he was unwilling to stay in a football game after he broke his finger. These labels helped to reinforce the sense that being tough and aggressive was an important part of being masculine.

The focus on aggression in sports increased its salience throughout much of the informal peer culture in this school, largely because the high-status boys in the school were all athletes.

Other boys were often targets of this aggression, either in the form of verbal insults and ridicule or in the form of physical attacks. Typically, if a boy failed to treat the initial insult as non-serious by responding in a playful or ritual manner, the insult exchange was likely to escalate into a more ruthless form of insulting.

A little later on in lunch, Phil was called a vasectomy girl, a V.G., and then that was changed to a valley girl and then back to a vasectomy girl again. He took this very personally and when it was done, he stood up and acted like he was going to be aggressive to whoever called him that. Jeff, Don, and Denny all took turns. They were somewhat scared of him in that they feared being hit by him, but at the same time, they were laughing and trying to keep their distance so that they could call him these names. [Steve's notes]

These boys were able to come up with certain labels that caused Phil to loose his cool and respond aggressively rather than playfully. The fact that all of these labels were potential threats to Phil's masculinity and especially to his masculine sexuality suggests that this is an area in which adolescent boys' insecurity can be easily tapped.

Given that the messages to be aggressive were often closely tied to one's masculinity, it is not surprising that the aggressive orientation learned in other contexts carried over into boys' newly formed relationships with girls. There is some evidence that boys did not hold an impersonal or aggressive stance initially and in fact were somewhat sensitive to the appropriate atmosphere for having sexual relations. However, the pressures within the peer culture to appear to be sexually competitive and aggressive often transformed these initial sensitivities into a much more impersonal orientation toward girls as seen from these notes.

Sam was acting as a messenger from Hank to the girls. They wanted him to come down to their group but he didn't want to. Joe told Hank that he was crazy not to; that she [Cindy] might want to fuck him on the other side of the school. Hank said he [Joe] was stupid; that wasn't going to happen and that nothing was going to happen. He added that it might if they were alone, but not with everyone around. Someone said that he didn't know how and didn't even want to fuck her. Hank got mad and said, "I'll fuck her anytime—right here, right now, anytime, anyplace." [Steve's notes]

At first Hank indicates that the public setting of the school is not realistic for sexual intercourse. However, after someone challenges him regarding his sexual abilities and interests, he moves to a much more impersonal and aggressive stance regarding sexuality, where timing and location become irrelevant. Since Hank has developed a reputation for being tough and competitive, it is not surprising that he responds so strongly when accused of lacking sexual knowledge and interest. It is likely that Hank's reaction is based largely on fear of losing status among his peers. It could also reflect an underlying insecurity in this new arena of sexual performance. At any rate, the sensitivity which Hank initially demonstrated is replaced with a much more impersonal stance toward sexuality where the feelings of girls are disregarded in the attempt to demonstrate one's sexual abilities.

One form which sexual rivalry took involved competitive insulting regarding the appearance of each other's girlfriends. In these competitions, even the most popular girls in the school were found to have serious appearance flaws, while other girls were accused of looking like sluts or whores.

Hank pointed toward the parking lot and said, "There's Kim. She's nasty." Eric said that she wasn't and that he thought she looked good. Hank said no, she piles all that makeup on and looks like a whore. He kept repeating "a whore" while Eric tried to tell me and/or Hank that she wasn't. During all this time Joe was going from our group back to the group of girls. Now he came up and lay down on top of the wall. He said, "Ah, it's just lust, just lust." Eric said that's why Joe was after Tammy. Joe said he was right and Hank said, "She's got a great body, but a nasty face." [Steve's notes]

Conversations such as this reinforce boys' tendency to objectify girls, judging them on superficial criteria and promoting a view of them as sexual objects rather than sexual actors. However, while girls are often expected to be sexual objects, it is important that they not draw *too* much attention to their sexuality. Furthermore, the few girls that were reported to actually make sexual advances toward boys received one of the most negative labels, that of "bitch."

Another way in which sexual rivalries were carried out was through defending one's "sexual property." While it was not acceptable for girls to make any sexual advances, the rivalry orientation made it acceptable for boys to make sexual advances towards other boys' girlfriends as well as their own as shown in this next episode:

> Perry and Richard walked over behind Tammy, and Perry acted like he was grabbing her bottom. Richard went ahead and actually did it. She turned around, but didn't retaliate in any way. They came back over to the table and retold what had happened. The point they stressed was that Carl (who was going with Tammy) was standing there when they grabbed her. After Richard grabbed her, Carl took a step toward Richard and said his name. Richard stuck his chest forward and said, "What?" Carl just backed down. Consensus was that Carl was a pussy. [Steve's notes]

Even though Carl makes some initial attempt to defend his girlfriend from unwelcome sexual advances, he is criticized for not continuing to stand up to a possible confrontation with Richard. However, no criticism is raised toward Richard for making a sexual advance towards someone else's girlfriend. Episodes such as this serve to reinforce a view that boys can and should be sexually aggressive and promiscuous. Girls, on the other hand, are expected to be sexually passive and monogamous. Furthermore their rights can be violated as part of these displays of masculine rivalry.

As boys become more and more concerned with displaying an aggressive, active sexuality in front of other boys, girls are often caught in the position of being treated as sexual objects.

> Cindy came over to the table and wanted to know who was throwing stuff. She addressed herself to Eric. Eric grabbed her arms when she got close. Joe told her that he wanted to eat her and grabbed her waist. She told him to let go.

Joe said he changed his mind and walked away. Eric started pulling her down on his lap and told her, "Just a little more. I can almost see down your shirt." She got away and before she attacked Eric, Bobby called her over and started talking to her. She calmed down immediately. [Steve's notes]

While the boys in this episode might view their behavior as "playful" and "harmless," it is clear that Cindy is angered by it and does not view it that way. A boy from a different group senses her angry reaction and intervenes in such a way as to provide support and keep the interaction from escalating further.

While boys occasionally intervened in supportive ways such as this, they seldom were able to successfully change or modify the behavior of their male peers. When boys did comment on the crude or gross nature of another boy's behavior, they were generally ignored as in the following example:

Bobby got the attention of a girl who was sitting in another part of the cafeteria. When she looked at him he said that Kevin liked her and wanted to get to know her. Kevin just ducked down so that he couldn't be seen as well. Bobby kept this up and Johnny joined in. Then Joe joined in, saying "He likes you and wants your body. He wants your ass." Kevin said that was gross. Joe continued telling her that Kevin wanted to put his prick up her shithole. Bobby and Johnny stopped talking to the girl at this point. I don't think they wanted to be connected with Joe's comments. Joe turned to Eric and asked if he had heard him. Eric said "no" and Joe repeated it. [Steve's notes]

Joe appears to be using this interaction as an opportunity to show off his ability to make crude and aggressive sexual comments to a girl, since he makes a point of reporting his behavior to Eric. He is not willing to modify his behavior when Kevin tells him he is being "gross," because he sees more advantage in impressing other male peers with the extent of his "grossness." Joe's comments depersonalize Kevin as well the girl he is interested in and reduce the chances of a relationship starting. Since Joe's behavior is unaffected by Kevin's sanction, the only option left for those boys who have negative reactions to sexually aggressive talk is to distance themselves from the interaction.

All of these informal activities create taken-for-granted notions about male sexuality (Eder, Evans, and Parker 1995). Because activities such as insult exchange are so routine, the messages they convey are often seen as being "natural" orientations toward sexuality and are seldom questioned. Boys in medium-high-status groups were less likely than those in the higher- or lower-status groups to engage in aggressive sexual behavior and, in general, were more sensitive to the concerns of girls. While they sometimes intervened on the behalf of girls, offering them support, they were more likely to distance themselves from such behavior. Messner (1992), in his study of older male athletes, also found that males who disapproved of the sexist language of other males tended to distance themselves from the jock culture rather than openly voice their complaints. Given the power of these norms within the most popular male subcultures and their link with school-sponsored forms of competitive aggression, few boys feel in a position to successfully challenge them.

GIRLS' RESPONSES TO AGGRESSIVE SEXUALITY

The competitive orientation toward sexuality which was being shaped within certain male subcultures in this school depends, as we have seen, on viewing girls as sexual objects versus sexual actors. One way in which boys (and some girls) reinforce the negative view of girls' active sexuality is through the labels of "slut" and "whore." While these labels imply promiscuous sexual behavior on the part of girls, they were widely used for many reasons. Lees (1993) has found these and similar labels applied to girls for being seen with several different boys, for dating many boys, for talking assertively to boys, as a means of self-defense, as well as for being single and thus available to any interested boy. In other words, sexual labeling is used to keep girls from being too independent as well as from being non-monogamous.

Girls at the school we studied were often faced with having to defend themselves against these and similar sexist labels. Steve observed cases in which boys would walk over to a table where girls were sitting at lunch and accuse someone of being a "slut" or "whore." In one case, Joe and Hank called a girl a "slut-face" and asked her if her rates had gone down, or if they were still a quarter. They also told her they knew she'd "fuck any guy in the school." Her only comeback early on was to say something about how they couldn't find Hank's IQ. Hank responded to this by saying, "Oh, that's really gay." Finally, she said, "Fuck you," at which point the boys backed off and left her alone.

Girls who were upset by boys' comments or did not have good initial responses were often subject to more harassment than girls who were more skilled in insult exchange. Andrea was a sixth grade girl with strong insulting skills. One day she was collecting money for a candy sale and had five or six dollars in an envelope. Walter, a former boyfriend and current friend, made a few comments about her collecting money as a prostitute. She responded to him by saying that she "wasn't that low and wasn't that cheap." Then she challenged Walter, saying now that he brought it up she remembered that he owed her some money. Walter replied saying, "I don't owe you anything. You enjoyed it, didn't you?" He then gave her a nickel, and Andrea said, "Well, I'm not that cheap."

Because of Andrea's verbal skills, she was able to keep the insulting at a playful level. Also, the high degree of rapport between Andrea and Walter made this exchange a less intimidating one. However, while some traditional views of sexuality are being mocked here, Andrea still takes on the role of prostitute to do so. Thus, the whore label itself is not being challenged within this exchange. Often by participating in insult exchanges, girls as well as boys are simply reinforcing the negative and limited roles associated with these sexual labels.

Andrea also announced to her friends one day that if anyone called her a slut or a whore they wouldn't be around long enough to say it again. Then she related a story about how she had punched a boy for calling her a bitch. Andrea's physical size and strength gave her a definite advantage in exchanges with boys her age. Generally, boys were careful not to insult those girls who were taller or larger than they so as to avoid the humiliation of being beaten up by a girl.

Those girls who lacked the advantage of physical size and strength had to rely solely on their verbal skills. Besides participating in the exchange in a playful way, some girls skillfully directed the content of the exchange into a non-sexual domain. For example, one day a girl stopped by the boys' table because she had heard that one of the boys was interested in going with her.

> She [Tammy] stopped at our group to say "hi" and waited
> until Richard said "hi" as well. She stood there smiling and

finally Richard said, "Well, what do you say—yes or no? Are you going to go with me? Come on and go with me." Sam then said, "Yeah, go with him. He just wants some." Tammy got mad and tried to hit Sam saying, "I'll give you some." She then turned and walked away from the group. Richard never got his answer. [Steve's notes]

Tammy offers a very effective response to Sam's sexual reference to Richard "wanting some" by transforming the meaning of "some" to her physical attack on Sam when she says "I'll give you some." This strategy is highly effective, because the sexual arena is currently based on males having more power than females, giving males the advantage in many sexual exchanges. For example, Spender (1980) reports that there are only a few labels for males who have multiple sexual partners while there are 220 different labels for females, most of which are negative. By switching the content of the exchange to a non-sexual one, Tammy not only successfully defends herself but also does not reinforce negative and limiting sexual messages for females.

GIRLS' PARTICIPATION IN REINFORCING MALES' SEXUAL ATTITUDES

While girls clearly did not benefit from the gender messages reinforced through informal talk, at times they participated directly in such talk. For example, they were almost as likely as boys to label other girls as sluts. In addition, they often gave negative labels to boys who violated male norms by associating with girls rather than with boys. One boy who spent much of his lunch period with a group of girls was often taken advantage of and bullied into doing favors for them. On one particular day many of the girls in this group joined in on calling him a faggot, yelling at him to leave another boy alone since they knew he was after his body. The fact that this boy had crushes on many of the girls in his class was completely ignored when these girls accused him of not being normatively heterosexual.

On another occasion a seventh grade boy who was sitting with a group of girls was collectively insulted by the group members. One girl began the insulting exchange by asking, "Do you feel weird sittin' around with a bunch of girls?" To which one girl responded, "No, he feels right at home," and another girl added "You're around your own kind." The boy finally responded by saying, in reference to the last comment, "That would make you guys bad," implying that badness, not femininity, is what they shared in common.

These same girls also insulted this boy by implying he was not sexually virile. This insult grew out of a series of threats to get the boy to rejoin their group, the last threat being "Jim, c'mere or I'll do something. I'll ruin your family life." Another girl picked up on this theme and said, "How come he don't ruin your family life—is he sterile?" to which the first girl replied, "Well, he's never gotten me pregnant yet so maybe he is." Other girls made similar insults to boys who sat with them, implying they were not as sexually potent or as well equipped as other boys. For example, one day a sixth grade boy complained about getting hit somewhere important twice before that day. An eighth grade girl, jokingly replied, "Oh, do you have anything worth getting hurt?"

It is ironic that girls would insult boys for being less masculine because of sitting with them or not being as potent sexually. However, girls as well as boys are exposed to traditional gender beliefs. These girls seemed to sense the same vulnerable concerns in boys that other boys did and made them the content of their insults. In other words, girls as well as the boys did not always reflect on the implied meanings behind their remarks and the ways in which these remarks further contributed to the current social hierarchy with male-oriented, tough, and sexually aggressive boys at the top.

One other way in which girls contributed indirectly to sexual aggression is through the female peer culture's focus on appearance and attractiveness (Eder, Evans, and Parker 1995). To some extent this focus was promoted through extracurricular activities such as cheerleading. But the girls themselves also reinforced this concern, with appearance being one of the most frequent topics of gossip among girls. By continually making negative remarks about the appearance and dress of other girls, many girls added to their own concerns in this area. As long as girls place much of their attention on seeing themselves as physical objects, it is easier for them to be objectified by the males in their lives.

DISCUSSION

Athletics and especially combat sports such as football and rugby were introduced in schools in the late 1800s and early 1900s as a means to develop "manliness" and to offset an environment that was perceived to be overly feminized (Dunning 1986; Messner 1990). They were also justified as training grounds for war. Today, rule-governed aggression is still believed to be useful to organizations due to the forceful energy it mobilizes according to Lyman (1987). Thus, athletics in schools today may be there as much to socialize males for corporate life as for combat in war. Also, by placing winning above the welfare of the opposing team members, teaching boys to be aggressive offers schools a competitive advantage in current sports rivalries which are often the focus of considerable community interest.

We have seen, however, that the coaches' attempts to channel the aggressiveness of boys and restrict it to the sports arena turned out to be ineffective. Instead, its high value in the top peer group resulted in aggression being one of the primary bases of informal status among the boys. Also, because it was strongly associated with masculinity by both the coaches and boys, avoidance of tough behavior could lead to challenges regarding one's masculinity.

It should be noted that while not all boys in the school displayed tough behaviors, these behaviors tended to be widely valued by most of the boys. Boys in the top social group displayed toughness on a regular basis since they were constantly vying for status within their peer group. While boys in the medium-high groups did not engage in as much insulting or physical fighting, they admired the toughness and defiance of boys in the elite group. Boys in the lower social groups also displayed their toughness but they tended to be feared more than respected by other boys. Since many of them did not participate in school-sponsored sports, they did not gain status through the legitimization of toughness as the most popular boys did.

One policy implication from these findings would be to eliminate particularly aggressive sports such as football and wrestling from public schools. These sports often link ruthless aggression with competition, promoting a violent orientation toward others. Schools could still offer other sports which emphasize self-challenge such as track, gymnastics, and swimming as well as less aggressive team sports. More creative outlets for expressing aggressive energy such as martial arts and drama could also be offered through school and other community organizations. While some might consider these suggestions to be extreme, some action is needed to change the way in which public schools currently teach boys to pursue winning and success regardless of the harm they inflict on others. As things now stand, we are training young men to hurt others in order to get ahead in life (Messner 1990).

This training clearly carries over into their relationships with girls where a focus on aggressive competition also prevails. By teaching boys that the feelings and injuries of others are not as important as winning or scoring, boys are being socialized into a culture of sexual aggression and harassment. Stein's (1993) nationwide study of sexual harassment in public schools and our study both provide strong evidence that sexual aggression is an extension of other forms of aggression and harassment in schools.

It is crucial that boys be shown other models for sexual behavior that do not rely on a competitive framework. They also should be encouraged to examine their daily language routines, like insulting and teasing, in order to identify potentially sexist remarks. Since many acts of prejudice occur due to a lack of awareness, it is critical that boys find out how others interpret their comments as well as have occasions to examine different potential meanings among themselves.

While it is essential that attempts are made to reduce the amount of sexual harassment girls face in public schools, it is also important to offer girls more strategies for responding to sexist insults. In her study of high school girls, Lees (1993) found that the most common response to sexual insulting was to deny the label as applying to them without challenging the implied double standard. Other responses included trying to ignore boys or their comments and actively challenging boys by calling them names. Although this last strategy is the most assertive, it was only moderately successful because there are fewer negative labels for males and because girls who did insult boys were often negatively labeled for this behavior.

In the analysis of the AAUW nationwide sample, most students (75 percent) responded to harassment through some type of avoidance behavior such as cutting class or skipping school, dropping a course or activity, or avoiding certain places or people at school (Lee et al. 1995). Girls were more likely to report using some type of avoidance behavior and were also more likely to report having some type of psychological problem, such as difficulty sleeping or loss of appetite, as a result of being harassed. While many students who were harassed reported engaging in some form of harassment themselves,[2] girls were more likely than boys to be exclusively in the victim role (31 percent versus 7 percent).

Clearly, girls are in need of more strategies for responding to sexual harassment. While it is important to teach girls that they can state when their rights are being violated, girls often face further harassment if they appear too formal and may be called names such as "Little Miss Priss." One general response which girls could use is to turn the conversation back on the insulter by saying, "Did you hear what you just said? What did you mean by that?"

Some girls have found creative ways to use language when responding to insults. One creative approach is to disarm the insulter through exaggeration and/or self-mocking. For example, to the insult of being labeled a slut, one middle school girl suggested responding like this: "Oh, you've offended me so deeply. I'm so terribly hurt that you would think such a thing about me." Another strategy shared by a teenage girl was to confuse boys who insulted her by using what she called "psycho babble." When insulted, she would turn to the boy and ask questions such as "Why do you feel the need to express your turmoil by being aggressive to people you don't know?" or "Do you need mental health?"

Yet another useful strategy is to transform the meaning of an act or comment into a non-sexual domain as seen in an earlier example when the girl changed the meaning of "some" from a sexual one to a physical attack on the boy who was insulting her. A high school girl described how she and her friend responded to some boys who were making lewd pelvic thrusts in their dorm windows during a drama camp. The girls transformed the meaning into inept attempts at skiing which they playfully imitated throughout the rest of their week at camp.

Realizing that sexual aggression is closely related to other forms of verbal aggression and abuse, many schools are beginning to teach children conflict resolution skills in the elementary grades. Other concerned adults in our community and I have started a student action group called KACTIS, Kids Against Cruel Treatment in Schools (Eder 1995). This after-school group brings together youth from different elementary schools to talk about the problem of ridiculing others and engaging in other forms of cruelty. Specific skills and strategies such as assertive expression of anger and intervening with humor are introduced. Students are encouraged to incorporate these skills when using role play to creatively arrive at new strategies for dealing with conflict and for confronting youth who are ridiculing or harassing others. In working with this group and from conducting this study, it is clear that certain alternative strategies are likely to be more effective than others. For example, it is evident that an important component of student peer culture is humor, being able to get others to laugh.

In KACTIS, students have learned how to use humor creatively to defuse the tension surrounding bullying episodes and get bullies to stop without making them more aggressive (Eder 1995). In one role play episode the "bully" was keeping other students from using a water fountain. The "intervener" tried a humorous response saying, "If you don't let them get a drink of water, they might die of thirst," after which the other students pretended to collapse on the floor, holding their throats in an exaggerated show of thirst. The bully left the scene saying, "You people are pathetic!" One important aspect of humorous responses is that bullies can more easily "save face" as they give up their aggressive behavior, and humor is much more likely to be effective.

When informal strategies fail, students also need to have adults to turn to who are prepared to deal with sexual harassment in effective ways. Too often officials to whom girls end up reporting incidents of harassment are well meaning, but ineffective. One hopes that, as adults begin to take the complaints of girls more seriously and respond to them more effectively, girls will no longer need to resign themselves to sexual harassment as a normal part of school life.

Sexual aggression in schools is not a problem that will go away on its own. Neither is it a necessary part of "growing up" and learning how to toughen up in order to face the "real world." As long as school attendance is mandatory, schools should be safe places in which students do not have to confront sexual aggression and other forms of harassment on a daily basis. Real and lasting changes will require us to rethink some basic values of this society which until now have focused on the importance of preparing boys and other youth for an aggressive workplace. Meanwhile, it is important that we offer students opportunities to become more informed and better prepared to deal with the realities of sexual aggression in their schools.

NOTES

1. I would like to thank Stephen Parker, Catherine Evans, and Stephanie Sanford for the assistance with data collection, coding, and analysis. This research was supported in part by a grant from the National Institute of Mental Health.

2. Given the way this question was phrased, it is impossible to determine if students harassed others prior to being harassed themselves or if this was a response to being harassed as Lees (1993) found in her study.

REFERENCES

Connell, Robert. 1987. *Gender and Power*. Stanford: Stanford University Press.

Connell, R., D. Ashenden, S. Kessler, and G. Dowsett. 1982. *Making the Difference: Schools, Families, and Social Division*. Sydney: Allen and Unwin.

Corsaro, William. 1992. "Interpretive Reproduction in Children's Peer Cultures." *Social Psychology Quarterly* 55:160-77.

Corsaro, William. 1988. "Routines in the Peer Culture of American and Italian Nursery School Children." *Sociology of Education* 61:7-14.

Corsaro, William, and Donna Eder. 1990. "Children's Peer Cultures." *Annual Review of Sociology* 16:197-220.

Corsaro, William, and Donna Eder. 1994. "The Development and Socialization of Children and Adolescents." Pp. 421-451 in *Sociological Perspectives on Social Psychology,* edited by K. Cook, G. Fine, and J. House. New York: Allen and Bacon.

Dunning, Eric. 1986. "Sport as a Male Preserve: Notes on the Social Sources of Masculine Identity and Its Transformations." *Theory, Culture, and Society* 3:79-90.

Eder, Donna. 1985. "The Cycle of Popularity: Interpersonal Relations Among Female Adolescents." *Sociology of Education* 58:154-65.

Eder, Donna. 1990. "Serious and Playful Disputes: Variation in Conflict Talk Among Female Adolescents." Pp. 67-84 in *Conflict Talk: Sociolinguistic Investigations of Arguments in Conversations*, edited by A. Grimshaw. Cambridge: Cambridge University Press.

Eder, Donna. 1991. "The Role of Teasing in Adolescent Peer Culture." Pp. 179-197 in *Sociological Studies of Child Development, Vol. 4*, edited by S. Cahill. Greenwich, CT: JAI Press.

Eder, Donna. 1995. "Making Conflict Resolution Part of Peer Culture." Paper presented at a Conference on Youth 2000. Middlesbrough, England.

Eder, Donna, and Janet Enke. 1991. "The Structure of Gossip: Opportunities and Constraints on Collective Expression Among Adolescents." *American Sociological Review* 56:495-508.

Eder, Donna, with Catherine Evans, and Stephen Parker. 1995. *School Talk: Gender and Adolescent Culture*. New Brunswick, NJ: Rutgers University Press.

Eder, Donna, and Stephen Parker. 1987. "The Cultural Production and Reproduction of Gender: The Effect of Extracurricular Activities on Peer Group Culture." *Sociology of Education* 60:200-13.

Goffman, Erving. 1974. *Frame Analysis*. New York: Harper & Row.

Kessler, S., D. Ashenden, R. Connell, and G. Dowsett. 1985. "Gender Relations in Secondary Schooling." *Sociology of Education* 58:34-47.

Larkin, June. 1994. "Walking Through Walls: The Sexual Harassment of High School Girls." *Gender and Education* 6:263-280.

Lee, Valerie E., Robert G. Croninger, E. Linn, and Xianglei Chen. 1995. "The Culture of Sexual Harassment in Secondary Schools." (Unpublished paper)

Lees, Sue. 1993. *Sugar and Spice*. London: Hutchinson.

Lyman, Peter. 1987. "The Fraternal Bond as a Joking Relationship." Pp. 148-163 in *Changing Men: New Directions in Research on Men and Masculinity*, edited by M. Kimmel. Newbury Park, CA: Sage.

Messner, Michael. 1990. "When Bodies are Weapons: Masculinity and Violence in Sport." *International Review for Sociology of Sports* 25:203-217.

Messner, Michael. 1992. "Like Family: Power, Intimacy, and Sexuality in Male Athletes' Friendships." Pp. 215-237 in *Men's Friendship*, edited by P. Nardi. Newbury Park, CA: Sage.

Parker, Stephen. 1991. *Early Adolescent Male Cultures: The Importance of Organized and Informal Sport*. Ph.D. dissertation. Department of Sociology, Indiana University, Bloomington, IN.

Spender, Dale. 1980. *Man Made Language*. London: Routledge & Kegan Paul.

Stein, Nan. 1993. "No Laughing Matter: Sexual Harassment in K-12 Schools." Pp. 313-324 in *Transforming a Rape Culture*, edited by E. Buchwald. Minneapolis: Milkweed Editions.

Thorne, Barrie. 1993. *Gender Play: Boys and Girls in School*. New Brunswick: Rutgers University Press.

CHAPTER 5

Issues of Race and Gender in the Educational Achievement of African American Children[1]

Cynthia A. Hudley

The *Brown vs. Board of Education* decision in 1954 affirmed the inherent inequality of the doctrine of separate but equal in American education. At that time, the removal of the barriers of *de jure* segregation from the nation's classrooms was presumed to insure an equal education for all. Yet in the more than 40 years since the *Brown* decision, the evidence is mounting that inner-city, low-income, minority children are receiving an education that is distinctly inferior to that received by middle-class, white, and suburban students.

For example, African American students in public schools are more likely to be enrolled in vocational or general track than in college–prep classes (Oakes 1985). In these academically unchallenging classes, students are rarely taught the critical thinking skills necessary to successfully complete a four-year college education (Irvine 1990). Further, schools in poor, nonwhite areas are more often staffed by less experienced and more poorly prepared teachers who are working without basic instructional support services such as computer labs, science labs, and foreign-language instruction (Oakes 1985). Thus, schooling for urban minority youth seems most often characterized by deficient academic opportunities.

Available evidence also indicates that urban minority youth are most likely of all children to encounter severely limited life chances. Explosive increases in unemployment and violent crime coupled with a general lack of social services and decent housing for citizens in urban areas have created an excessively harsh climate in which minority children, and especially African Americans, will grow to adulthood (Ascher 1991). These devastating conditions must be navigated by children in perhaps the most vulnerable period of human development for the establishment and maintenance of appropriate patterns of school achievement and adjustment—middle childhood (Brooks 1984).

CURRENT LEVELS OF SCHOOL ACHIEVEMENT
This daunting combination of restricted academic opportunities and limited life chances provides a context for interpreting the low levels of academic achievement and persistence observed among many African American youth. African American children as a group consistently achieve at levels below their white and Asian counterparts, as measured by traditional indices (e.g., standardized test scores, GPAs, college entrance and completion) (Irvine 1990). In 1992, the percentage of African American students who met minimum performance standards as established by the National Educational Goals Panel ranged from a low of 3 percent for 8th grade mathematics achievement to a high of 16 percent for 12th grade reading achievement (National Education Goals Panel 1995). This contrasts with 44 percent for Asian students and 32 percent for white students in math achievement. Comparable data for reading achievement are 39 percent for Asian students and 43 percent for white students. Measures of science achievement also indicate disturbingly low levels of proficiency among African American students (National Education Goals Panel 1995).

African American students are also especially likely to leave secondary and post-secondary academic institutions without completing a diploma (Irvine 1990). In 1993, the high school dropout rate for African American teens was double that of whites (National Education Goals Panel 1995). In 1992, although 45 percent of African American high school graduates enrolled in college, fewer than 15 percent of African American high school graduates had completed a 4-year degree by age 29. Fewer than 3 percent overall had completed graduate or professional training (National Education Goals Panel 1995).

GENDER AND ACHIEVEMENT
Among low-income African American youth, males are more likely than females to experience alarming levels of educational failure and school adjustment problems. These young men are more likely

than either white males or females of any race to drop out of school before the completion of high school (Reed 1988). Those enrolled in school are suspended at rates more than twice that of African American females or white males (Reed 1988). Further, while enrollment in post-secondary education programs during the 1980's was declining 1.1 percent for African American females, the decline was greater than 6 percent for African American males (Reed 1988).

Educational failure is mirrored in subsequent employment status and life outcomes. Unemployment rates among high school dropouts aged 20-24 are more than three times higher for African American males than for white males, while the ratio between African American and white females is near parity (Narine 1992). Instead, African American young men are enmeshed in the criminal justice system. African American male youth are detained in juvenile detention centers at rates nearly triple those for white male youth (Dembo 1988); overall, one in four African American male adolescents is either incarcerated or on parole (Narine 1992).

High unemployment and incarceration rates also have formidable consequences for African American females. Joblessness is a powerful deterrent to marriage, and frequent incarceration reduces opportunities to establish stable, long-term adult relationships. Thus, African American females are most likely to become impoverished single parents, and an estimated 86 percent of all African American children spend some of their life in a female-headed family (Ascher 1991). Most troubling, these female heads of households are often unmarried teens with little education and no means of economic support. In 1989, 92 percent of new African American teenage mothers were unmarried (National Center for Health Statistics 1991), and teen mothers are more than five times as likely to drop out of school as are young women who have not given birth (Freeman and Rickels 1993). Children of African American teen mothers are three times more likely to be raised in poverty than children of any other race or family composition (Simms 1986). Finally, communities in which men pursue dangerous, illegal lifestyles and transient family relationships are highly problematic for the development of the male child (Edelman 1987) and especially likely to perpetuate the cycle of teen pregnancy and impoverished, single-parent households (Freeman and Rickels 1993). These data indicate that the educational difficulties of African American children have a profound impact on their lives into adulthood and on the lives of their children and communities as well.

Although the economic status of African American adults is equally perilous for both males and females, early predictors of economic hardship seem to vary by gender. For women, early childbearing seems to be a significant risk factor. For men, the risks center on early academic achievement and subsequent employment status. Thus, negative consequences of difficulties with schooling are apparent for African American men at an especially early age and tend to persist in school and throughout their lives.

EDUCATING AFRICAN AMERICAN BOYS

This disparity in life chances, educational opportunities, and achievement outcomes has prompted some academics, politicians, and community members to advocate a return to a segregated model for the education of African American boys, as exemplified by public school programs in Detroit, New York, and Baltimore (Ascher 1991). The overall goal of these race- and gender-specific programs is one of empowerment. As the children are provided with the academic opportunities necessary to ensure their success in the larger society, they are also provided with the coping skills and achievement motivation which should insure that they will proceed along the path to success as they develop to adulthood. By changing the ways in which African American boys are schooled, these programs aim to break the cycle of poverty, illegal behavior, and absentee fatherhood which characterizes the lives of far too many of these youth.

The programs, though highly diverse in their individual approaches, all share a set of core beliefs around which they are organized: the importance of male role models, the need for a rigorous Afrocentric curriculum, an emphasis on academic values, and the creation of a safe and orderly classroom environment through the display of appropriate social behavior (Ascher 1991). African American male teachers and other successful individuals are present in these classrooms to serve as positive images of African American male adults. Such role models are typically limited in both the communities and media images available to these young people (Irvine 1990). An intellectually challenging Afrocentric curriculum focuses on the central role of these children's ancestors in the development of human civilization. Further, this culturally relevant material is delivered in an instructional setting tailored to an

African cultural frame of reference (Irvine 1990) that emphasizes personal relations, cooperative activities, and a climate of mutual respect. Academic rigor and social competence are believed to instill personal discipline and values that prize academic tasks and achievement as goals of the highest priority. The underlying premise is that culturally relevant curricula and instructional methods, coupled with intellectual challenge, a redefinition of male identity, and a safe, orderly environment, will enhance these students' self-esteem and achievement motivation. These affective changes, in turn, should serve to significantly improve students' long-term academic achievement.

Proponents of segregated educational programs see these reforms as analogous to the movement for single-sex education for women. Data on classroom environment have sometimes suggested that women receive less attention from teachers, interact with fewer successful female peer models, and undertake a restricted range of curricular opportunities in coeducational settings (Lockheed and Klein 1985; Riordan 1990). Thus, single-sex schooling serves to bolster self-confidence, increase educational opportunities, and develop leadership among women students (Riordan 1990). In a similar vein, traditional education programs are believed to devalue the ability and identity of African Americans, boys in particular (Reed 1988; Steele 1992). Such devaluing, in turn, may cause this group of students to reject achievement striving (Hudley and Graham 1995) and to de-emphasize school achievement when constructing their cultural and personal identities (Fordham and Ogbu 1986). Thus, race and gender specific schooling may enhance motivation, self-confidence, and achievement among African American boys in a manner analogous to the documented benefits of single-sex schooling for women.

However, race specific, single-sex programs are highly controversial educational remedies for the underachievement of African American males. Groups ranging from the NAACP to the National Organization of Women have spoken out against these reforms, fearing that they promote gender and racial discrimination and limit diversity among both students and faculty (Narine 1992). There is no body of empirical data comparable to that for women in single-sex environments which documents the immediate consequences and long-term effects of segregated schooling for African American boys and communities. However, at least one recent empirical investigation (Hudley 1995) has begun to examine the short-term outcomes of segregated educational programs.

EXAMINING THE IMMEDIATE CONSEQUENCES OF SEGREGATED SCHOOLING

Recently, I examined some effects of separate schooling for a group of African American boys attending a middle-school (grades 6-8) program designed specifically to enhance their academic achievement and school adjustment. These boys attended the regular school but were enrolled in a separate, self-contained academic classroom for African American boys, taught by an African American male teacher.

The Program

In Southern California, where this research was conducted, the county office of education has established an administrative structure to support individual classrooms on comprehensive elementary and secondary school campuses across the county. The policy of housing self-contained classrooms on comprehensive public school campuses was an initial attempt to make the segregated program less vulnerable to legal challenge. At the program's inception, each of these classrooms provided academic instruction for up to 25 African American male students deemed to be at-risk for failure within their current school environment. The county office paid for an additional teacher, an African American male, and a classroom aide to staff the program and provided specialized inservice training for these staff people. Matching funds were also provided to purchase supplementary curriculum materials.

The middle school where this study was conducted furnished physical space, necessary equipment, curriculum materials, and students experiencing motivation and/or behavior problems. These students received their academic instruction (i.e., English, math, social studies, science) within the self-contained classroom and were enrolled in mainstream classes for their physical education instruction and an elective. Staff, in collaboration with the author, developed a curriculum to meet the unique needs of this targeted population in a segregated environment. Based on evidence from previous research (Irvine 1990; Boykin 1986; Brown, Palincsar, and Purcell 1986) we modified and supplemented the materials provided by the district in order to emphasize:

- The history and culture of both ancient and modern civilizations on the African continent.
- The contributions of African Americans to the political, social, economic, and technological development of this country.
- The analysis of current social and political issues and problems, including the impact of racism, classism, and sexism on all members of American society.
- The rights and responsibilities of individual citizens in a democratic society.

This curriculum comprised the basic instructional materials for core courses i.e., social studies, science, math, and language arts. For example, students read literature by African, African American, and Afro-Caribbean authors as part of their language arts curriculum. Math problem-solving activities included calculations of differential income, longevity, population distribution, and other factors which were presented as a function of gender and ethnicity. The data were gathered from government publications as research projects conducted by students at either their school or public library.

The material was presented by means of a variety of teaching techniques, with an emphasis on cooperative and collaborative learning. Instructional goals focused on the development of higher-order thinking and critical analysis skills through the use of tasks requiring problem-solving and independent research, as described previously. Behavior management techniques were developed to complement the instructional setting. For example, student-of-the-week awards and daily opportunities for students to select a preferred activity stressed positive reinforcements, student choice, and recognition of student efforts and improvement. By providing a teacher who serves as a role model, curriculum and instruction that stresses their ethnic heritage, and an environment that provides a safe yet intellectually challenging haven from the negative influences of the street, this school program substantially redefined the typical instructional context for these boys.

The Study

The research focused on students' perceptions of their own intellectual and social competence and their perceptions of the emotional and social support provided by others in their lives. I compared the perceptions of these youth and those of an equal number of African American boys who continued in the regular (i.e., mainstream) instructional program at the same school.

One useful theoretical perspective for analyzing the impact of educational programs is a "goodness of fit" model. Such a model estimates an individual's success in a given context by assessing the demands present in the environment and the personal characteristics of the individual. In essence, successful adjustment requires congruence between the individual and the demands of a given context (Lerner, Baker, and Lerner 1985). When a person's behaviors, abilities, interests, and motives match the role requirements, expectations, and rewards available in a given environment, personal adjustment should be successful and levels of stress in that context should be minimal (French, Rodgers, and Cobb 1974). It is this congruence that defines the concept of "goodness of fit," and this person-environment fit either promotes or constrains the growth and development of the individual.

In examining the immediate consequences of separate schooling, a goodness-of-fit model would predict that school adjustment should be optimized when the demands of the educational context are compatible with the characteristics of the students served in that context. Mainstream academic programs may be less than compatible with African American males for a variety of reasons. The largely white female faculties (Jones-Wilson 1990) may present expectations and rewards that are inconsistent with the needs and behaviors of these students. These white females are also unable to serve as successful role models for African American males, given the discrepancies in both gender and ethnicity. Further, the traditional curriculum offerings pay scant attention to the contributions and concerns of people of African descent (Irvine 1990). Therefore, school assignments may depress the achievement motivation of African American students because they lack relevance to these children's experiences. This possibility is supported in the achievement motivation literature, which suggests that student interests may be strongly related to their achievements (Schiefele, Krapp, and Winteler 1992).

Thus, changes in the context of schooling that accommodate the characteristics, values, and interests of the learners in the educational process should significantly enhance the goodness of fit between learner and schooling environment. This enhanced fit should, in turn, promote school adjustment and achievement. Therefore, my study hypothesized, in line with a goodness of fit model, that the young men enrolled in this special program should demonstrate significantly greater school adjustment than the comparison group of boys who remained in the regular education setting.

The dimensions of school adjustment assessed in this study were perceptions of social support from significant others, self-reports of academic competence, beliefs about the importance of academic pursuits, and school reports of academic and behavioral adjustment. The measure of perceived support from significant others assessed how much students felt that a teacher, a parent, a friend, and a classmate treated them in a kind and caring manner. I anticipated that the African American teacher and the fellow classmates in the experimental program would be perceived as especially supportive, since the program specifically emphasized the development of meaningful bonds between African American men. In a similar vein, I expected features of the experimental program to enhance beliefs about personal competence and the importance of academics. The curriculum materials highlighted African culture as well as the accomplishments of notable African Americans, while the instructional strategies highlighted students' academic and personal achievements. Further, the content of class assignments was personally relevant, and often assignments could be chosen by students from among a range of topics. Together these features were expected to demonstrate to students that academic achievement was not only possible for them and others of their ethnicity but also personally advantageous. If the program succeeded in producing such beliefs, students should be more likely to pursue academic achievement regularly and appropriately, and they should perceive academic achievements to be both useful and attainable. Thus students in the experimental program were also expected to be more likely to earn higher grades, accumulate fewer suspensions, and to attend school more regularly than students in the regular program.

This research assumes that affective, motivational, and behavioral factors, which are deliberately stressed in the experimental instructional program, are causally related to improvements in academic achievement for this population (Haynes and Comer 1990). Further, self-perceptions of competence and support are presumed to be necessary, though not sufficient conditions for subsequent increases in academic achievement for program participants. Measuring the affective and motivational consequences of separate schooling is thus a necessary first step in the development of a model of the effects of separate schooling.

The Evidence
The findings demonstrated that the experimental program benefitted its participants in several domains. The assessment of perceived social support from significant others revealed group differences in perceptions of teachers and classmates. Students in the self-contained classroom rated their teacher as caring, fair, helpful, and interested in them as a person. Ratings from students in the mainstream program, who were asked to rate "their favorite teacher," were significantly lower than those in the self-contained class (M's = 2.77 vs 3.37 on a 4-point scale). Self-contained class students were also more likely than mainstream students to report that their classmates were friendly, liked them as they are, did not make fun of them, and paid attention to what they said. In addition, perceived teacher support correlated with classmate support at a substantially higher level for students in the self-contained class (r = .53) than for comparison group students (r = .18). Thus, students in the experimental, self-contained class perceived their teacher and classmates as friendly and accepting of them and their ideas, suggesting that the overall classroom environment functioned as a supportive context to which all members contributed. This perception of social support was not true for the comparison students in the mainstream classrooms.

Perceived competence ratings differed for the two groups as well. Students in the self-contained classroom perceived both their general intellectual ability and their social competence to be significantly higher than did students in the regular program. In addition, one of the ten subscales of the *Self-Perception Profile* directly measured children's perceptions of their global self-worth. This subscale correlated significantly with perceived intellectual ability and physical appearance for both groups; however, the relative strength of the correlations with intellectual ability and physical appearance was reversed for the two groups of students. For students in the self-contained class global self-worth was more highly correlated with general intellectual ability (r = .86, p = .01) than with physical appearance (r = .59, p = .05). The opposite pattern was true for comparison students: for self-worth and intellectual ability, $r = .56$, $p = .05$; for self-worth and physical appearance, $r = .83$, $p = .01$. Rather than perceiving their academic competence to be inimical to their social competence, the young men in the self-contained class saw intellectual ability as more integral to their feelings of self-worth than did comparison students.

School records of achievement, behavior, and attendance revealed small but interesting differences between the two groups of students. Academic grades and days of suspension slightly favored the self-contained classroom. Absences were greater in the self-contained class; however, group averages were influenced by a small number of students who rarely attended school. The self-contained class enrolled five students who were each absent at least 26 days out of the school year (range 26-48 days). In the mainstream classes, two students also displayed extreme absenteeism (54 and 43 days, respectively), and five others were absent more than ten days (range 11-17). Interestingly, several of these comparison students were often observed by the researcher on campus but not in class. Each group also contained students with regular attendance (less than nine absences during the school year): eleven in the self-contained class and seven among the regular students. Thus the self-contained class had twice as many students with regular attendance as with excessive absenteeism (11 vs. 5 students), but regular attendance and high absenteeism were evenly represented among students in the regular classes (7 students in each category).

Absenteeism also had strikingly different effects on ratings of perceived competence for the two groups of students. For students in the self-contained class, the number of days they were absent from school correlated significantly (all p's $< .05$) with their ratings of their general intellectual ability ($r = -.71$) and their ratings of their perceived competence in reading ($r = -.76$), math ($r = -.61$), writing ($r = -.71$), and spelling ($r = -.79$). In contrast, attendance records of students in regular classes were not significantly related to ratings of general intellectual ability or perceptions of competence (r's ranged from .03 to .19, ns.).

Although a number of students in the self-contained classroom attended school irregularly, perceptions of academic competence were strongly related to attendance. Apparently for some high-risk youth, the person-environment fit with the experimental program was as poor as had previously been the case with the mainstream program of instruction. Perhaps academic programming was not the primary source of the mismatch between school and learner. For example, these students may have had to meet family pressures for economic support or childcare. Alternatively, they may have engaged in activities (e.g., involvement in the drug trade) or held beliefs (e.g., schooling is for whites) that precluded school attendance. However, the majority of youth in the self-contained class demonstrated both regular attendance and a strong commitment to their own intellectual competence. For these youth, the match between learner and educational program was a good one.

Thus the experimental program seems to have created a cadre of academically confident young men who supported one another's achievement strivings. These young men's perceptions of mutual support for academic competence stand in stark contrast to findings that peer pressure among African American males works to discourage academic achievement because such strivings are seen as the province of whites (Fordham and Ogbu 1986). For students enrolled in this program which emphasizes the accomplishments of people of African descent, being smart clearly does not equate with acting white.

The role of the teacher may have been central to the development and maintenance of a safe, intellectually challenging class environment that supported the achievement strivings of these young men. Research on school reform is consistent with such an interpretation, suggesting that the quality of interpersonal interaction within classrooms, rather than structural features (i.e., general school policies, student demographic characteristics), seems to best account for student success (Pauley 1991). Although a variety of school adjustment measures indicated positive changes in self-perceptions and behavior, important domains of school-relevant beliefs and behavior appeared to be unchanged. Students in the self-contained class did not rate intellectual and academic competence as any more important than did comparison students. Neither did classroom grades discriminate strongly between the two groups. These findings may be reflections of the economic and socio-political conditions that exist in America's cities. Residents of inner-city communities, including those who have completed high school, are often unable to successfully translate academic credentials into economic advantage due to such factors as racism, inaccessibility of jobs, job ceilings for certain groups, and deficient academic preparation (Narine 1992).

Inner-city minority youth are more often confronted with male role models who are either underemployed or engaged in an extralegal economy to meet their basic subsistence needs. Thus it is no surprise to discover that these young minority men perceive education as not causally related to securing life success (Cullen 1991; Weis 1985). The data reported here are completely consistent with prior research in suggesting that a school-based program is unable to overcome, in a single year, the incredibly strong contrary evidence regarding the importance of schooling for these young men.

IMPLICATIONS FOR PUBLIC POLICY
The Search for Long-term Consequences
The relatively sparse data currently available on race- and gender-segregated schooling suggest that proximal effects are positive for African American boys enrolled in these programs. Both the quantitative data reported here concerning a self-contained classroom and a wealth of anecdotal reports describing separate schools (Ascher 1991; Narine 1992; "Detroit's African-Centered Academies" 1994) describe boys who are achieving well and feeling good about themselves, their culture, and their futures. What educators currently lack is a coherent body of longitudinal data that estimates the distal effects of the full range of program models on participants, communities, and schools.

How will young men educated in separate schools fare in their long-term educational attainment and subsequent life achievement? For example, one wonders if separate public schools will be adequately resourced and provide a sufficiently broad curriculum to equip their students to enter the sophisticated, global economy of the twenty-first century. Public support for education and public commitment to race-based programs to redress inequality continue to wane, as evidenced by recent Congressional action to cut education funding (Shapiro 1995) and Supreme Court decisions to limit affirmative action programs (Price 1995). Thus, the political will to implement necessary investments in information technology, laboratory facilities, and physical plants dedicated to the education of a single group may not be forthcoming. In the absence of equivalent educational settings, separate but equal will continue to be a false promise. However, without adequate documentation of student outcomes, the necessary investments in gender- and race-segregated environments may be an inappropriate use of scarce resources. One possible compromise may be the self-contained classroom model, which allows segregated programs to share physical facilities with comprehensive school programs.

What of the consequences of race- and gender-segregation for peer relations? The limited data available to date suggest that separate schooling engenders supportive peer networks among participants (Hudley 1995). However, there are no data presently available that assess the stability of these networks or the relationships between these students and those educated in other settings. We do not know the extent to which these friendship networks forged in schools mediate antisocial behavior and peer-directed aggression in nonschool settings. One of the greatest potential benefits of separate schooling is the development of nonviolent peer relations and an end to the reliance on antisocial behavior to win the esteem of peers (Anderson 1994; Dembo 1988). Separate schooling might allow young African American men to form both same-age and cross-age friendships with achievement-oriented males who would serve as both peers and role models. These networks, in turn, may support long-term social, economic, and political co-operation which might ultimately empower communities and create a significant cadre of leadership for African Americans. However, research is limited on the actual accomplishment of these potential benefits (Moore and Smith 1992).

Another unanswered question is the impact of separate schooling on cross-sex relationships. For example, will boys in segregated programs be more or less likely to pursue inappropriate sexual contact with young females? Self-esteem and school attendance appear to increase for program participants (Hudley 1995), and defining manhood in socially and sexually appropriate ways is a central tenet of the program curricula (Narine 1992). Thus one might expect reduced rates of teenage pregnancy and higher rates of stable, two-parent families among program participants, if sexual contact and family formation are delayed beyond the high school years (Moore and Smith 1992). Or, as critics of single-sex schools have always contended, will interactions between the sexes occur in unsafe, unsupervised situations and sexual stereotypes be perpetuated due to lack of contact between the sexes (Riordan 1990)? The implications for cross-sex and family relations are as yet unknown but of critical importance for the African American community.

Perhaps the most compelling question relative to educational policy is understanding how race and gender segregated schools will affect overall public education (Moore and Smith 1990). For example, the proportion of African American teachers is perilously low and declining steadily (Garibaldi 1991), which calls into question a policy of siphoning off male teachers for segregated programs. Do not African American girls and students of all backgrounds benefit from exposure to African American male role models? African American males have important contributions to make to the development of attitudes and values of all children. In our culturally pluralistic society, the presence of these men as legitimate authority figures in the lives of all children may be a useful antidote to the development of racist attitudes.

Further, the academic and motivational consequences of separating African American girls from their male peers and teachers are largely ignored in the debate over resegregation. However, the potential benefits of race- and gender-specific classrooms and schools for boys must be balanced against possible damage to other students, including African American females. If segregated programs are an attempt to protect students from a potentially hostile, inappropriate learning environment, African American girls should merit no less attention than boys. For example, teachers view African American girls as well as boys more negatively than positively (Washington 1982), and teacher perceptions have been found to significantly impact student outcomes (Hudley 1993). Further, African American girls perceive their teachers as treating them in ways consistent with low expectations (e.g., unsolicited help in class, emphasis on following rules) (Marcus, Gross, and Seefeldt 1991). These girls face equally daunting educational risks and should not be jeopardized by educational programs that pit the success of one group of children against other groups.

Other Evidence on Single-sex Education
These and many pressing questions remain to be answered. Limited insights are available from comparisons of the effects of single-sex and coeducational Catholic high schools (Bryk, Lee, and Holland 1993; Riordan 1990). Among minority students enrolled in Catholic schools, both boys and girls in single-sex environments outperformed

their peers in coeducational settings on a variety of measures. On standardized tests, minority males achieved at approximately three fourths of a grade level above their peers in coeducational schools after adjusting for cognitive ability and socio-economic status (Riordan 1990). One possible explanation is that these boys take more academic coursework and complete more homework in single-sex Catholic high schools and are less likely to enroll in vocational courses (Bryk et al. 1993). For girls in single-sex schools, the advantage in test scores approached a full grade level, perhaps because girls in single-sex schools were more likely to associate with academically oriented peers and to express a positive interest in academics (Bryk et al. 1993). Both minority boys and girls in single-sex Catholic schools report higher levels of self-esteem and internal locus of control than their peers in coeducational settings. Interestingly, the only students who seem to benefit from coeducation, both academically and affectively, are white males. Yet, the most robust tradition of single-sex schooling was found among elite private institutions (Slaughter and Johnson 1988) and highly regarded public secondary schools (e.g., Boston Latin School) (Riordan 1990), both of which traditionally served white males.

RECOMMENDATIONS AND CONCLUSIONS

As our country faces the reality of global economic competition, we face the concomitant necessity of successfully educating all who are capable. The nation can no longer discard the talents of undereducated members of society and remain economically viable. Thus, urban minority youth represent a constituency whose fate will help shape the future of this country. The data discussed here provide a strong impetus for the continued development and evaluation of race- and gender-specific educational programs. However, these programs should be investigated in the context of multiple models of school reform. Fortunately, public education is undergoing reform at a pace unprecedented in this century.

School-based efforts to enhance the achievement of minority children have traditionally focused on two broad constellations of factors that appear to influence achievement outcomes. One set of factors can be loosely grouped under the rubric of school climate: those structural features, organizational policies, and management practices that determine the school-wide interpersonal context (Edmonds 1986). Among such reform efforts, extensive attention has been given to the deleterious effects of tracking on students of both genders (Vanfossen, Jones, and Spade 1987; Oakes 1985) and the search for alternative means of curricular organization. More recently, the paradoxical effects of school desegregation for African-American children have been actively debated by researchers, parents, and policymakers (Willie, Garibaldi, and Reed 1991). Reform efforts have been undertaken to forge collaborative relationships among diverse student groups (Perry and Fraser 1993) as well as between minority students and communities and Anglo teachers and administrators (Comer 1980). Further, the escalating shortage of African American teachers has been deplored repeatedly, with increasing alarm and a variety of proposed reforms for teacher recruitment and training (Garibaldi 1991).

The greatest amount of attention over the longest period of time, however, has undoubtedly been devoted to alterations in classroom curriculum and instructional practices (Stringfield and Yoder 1992). Compensatory education, such as Chapter 1 programs, has a lengthy history of providing supplemental curricula and materials, diagnostic/prescriptive services, and additional classroom staff in an effort to remediate the deficits of economically disadvantaged students (Slavin 1987). Accelerated education programs (McCarthy and Levin 1992) begin from the opposite premise. Students are assumed to be capable of high levels of achievement, and the curriculum enhances thinking skills and motivation by providing relevant and challenging materials and instruction. Culture specific curricula, such as Afrocentric education for African American students and multicultural curricula in ethnically diverse schools are other active arenas for reform efforts in teaching and learning.

Estimating the usefulness of separate schooling for African American males will be best accomplished against this backdrop of multiple reform efforts. African American boys are a highly diverse group of individuals as are all students. Some students might well benefit from sex- and gender-segregated public education, as has been documented for Catholic education (Riordan 1990). On the other hand, some students may be better served by alterations in curriculum (e.g., more personally relevant or challenging) and instruction (e.g., more collaborative projects). For yet others, alterations in school climate (e.g., increased parental presence on campus) may provide the greatest academic benefits. Research must explore the aptitude-by-treatment interaction in the search for an optimal education for all children.

For example, I have recently investigated the motivational consequences of a dropout-prevention program that operates in a predominantly African American middle school (Hudley in press). This elective class offered group counseling, study skills instruction, and career awareness. Instruction was provided by the students' guidance counselor, an Anglo male, as part of a pilot program funded by the California State Department of Education. The class enrolled both males and females in equal numbers, and all students scored significantly higher on measures of intrinsic motivation for academic tasks and perceived academic competence than a comparison group of students who did not receive such instruction. This program successfully serves children of both genders and shows clearly that resegregation is not the only viable alternative for enhancing the achievement motivation of African American youth. However, race- and gender-specific programs may be best for some children.

We must therefore carefully consider the interactive effects of multiple reform strategies that occur simultaneously. For example, are the apparent benefits of race- and gender-specific programs due to their segregated environment, a changed relationship with the teacher, a more culturally relevant and challenging curriculum, or the unique interactive effects of all elements working in tandem? Would the same benefits accrue to girls in a similarly segregated program? Is this the best combination of reform elements for the enhancement of academic competence for these students, or is some other model as effective or more so? In sum, I remain cautious in my belief about the efficacy of segregated education programs as a solution to the underachievement of African American children. I would encourage the careful longitudinal and comparative study of a rich and diverse mix of these and other reform efforts. Each of our children deserves no less.

I would end with a cautionary note on the potential effectiveness of school-based solutions to macrosocial problems. The condition of African Americans and other minorities in America's inner cities is best characterized as deplorable. Problems of economic isolation and poverty, homelessness and substandard housing, crime and violence, racial discrimination, and a host of other ills continue to besiege the urban poor. When we realize that an equivalent education for African Americans and whites does not erase a substantial differential in either earnings or opportunities (Hacker 1992), it becomes clear that educational programs are no panacea.

If optimal personal development is truly the goal, we must see that all of our children are well educated and also provided with meaningful opportunities to achieve academic and career goals to the fullest extent of their abilities. We as a society must summon the collective will to improve not only the education but also the full context for development provided for the marginalized residents of our inner cities.

NOTES

1. This research was supported in part by a University of California Academy Senate General Research Grant. Appreciation is extended to the faculty and students who participated in this study as well as to research assistants Steve Edwards and Dan Dimmit.

REFERENCES

Anderson, Elijah. May 1994. "Code of the Streets." *Atlantic Monthly* 273: 81-94.

Ascher, Carol. 1991. *School Programs for African American Male Students* [Trends and Issues No. 15, Institute for Urban and Minority Education]. New York: ERIC Clearinghouse on Urban Education.

Boykin, A. Wade. 1986. "The Triple Quandary and the Schooling of Afro-American Children." Pp. 57-92 in *The School Achievement of Minority Children*, edited by U. Neisser. Hillsdale, NJ: Erlbaum.

Brooks, Robert. 1984. "Success and Failure in Middle Childhood: An Interactionist Perspective." Pp. 87-128 in *Middle Childhood: Development and Dysfunction*, edited by M. Levine and P. Satz. Baltimore, MD: University Park Press.

Brown, Ann, Annmarie Palincsar, and Linda Purcell. 1986. "Poor Readers: Teach, Don't Label." Pp. 105-143 in *The School Achievement of Minority Children*, edited by U. Neisser. Hillsdale, NJ: Erlbaum.

Bryk, Anthony, Valerie Lee, and Peter Holland. 1993. *Catholic Schools and the Common Good*. Cambridge, MA: Harvard University Press.

Comer, James. 1980. *School Power*. New York: Free Press.

Cullen, Cecelia. 1991. "Membership and Engagement at Middle College High School." *Urban Education* 26:83-93.

Dembo, Richard. 1988. "Delinquency Among Black, Male Youth." Pp. 129-165 in *Young, Black, and Male in America: An Endangered Species*, edited by J. Gibbs. Dover, MA: Auburn House.

"Detroit's African-Centered Academies Disarm Skeptics, Empower Boys." 1994. *Black Issues in Higher Education* 10(February):19-21.

Edelman, Marion. 1987. *Families in Peril: An Agenda for Social Change*. Cambridge: Harvard University Press.

Edmonds, Ron. 1986. "Characteristics of Effective Schools." Pp. 93-104 in *The School Achievement of Minority Children*, edited by U. Neisser. Hillsdale, NJ: Erlbaum.

Fordham, Signithia, and John Ogbu. 1986. "Black Students' School Success: Coping with the Burden of 'Acting White'." *Urban Review* 18:176-206.

Freeman, Ellen, and Karl Rickels. 1993. *Early Childbearing*. Newbury Park, CA: Sage.

French, John, Willard Rodgers, and Sidney Cobb. 1974. "Adjustment as Person-Environment Fit." Pp. 316-333 in *Coping and Adaptation*, edited by G. Coelho, D. Hamburg, and J. Adams. New York: Basic Books.

Garibaldi, Antoine. 1991. "Abating the Shortage of Black Teachers." Pp. 148-158 in *The Education of African-Americans*, edited by C. Willie, A. Garibaldi, and W. Reed. Westport, CT: Auburn House.

Hacker, Andrew. 1992. *Two Nations: Black and White, Separate, Hostile, Unequal.* New York: Scribner's.

Haynes, Norris, and James Comer. 1990. "Helping Black Children Succeed: The Significance of Some Social Factors." Pp. 103-112 in *Going to School: The African-American Experience*, edited by K. Lomotey. Albany, NY: State University of New York Press.

Hudley, Cynthia. 1993. "Comparing Teacher and Peer Perceptions of Aggression: An Ecological Approach." *Journal of Educational Psychology* 85:377-384.

Hudley, Cynthia. 1995. "Assessing the Impact of Separate Schooling for African-American Male Adolescents." *Journal of Early Adolescence* 15:38-57.

Hudley, Cynthia. (In press). "Effects of Alternative Educational Programming on Intrinsic Motivation Among Ethnic Minority Adolescents." To appear in *At-Risk Youth: Theory, Practice ,and Reform*, edited by R. Kronick. New York: Garland.

Hudley, Cynthia, and Sandra Graham. April, 1995. "Adolescents' Perceptions of Achievement Strivings." Paper presented at the annual meeting of the American Educational Research Association, San Francisco, CA.

Irvine, Jacqueline. 1990. *Black Students and School Failure: Policies, Practices, and Prescriptions*. New York: Praeger Publishers.

Jones-Wilson, Faustine. 1990. "The State of African-American Education." Pp. 31-51 in *Going to School: The African-American Experience*, edited by K. Lomotey. Albany: State University of New York Press.

Lerner, Jacqueline, N. Baker, and Richard Lerner. 1985. "A Person-Context Goodness of Fit Model of Adjustment." Pp. 111-135 in *Advances in Cognitive Behavioral Research and Therapy* (Vol. 4), edited by P. Kendall. Orlando: Academic Press.

Lockheed, Marlaine, and Susan Klein. 1985. "Sex Equity in Classroom Organization and Climate." Pp. 198-217 in *Handbook for Achieving Sex Equity Through Education*, edited by S. Klein. Baltimore: Johns Hopkins University Press.

Marcus, Geoffrey, Susan Gross, and Carol Seefeldt. 1991. "Black and White Students' Perceptions of Teacher Treatment." *Journal of Educational Research* 84:363-367.

McCarthy, Jane, and Henry Levin. 1992. "Accelerated Schools for Students in At-Risk Situations." Pp. 250-263 in *Students at Risk in At-Risk Schools*, edited by H. Waxman, J. Walker de Felix, J. Anderson, and H. P. Baptiste. Newbury Park, CA: Corwin Press.

Moore, Elsie, and A. Wade Smith. 1992. "Positive Segregation?: The Consequences of Separate Schools for African-American Males." *The National Alliance of Black School Educators Journal* 1:16-21.

Narine, Marcia. 1992. *Single-Sex, Single-Race Public Schools: A Solution to the Problems Plaguing the Black Community?* [ERIC Document Reproduction Service No. ED 348 423]. Springfield, VA: ERIC Document Reproduction Service.

National Center for Health Statistics. 1991. "Advance Report of Final Natality Statistics. *Monthly Vital Statistics Report*, 40(8 Suppl.). Hyattsville, MD: Public Health Service.

National Education Goals Panel. 1995. *1994 National Education Goals Report*. Washington, DC: U.S. Government Printing Office.

Oakes, Jeannie. 1985. *Keeping Track: How Schools Structure Inequality*. New Haven, CT: Yale University Press.

Pauley, Edward. 1991. *The Classroom Crucible: What Really Works, What Doesn't, and Why*. New York: Basic Books.

Perry, Teresa, and James Fraser. 1993. "Reconstructing Schools as Multiracial/Multicultural Democracies: Toward a Theoretical Perspective." Pp. 3-24 in *Freedom's Plow: Teaching in the Multicultural Classroom*, edited by T. Perry and J. Fraser. New York: Routledge.

Price, Hugh. July 2, 1995. "Unacceptable, Divisive, and Cynical." *The Los Angeles Times*, p. M5.

Reed, Rodney. 1988. "Education and Achievement of Young, Black Males. Pp. 37-96 in *Young, Black, and Male in America: An Endangered Species*, edited by J. Gibbs. Dover, MA: Auburn House.

Riordan, Cornelius. 1990. *Girls and Boys in School: Together or Separate?* New York: Teachers College Press.

Schiefele, Ulrich, Andreas Krapp, and Adolph Winteler. 1992. "Interest as a Predictor of Academic Achievement: A Meta-Analysis of Research." Pp. 183-212 in The Role of Interest in *Learning and Development*, edited by K. A. Renninger, S. Hidi, and A. Krapp. Hillsdale, NJ: Erlbaum.

Shapiro, Harold. July 2, 1995. "Fuel Faith in the Power of Learning." *The Los Angeles Times*, p. M5.

Simms, Margaret. 1986. "Black Women Who Head Families: An Economic Struggle." Pp. 141-152 in *Slipping Through the Cracks: The Status of Black Women*, edited by M. Simms & J. Malveaux. New Brunswick, NJ: Transaction Books.

Slaughter, Diana, and Deborah Johnson. 1988. *Visible Now: Blacks in Private Schools*. Westport CT: Greenwood Press.

Slavin, Robert. 1987. "Making Chapter 1 Make a Difference." *Phi Delta Kappan* 69:110-119.

Steele, Claude. April, 1992. "Race and the Schooling of Black Americans." *Atlantic Monthly* 269:68-78.

Stringfield, Sam, and Nancy Yoder. 1992. "Toward a Model of Elementary Grades Chapter 1 Effectiveness." Pp. 203-221 in *Students at Risk in At-Risk Schools*, edited by H. Waxman, J. Walker de Felix, J. Anderson, and H. P. Baptiste. Newbury Park, CA: Corwin Press.

Vanfossen, Beth, James Jones, and Joan Spade. 1987. "Curriculum Tracking and Status Maintenance." *Sociology of Education* 60:104-122.

Washington, Valora. 1982. "Racial Differences in Teacher Perceptions of First and Fourth Grade Pupils on Selected Characteristics." *Journal of Negro Education* 51:60-72.

Weis, Lois. 1985. *Between Two Worlds: Black Students in an Urban Community College*. Boston: Routledge.

Willie, Charles, Antoine Garibaldi, and Wornie Reed. 1991. *The Education of African-Americans*. Westport, CT: Auburn House.

CHAPTER 6

Gender Equity and the Organization of Schools

Valerie E. Lee

GENDER ISSUES IN RESEARCH ON GENDER AND SCHOOLING

A Point of Departure

For readers to evaluate the validity of research and other expository writing, I suggest that it is useful to know the viewpoint of the writer. The general focus of my research and writing is on school organization, particularly how the organization of secondary schools influences their students' educational progress. Although educational researchers typically take students' race, ethnicity, family social class, and gender into account in their analyses, sociological research that focuses on educational equity infrequently centers on gender differences. In any single study, the focus would typically be on one social dimension. In this chapter, I describe my several studies that focus on educational equity by gender. These studies, mostly quantitative in nature and generalizable to a broad population from which the samples are drawn, represent the source of my thoughts and conclusions reported here. The boundaries of these studies are laid out later in the chapter.

A Hot Topic

Issues of gender and education have moved to the front burner recently. Together with larger societal reasons for this new-found prominence, three recent and widely circulated publications have brought the issues into the public consciousness. One is the 1992 report by the American Association of University Women (AAUW), *How Schools Shortchange Girls*. Launched in a blizzard of publicity, the report aimed to raise America's consciousness (and conscience) about gender equity in educational settings. Myra and David Sadkers' 1994 book, *Failing at Fairness: How America's Schools Cheat Girls*, has also drawn public attention to gender issues in schools. The AAUW report and the Sadkers' book were followed by Peggy Orenstein's 1994 book, *School Girls: Young Women, Self-Esteem, and the Confidence Gap*, written with the sponsorship of the AAUW. These writings did not just drop out of the sky, of course. They are embedded in a substantial (if not always solid) base of more scholarly and frequently theoretical work on gender. What is a short list of major issues about gender equity and schools that may be drawn from these books? I raise only a few of the many possible ones and organize this chapter around them. Although I state these issues as facts, later in the chapter readers will see that I question some of these "facts."

- *Issue 1: Gender Differences in School Achievement.* Girls are not doing as well in school as boys, particularly in the areas of mathematics and science. In these discussions, little attention is directed toward educational outcomes on which girls might be favored. That is, gender equity is viewed as a one-sided phenomenon, with boys consistently outperforming girls.

- *Issue 2: Gender Issues in Classroom Treatment.* Girls do not receive fair treatment in schools. Teachers focus most of their efforts on boys and either systematically ignore or actively discriminate against girls. Girls' contributions in class discussion are disregarded or undervalued. There is a general feeling that boys fare better in schools than girls and that discrimination in classroom treatment is a major factor.

- *Issue 3: Gender and Self-Esteem.* Girls lose self-esteem as they mature and advance through the educational process. This is seen largely as a function of the schooling process, with a systematic undervaluing of the way girls think, learn, and react. At the very least, even if schools are not the primary source of the problem, they are seen as responsible for correcting it.

- *Issue 4: Instructional separation or integration?* Because of the inherent inequity seen in the educational system as it relates to its female clients, a desirable solution (for either the short or the long term) is to educate girls in educational settings where the genders are separated. These settings can take the form of either single-sex schools or single-sex classes (especially for math and science). This type of separation is seen as particularly beneficial to girls, especially if it involves same-sex role models as principals and teachers. Single-sex effects on boys are usually not considered (except, perhaps, for Afrocentric all-male academies, where the lack of male role models is a major issue, or in all-male publicly funded colleges such as VMI or the Citadel).

HOW MY RESEARCH RELATES TO THESE ISSUES
Boundaries
Among the myriad issues relating to the education of females, I discuss only a few (I hope, interesting) ones. Instead of reviewing the full research base on these issues, I draw on my own research and conclusions about them (based on empirical evidence).[1] My intention is not to provide details about the design and findings of these studies, most of which have been published elsewhere, but rather to summarize the findings of these studies that relate to the issues spelled out above. There are some clear drawbacks to this approach. The studies may seem incomprehensible in snippets, and the conclusions I draw may not seem well supported. Besides the limitation of this approach, there are also several boundaries to what my research brings to these issues.

For example, in this chapter I draw only on gender studies that focus on the educational development of students—and exclude those targeted on teachers and principals. A second constraint is methodological. Most of my research is quantitative in nature. That means that some may feel that it lacks the richness of case studies or ethnographies of educational settings. Other boundaries are location and approach. The focus of most of my studies has been on schools, and my approach is sociological rather than psychological (i.e., a focus on groups rather than on individuals). In the language of research, this relates to the units of analysis. Typically my work focuses on students "nested" in schools. This leads me to explore such psychological or attitudinal issues as self-esteem less often than academic behaviors (such as engagement with school) and academic outcomes (especially achievement).

Another boundary concerns students' educational level and age. Most of my research has focused on high schools. Thus, the issues I explore involve adolescent girls and boys (or is it "men and women"?). The obvious confusion we face in talking about students in their teenage years is more than semantic. Are they children? Though they are certainly someone's children, this term seems pejorative. "Boys and girls" feels a bit insulting, but "men and women" does not seem quite appropriate. My usual solution is to use the generic "student" when possible or "young men and young women." Clearly, adolescents are on the boundary of childhood and adulthood. What we call them is surely a function of how we think about them. Linguistic difficulties are related to the very identity of an adolescent.

Gender, Academic Outcomes, and Equity

A recent study, sponsored by the AAUW, investigated school climate and its effects on girls' and boys' educational outcomes: engagement with school and achievement in reading, mathematics, science, and social studies (Lee, Chen, and Smerdon 1995). The work constitutes a part of AAUW's second-stage research agenda: to explore issues of school climate that affect girls' school success, particularly in the middle school years. We studied 8th graders, using data from the base year of the National Educational Longitudinal Study (NELS:88), a large national database of students and schools collected by the U.S. Department of Education.

Rather than detailing our findings about school climate here, I want to highlight how gender equity has *not* always been, but (I suggest) should be, defined. The AAUW "Shortchanging Girls" report (1992:2) states that, "Whether one looks at achievement scores, curriculum design, self-esteem levels, or staffing patterns, it is clear that sex and gender make a difference in our nation's public elementary and secondary schools. There is clear evidence that the educational system is not meeting girls' needs." This statement, the tenor of the report, the publicity surrounding its release, and the public discussions thereafter suggest that girls are being systematically "shortchanged" by the American educational system.

There is a lot of truth to this statement and a lot of research to support it. Although I do not wish to understate the problems girls face in the educational system, I also want to point out that not all educational outcomes show disadvantages for girls (as the statement would imply). The first step in our gender and school climate study was to examine observed gender differences in achievement and engagement for U.S. 8th graders—including no statistical adjustments. We certainly found gender differences that favored boys for some educational outcomes (namely achievement in social studies and science). There were, however, gender differences of equal or greater magnitude favoring girls—in reading achievement and engagement with school. Surprising to some was a non-finding: there were no observed gender differences in mathematics achievement for a large and nationally representative sample of students of this age.

My point here is a simple one, and it targets definitions. Gender equity in education should be defined as the absence of gender differences in educational outcomes. It should not be restricted to only those outcomes on which girls are disadvantaged. In some cases, boys are disadvantaged. Happily, there are some outcomes (for example, mathematics achievement at the end of the 8th grade) where there are no gender differences.[2] A lack of stratification in educational outcomes by gender is a positive finding, and more should be made of it. Gender differences in any educational outcomes are troubling. I suggest that gender differences that disadvantage boys in reading are just as problematic as those disadvantaging girls in science. Why shouldn't we pay attention to all of these? I argue, quite simply, for a "gender-neutral" definition of gender equity. Politicizing the gender question—which often paints girls as victims in an unjust world—is unfortunate. Inequity and injustice are wrong, period.

Gender and Classrooms

The theme of the Sadkers' book—systematic bias in the treatment of girls in American classrooms—is also spelled out in detail in the "Shortchanging" report. "From grade school through graduate school female students are more likely to be invisible members of classrooms. Teachers interact with males more frequently, ask them better questions, and give them more precise and helpful feedback," the Sadkers state on the opening page of their book. This type of sexism is important to document, and I do not question the general findings. The fact is that in most educational settings, girls' ideas and contributions are undervalued and given less credence.

There is considerable empirical support for these findings about "sexism in classrooms." Rather than question the finding, my concern in raising it lies in what is sometimes offered as a solution to this problem. Quite a lot of my work compares students in single-sex and coeducational schools (all private schools, but large and random samples of schools of this type). A particularly relevant study describes results of systematic observations in classrooms (English, mathematics, science, and history) in 21 elite secondary schools (Lee, Marks, and Byrd 1994). By definition, the gender-discriminatory classroom interactions typically reported in research could occur only in coeducational settings. The aim of our study, reflected in its design, was to explore the nature and prevalence of sexism in high school classrooms. Because our study focused on gender, we felt it was useful to study single-sex and coeducational classroom settings. Thus, we observed several classrooms in each of seven girls' schools, seven coeducational schools, and seven boys' schools—86 classrooms in all.

Some findings support the Sadkers' contentions. We found the type of sexism the Sadkers describe, which we labelled "gender domination," in many classrooms in coeducational schools (particularly in science classes). The argument here relates to what some see as a remedy for this phenomenon: to separate the instruction of boys and girls into single-sex classrooms (or schools). Besides the sexism in coeducational classrooms, our study found a considerable amount of sexism in single-sex classrooms. However, it was of a different type. Rather than gender domination, which can only occur when both genders are present, we found a type of sexism we called "gender reinforcement" quite prevalent in both boys' and girls' schools. Another type, "embedded discrimination," was observed in all three types of schools,[3] but it was more common in single-sex classrooms. Sex-role stereotyping was almost absent from the coeducational classrooms, but we saw many examples of this type in both boys' and girls' schools. Several instances of one very troubling type of sexism, "explicitly sexual incidents," were observed only in boys' schools.

A few other findings are relevant here. One relates to the types of classes where we observed incidents of sexism. In boys' schools, most sexism was in English classes; in coeducational schools, most (but not all) incidents were in science classes (especially Chemistry). Sexism in girls' schools was rather evenly distributed across subject areas. Another had to do with the gender of the teacher. By design, single-sex schools seek out a gender match between teachers and students. Yet it was in these "matched" situations—where everyone in the classroom shared the same gender—where we found some of the most flagrant sexism (particularly in boys' schools). While recognizing the risk of confusing readers by drawing conclusions from a study without describing it in detail, I draw two major conclusions from the research I have just described:

- Sexism comes in many forms, only one of which is described in most research on gender and classrooms. Though it takes both genders to create a "gender domination" situation, the presence of both genders in a class seems to moderate other types (e.g., sex-role stereotyping);
- The single-sex classroom, particularly in public schools, seems to be a fast-growing reform idea. The charter school movement appears to allow single-sex public schools in many states. Although it may seem that these innovations represent a solution to the problems spelled out in the Sadkers' book, I suggest that they may create others. Later I expand on this point.

Another recent study about gender differences has relevant findings about classrooms (Lee and Burkam 1996). It was the first of a series of three studies sponsored by the National Science Foundation. In these studies we attempted to explain why there are gender differences in science achievement among 8th graders, why these differences favor boys, and particularly why the female disadvantage in science achievement for young adolescents is largest for the most able students (that is, the potential scientists of the future). The studies targeted two issues: the course and test item emphasis on science subject matter (life science vs. physical science) and the science classroom.

For 8th graders, science-based gender differences are located entirely within physical science achievement and, as suggested, most pronounced for students who do the best in school (that is, students who report having received mostly A's in science since

Grade 6). Because virtually all 8th graders take science, and the emphasis of their courses does not vary by gender (or by the gender of the teacher), differences in what and how many science courses students take—a typical explanation given for gender differences—could not explain these findings. We focused our investigation on the character of instruction in 8th-grade science. We were chagrined to learn that only a quarter of U.S. 8th graders (virtually all of whom take science) report having even one laboratory experience per week. Although the presence or absence of lab experiences was not related to student achievement in science (in analytic terms, there was no main effect for lab experience on achievement), there was a laboratory-by-gender interaction effect. The meaning of this interaction effect is as follows: although the lab experience had no effect on science achievement for boys, such experiences had a positive effect on girls' achievement. Our findings lead to another conclusion about classrooms, especially in science:

- Among young adolescents, the most able girls are the most disadvantaged in science achievement. As this is the pool from which future woman scientists are likely to emerge, this is important. Women are grossly underrepresented in physical science fields. The special importance of hands-on (i.e., laboratory) science experiences for girls is noteworthy. This argues for making sure girls are involved in laboratory classes, particularly in the physical sciences, and that they are encouraged into full participation in these settings. Again, I am not suggesting that this be accomplished in all-female settings.

Gender and Self-Esteem

My research says little about this outcome, mainly because I see self-esteem primarily as an attitude held by individuals about themselves, and not particularly amenable to direct intervention by schools. Within the educational world, I question the trend in gender-equity studies to pursue self-esteem as a "stand-alone" educational outcome. I regard self-esteem or, as it is commonly referred to, "self-concept" as an attitude that is developed as a byproduct of success in school, rather than a substitute for success. It could be simplistic, but I believe that when students experience solid and demonstrable success in school, their self-esteem will take care of itself. In my work I have not had much success in relating elements of the organization of schools to this outcome.[4]

My concerns here may be more political than empirical. I have noticed that Americans worry about raising the self-esteem of groups whom the educational system has failed badly: racial and ethnic minorities, children from poor families, and now girls. The assumption is that if we make such children "feel better about themselves," then they can learn. This kind of discussion, in my opinion, suffers from a confused causal order. I would argue that "feeling good about yourself" is a direct result of success. Thus, I recommend that researchers and the concerned public turn away from "self-esteem" as an independent outcome of the schooling process. In relation to gender equity, I fear that focus on this "affective" domain would be seen as uniquely important for females. I don't buy it--I'm a female, but I have not had too much trouble with my "self-esteem." My conclusion, grounded on personal beliefs and others' research, is simple:

- Self-esteem is not an appropriate educational outcome worth pursuing on its own. Our efforts are better directed to raising children's (here we speak of girls') performance. Children's self-esteem goes up when they are successful in school.

Single-Sex Schools, Yes or No?
I have made some reference to my research in this domain. It has taken me several years and a lot of introspection to decide where I stand on this issue. Before I lay out my own answer to this question, let me provide some context by describing the structure of the research, how it has evolved over time, and a short description of each study.

A Little History. In the United States, single-sex education at the elementary and secondary levels is available only in private schools. Systematically, Title IX enforcement has been evoked in efforts to close the last few public single-sex schools. Historically, education in the two types of schools where single-sex education is still alive—Catholic schools and elite private schools—was developed almost exclusively separate by gender. Tyack and Hansot (1990) describe the interesting history and demise of single-sex education in the public sector. Although my comments are most relevant for secondary schools, the same trend is observed for elementary schools. In fact, single-sex education is more common at the secondary than the elementary level (likely in recognition of and reaction to the development of adolescent sexuality).

For many interesting reasons, the trend has been in one direction: a steady decrease in the number of single-sex institutions. Although the rate of decline has slowed in recent years, no new single-sex schools have opened. Schools have either closed their doors entirely, opened them to the other gender (instantly doubling the pool of qualified candidates), or merged with an opposite-sex school to form a larger and more viable coeducational institution. Moreover, this trend has been somewhat selective. There are still proportionately more single-sex Catholic than independent secondary schools. There are also more girls' schools than boys' schools (resulting in a gender imbalance in coed-school enrollments). In the secondary school world it is unusual to have women principals; thus, the demise of girls' schools has resulted in a decrease in the proportion of women principals. Sometimes the conversions away from single-sex status are contentious, and some have landed in court and/or received lots of media attention. The fact is that today there is more support for single-sex education for girls than for boys, and this support is very much tied to the gender equity issues that undergird this book.

Catholic School Studies. My work on the topic of single-sex education began within my research about Catholic schools. Our first study used national data from the High School and Beyond (HS&B) study collected on 1982 high school graduates to compare students who attended single-sex and coed Catholic high schools (Bryk, Lee, and Holland 1993; Lee and Bryk 1986). Because we hypothesized that single-sex school effects could be different by gender, we analyzed data separately for males and females. All my single-sex research has followed this design. The conclusions of this first study were quite clear: on a number of educational outcomes (particularly achievement, educational aspirations, and less stereotypic attitudes about sex roles in the family), girls in single-sex Catholic schools were favored over their coeducational counterparts. For boys, there were very few differences between the two types of schools, once a series of statistical controls was introduced. For neither gender was coed school attendance favored. Effects of single-sex school attendance were either positive or neutral. These effects, while quite pervasive, were either small or moderate in absolute magnitude.

Because of the longitudinal nature of the HS&B data,[5] we were able to investigate whether the single-sex high school effects would be sustained once students were in college (almost all the HS&B Catholic school students were in college four years later). Although few of the students were in Catholic colleges, and even fewer in single-sex colleges, we found that many of the effects of attending single-sex high schools were sustained through college (Lee and Marks 1990). Young women who had attended single-sex Catholic high schools had higher aspirations for graduate school attendance (especially in fields that were then considered non-traditional for women); they held less stereotypic attitudes about women in the work place, and they had more positive attitudes about social responsibility. We were a bit surprised that high school effects would hold up through the college experience (although our friends and colleagues who attended all-girls' Catholic high schools were not). Again, effects were small to moderate in magnitude.

Thus, we felt we had a sturdy set of findings about the benefits of single-sex education for young women, accompanied by no negative effects (but no positive effects either) for young men. But did these effects accrue to students because of the particular nature of Catholic high schools? Because my research at that time was intensely tied up with Catholic/public school comparisons, it seemed at least possible that it could be the "Catholicness" of these schools as well as their single-sex organization that could account for these findings.

Independent School Studies. To explore this issue, I pursued similar research questions in the other major group of U.S. schools which offer the single-sex alternative, elite private or "independent" schools that belong to the National Association of Independent Schools (NAIS). Unfortunately, there were no publicly available data about these schools, as they comprise only a very small proportion of the American secondary school universe (5 percent or less). I collected data in a random sample of 60 independent secondary schools, stratified by gender organization—20 girls' schools, 20 boys' schools, and 20 coeducational schools. The information about sexism in classrooms described above (Lee, Marks, and Byrd 1994) was collected in 21 of the 60 schools we sampled. The data differed from that used in the Catholic schools in several ways. Although we were unable to conduct a longitudinal study, as HS&B was, we surveyed students, teachers, and school heads for each school. Rather than testing students, we used achievement data from SAT tests and pretest data from admissions tests. We visited 21 schools, seven of each type. Our visits included observations in 86 classrooms, interviews with student groups and all math and English teachers, interviews with school heads, and extensive field notes about the visits. We thus compiled a rich picture of life inside single-sex and coed independent secondary schools.

An early study using these data investigated the types of students who choose single-sex and coeducational independent schools. Although we had found very little difference in the demographic and academic characteristics of students in the three types of schools in the Catholic sector, there were more differences in independent schools. For both boys and girls, students who selected single-sex schools were more religious, were more likely to have had relatives with single-sex school experience or a history of private schooling, and to have attended single-sex elementary schools themselves (K-12 independent schools are quite common, particularly girls' schools). Single-sex girls' school students had somewhat lower entrance scores in mathematics. Boys' school students were more likely to have come in as transfers. Although both boys and girls reported choosing the school because of its single-sex status, smaller size, and availability of boarding facilities, they were as likely to cite a strong social as an academic reputation as a motivating factor.

Because of the relationships of religiosity and family history to the choice of single-sex schooling for both genders, we concluded that independent school students were more likely to choose single-sex schooling for its traditional than its opportunity structure. This finding was contrary to typical discussions of this subject in which girls' schools (in particular) are seen as providing opportunities for their students' development that might be constrained in a coeducational setting (a contention in the AAUW report and the Sadkers' book). Although that is always possible for individual students and schools, these findings did not support the opportunity structure motivation for girls selecting single-sex independent schools.

We also investigated the relative effectiveness of single-sex independent schools on a wide array of outcomes, following closely the design of the Lee and Bryk (1986) study in Catholic schools. Because results were not conclusive, we did not pursue publication for our work on "relative effectiveness." There was no special pattern for or against gender grouping for either gender; on some outcomes students in girls' schools did better than their coeducational counterparts, on others the reverse. The same non-pattern was true for comparisons among boys. Thus, we felt that we could give the "Which works best?" question only a very equivocal response within the elite private school sector. At the time, we were disappointed and perplexed by these findings; our earlier studies in Catholic schools favoring the girls' school experience were just not generalizable to the independent sector. We began to wonder why.

Catholic and Independent School Differences. All these studies and a lack of clear patterns made us wonder, "What is really going on here?" Several possible reasons for the inconsistency in findings between the two types of schools seem reasonable, although it is not possible to subject these explanations to rigorous empirical scrutiny with available data. One possible explanation relates to who goes to these schools—what sociologists call their "social location." It is clear that while Catholic high schools have traditionally served a largely middle-class or working-class (and overwhelming Catholic) clientele, increasingly these schools have come to serve more minority, disadvantaged, and non-Catholic students and families. Our research on Catholic schools, which includes Catholic/public comparisons, documents the particular effectiveness of these schools for disadvantaged students (Bryk, Lee, and Holland 1993). Their tuitions, while not trivial for families of modest means, are considerably lower than those in independent schools.

Independent schools, for the most part, have an upper-middle or upper-class clientele. Not only are many of these schools selective in academic terms, their high tuitions make them quite selective in economic terms. Independent schools are for the elite, while Catholic schools seldom are. Catholic schools thus offer the promise of social mobility to their students, while independent schools' social aims are more likely the maintenance of privilege (mobility for people at the top would only be downward). Such "social location" differences suggest that students in Catholic schools might seek out these schools for their opportunity structures, and this could be particularly true for girls. Our evidence suggests that this is not the case in independent schools, where families may be seeking them out for their traditional and/or status preservation aims.

The substantial social distance between families and students in the two sectors might also explain the differing roles of teachers. We found the teaching staffs in single-sex schools in both sectors to be well matched to their schools' gender compositions. Although female teachers in Catholic girls' schools may serve as potential professional role models for their students, it is unlikely that independent school students view any teacher—male or female—as a credible professional role model. Interviews in those schools suggested that although students respected their teachers as authority figures with subject matter expertise, students spoke with some disdain about "teaching" as a profession. In fact, students in these schools (male and female) were aiming only toward high-income professions. Unless their own mothers had high-paying and prestigious jobs (which was rare), their mothers' professional status was not respected. We heard references to their mothers' work as "little jobs."

Another reasonable explanation for the sector difference in findings resides in the schools' history. There is a differential picture of school selectivity and single-sex status within the two sectors. As mentioned, both sectors' history is dominated by single-sex organization at the secondary level. However, as coeducation began to take hold in the Catholic sector, these were established as schools with fewer resources, more often operated by parishes and dioceses than religious orders. Even today, most single-sex Catholic schools are either owned, operated, or sponsored by religious orders. Religious-order schools are the relative elites among Catholic schools. Overwhelmingly, then, the more prestigious Catholic high schools are single-sex schools operated by religious orders (for example, Sacred Heart or Jesuit schools). In the independent sector, some schools (particularly the more progressive ones) began as coeducational schools. In the wave of conversion to coeducation which swept the sector in the 1970s and 1980s, it was the most elite boys' schools that moved to coeducation—the Andovers, Exeters, Grotons, St. Pauls, and Choates. Although there are some exceptions, in the independent school world, the most elite schools are now coeducational—boys' schools that either started accepting girls or subsumed a girls' school.

Although these potential explanations for the differences in findings across the sectors may provide some intellectual satisfaction, a major problem remains. I suggest it is not possible to draw firm conclusions about the value of single-sex secondary schools as providing an opportunity structure for young women to take their rightful place in the professional or personal world. In personal terms, this conclusion has created a serious dilemma. In the most instrumental terms, I have a contract to write a book on this topic, and that was premised on a solid base of research on single-sex schools. What should I conclude? I've done a lot of research on this topic, so I must have learned something. I'm not inclined to throw myself into five or more years of research to learn more. So what do I say in this book? Let me offer a conclusion here, albeit a bit uncomfortably. I recognize that this conclusion is somewhat contradictory to those I have drawn in my research on this topic about a decade ago.

- In general, separating the secondary educational experience by gender, either in separate classrooms or separate schools, is not an appropriate solution to the problem of gender equity in educational settings, in either the short or the long run. Although separate-by-gender education may benefit particular students (usually, girls), or be beneficial to some in particular settings (perhaps in Catholic schools), the research basis for the benefits of single-sex education as a policy change is not solid.

TOWARD A BROAD THEORY OF GENDER EQUITY AND SCHOOL ORGANIZATION

What follows represents a series of speculations about what my research on single-sex schools, and other gender-equity research I have done, adds up to—what it all means. Although these speculations grow out of my own research and familiarity with the general body of research on gender equity and schools, they should be seen as personal speculations. A major benefit of the forum of a book chapter (compared to a journal article) is the ability to be somewhat more receptive to more speculative and subjective comments. I am taking advantage of this receptivity.

Gender and School Climate

To lay the groundwork for the approach I advocate, let me provide a bit more detail about a recent study I referred to above. The aim of that study, sponsored by the AAUW, was to identify the characteristics of school climate that are associated with high levels of engagement and achievement, together with the equitable distribution of these outcomes among 8th grade boys and girls (Lee, Chen, and Smerdon 1995). This paper was cited earlier to illustrate the direction of gender differences in educational outcomes for young adolescents. The paper used a rather new statistical method, hierarchical linear modeling, that reflected the nature of the research question. We were interested in the association of school factors with student outcomes, including how those outcomes are distributed by gender inside schools. This sort of research question and data structure—called, "school effects research"—characterizes much of my research.

The AAUW-sponsored study explicitly looks at gender gaps inside schools as functions of school organizational features. The study takes into account other personal characteristics of students besides their gender (race/ethnicity, social class, and academic background). We defined school climate along three dimensions: (1) composition and structure climate (average SES, minority concentration, school size, and sector); (2) teaching and learning climate (tracking, authentic instruction, teacher-student relations); and (3) normative climate (order and safety, academic press, parental involvement). In general, we found that these elements of school climate were more strongly related to achievement and engagement differences between schools than the so-called "gender gap" in these outcomes inside schools (which is how we defined gender equity in this study). Gender differences in educational outcomes are much smaller than those related to either race or class.

A few findings are noteworthy. There is generally more gender equity in smaller schools and in schools with a more academic orientation. Two findings were quite surprising. Although achievement in social studies is higher in schools with more positive relations between teachers and students, the gender gap is increased by this school climate factor. A similar finding relates to parent involvement. Schools with more parent involvement have higher gender gaps in mathematics. Both of these gender gaps favor boys. We usually think of parent involvement and positive relations between teachers and students as positive characteristics of schools, and in general these factors modestly increase achievement. But our findings also suggest some differential benefits to boys from teachers and parents. It is seldom thought that such generally positive organizational factors as parental involvement or teacher-student relationships could have differential (and not always beneficial) effects for some students. But with this kind of research design, and a large sample of students and schools, we were able to uncover some inequities that result from such school climate factors.

Some Organizational Characteristics of "Good" Schools
To lay more groundwork for the theory I want to propose, I move from the description of this study and momentarily away from research that focuses on gender. It is useful to describe in very general terms some findings from another series of studies that focus on school organization (but not in the context of gender). The studies investigate organizational effects on student outcomes, and all of them also consider social equity in some way (usually by social class). Though these ideas have grown out of our research on Catholic schools, my more recent work on school organization (within a school restructuring framework) has shown that these findings generalize to all schools.[6]

Several school organizational characteristics are associated with positive school outcomes. Very broadly defined, these outcomes involve a high average in terms of student achievement in a particular school, gains in achievement (or learning), or engagement with school, and also its equitable distribution within the school among students defined by their social background characteristics. My definition of equity, as mentioned earlier, suggests that educational outcomes should not be related to race, class, or gender. But equity should not arise because no one is learning. In more technical terms, a paired outcome of this sort might include a high school average gain in mathematics achievement (change in scores on the same math test between, say, 8th grade and 10th grade), and also a smaller "minority gap" or "gender gap" in the school (the difference in math gain between minority and white students or between girls and boys). We have come to call the high average achievement gain the effectiveness parameter and the low gender gap an equity parameter. Both are measured as characteristics of schools and of the students who attend them.

In a series of studies, my colleagues and I have searched for organizational characteristics of schools which are simultaneously related to the effectiveness and equity parameters—school characteristics that define "good" schools along those lines. Although not all of these characteristics were important in every study, several organizational features have emerged that show this characteristic pattern:

- Smaller school size;
- A constrained curriculum that is mostly academic in nature;
- A curriculum pattern that shows almost all students taking the same, mostly academic, courses (a core curriculum approach);
- Positive social relations among members of the school that define these schools more as communities than bureaucracies;
- A type of instruction that involves students in higher-order thinking, that is, characterized by constructivist teaching, and where students are encouraged and expect to become actively engaged in their learning;
- A pattern of this type of instruction that is pervasive across the school rather than isolated in particular classrooms where some teachers happen to know how and want to teach this way;
- A commonality among teachers in their beliefs in the ability of all their students to learn what they are taught, in the teachers' ability to "get through" to all their students, and in teachers' willingness to take personal responsibility for their students' learning.

What Does This Have to Do with Single-sex Schools?
I have asked readers to bear with me through many detours, describing many studies and some more general findings. Here comes the bottom line: Single-sex schools for girls often look this way.

Size. In our single-sex studies in both Catholic and independent schools, we have shown that girls' schools are somewhat smaller than either coed or boys' schools. Although all these private schools are small in comparison to public schools, girls' schools are relatively smaller yet. The schools themselves don't always see this as an advantage (after all, private schools need tuition dollars to make them go). But much of our research has shown that many other organizational factors on our list are simply easier to institute in smaller places.

Social Organization. Other studies I have done that examined gender issues in regard to teacher gender and principal gender have suggested that schools with female principals are quite different places (Lee, Smith, and Cioci 1993). The extant research is in substantial agreement: compared to their male counterparts, women principals exercise a more democratic and participatory management style, evidence a more personal leadership style, and focus more of their efforts on their schools' core technology than on management. It is also the case that among U.S. secondary schools, very few principals are women (around 10-15 percent).

One place that women principals are not in short supply is in girls' schools. In fact, when we tried to do a comparative study about the role of women principals in independent secondary schools, principal gender and school gender type were hopelessly confounded (Lee, Loeb, and Marks 1995): no boys' schools had women principals, only 10 percent of coed schools' principals were women, but 60 percent of girls' schools had women principals. I suggest that girls' schools are most likely to have women principals (and women teachers). Not by accident (and clearly related to the gender of the principal), girls' schools are more communally organized. Social interactions among administrators, teachers, and students are more informal and more prevalent. Principals are actively engaged in the learning aims of their schools. The aims of principals become the aims of their schools. We also know that girls' schools (and women teachers) are especially likely to espouse social justice as an explicit aim in their schools (Marks 1994). Thus, the equity findings discussed earlier—related to race and class as well as to gender—are more likely to accrue in girls' schools.

Academic Orientation. Although we have no direct evidence that girls' schools have more academic orientations than other types of schools, some indirect evidence seems applicable. Our findings from the Catholic school studies were that girls' school students had higher educational aspirations while still in high school and were more likely to plan graduate school in non-stereotypic fields (Lee and Bryk 1986; Lee and Marks 1990). Because the goals of almost all private schools (Catholic and independent) are academic, and because the curricula of these schools are almost always academic and virtually all students take only academic courses (they have no other choice), it is unlikely that the differences in this regard that we see among public schools would show up in the private schools where single-sex schooling is available. We did find, however, that in Catholic schools, girls' school students did significantly more homework, associated with more academically oriented peers, and took more math courses as well as having higher achievement in reading and science than girls in coeducational schools.

Instruction. Our studies have provided us with very little direct information about the quality or nature of instruction in single-sex schools. We do know that students in Catholic girls' schools reported higher quality instruction and gave their schools higher general ratings than their counterparts in Catholic coeducational high schools. We also observed more incidents of gender equity in girls' independent schools (particularly by male teachers) than in either coed or boys' independent schools. There is, thus, at least some indirect evidence to suggest that girls' schools have some advantage in the area of instruction.

FINAL COMMENTS
I admit to taking readers on a rather circuitous and lengthy journey. Because my conclusions about gender and school organization rest largely on the research I have done myself, it seemed important to provide a few details of the sources from which my conclusions and speculations have sprung. I suggest that proposed "solutions" to the problems of gender equity in American schools that advocate separating girls and boys for instruction, particularly in mathematics and science, are misguided. The research on single-sex schools (my own and others') should not be interpreted as favoring gender separation in educational settings.

Although the results of my research in the two sectors of private schools I have studied (Catholic and independent) have convinced me girls are seldom disadvantaged by being schooled in these separate settings, I think boys often are.[7] It is not possible, however, to offer separate-by-gender classes only for girls, without seriously damaging the coeducational balance in an individual school or in the entire sector. There are indications that supposedly coeducational settings that depart from a 50-50 balance toward larger proportions of boys have some negative effects on the girls in those settings (Lee, Marks, and Byrd 1994). This would be a logical result of offering single-sex schooling only for girls.

How should schools respond to differential performance by boys and girls? Separating instruction by gender is one response. It is often quite easy to accomplish, and it gives the impression of "really doing something" about the problems of gender inequity. As such, this solution might have some symbolic value. I suggest separate-by-gender classes (especially in math and science) represents a misguided approach. I think there is some danger in all-girls' classes in these subject areas. I have sometimes heard arguments that making these classes more "relational" or "nurturing" (a misguided interpretation of Carol Gilligan's or Nel Noddings' work) will make them better places for girls. Unfortunately, "relational" and "nurturing" are often interpreted as moving away from rigorous academics—as though girls couldn't take it (in our study of classroom sexism, we called this "wrapping Calculus in a pink ribbon"). I don't think that girls need this kind of "soft" touch to succeed. When we saw this kind of approach in some of the classrooms we observed, we classified this kind of approach as either "sex-role stereotyping" or "embedded discrimination." Separating the genders for instruction makes a basic assumption that boys and girls need or flourish under different instructional environments. My argument is that this often leads to a "soft touch" approach for girls. I don't agree that girls need a soft touch to succeed or flourish in school. The solution I propose is much more difficult. I suggest that it will also be considerably more effective. My solution to problems of gender equity in our schools is that they be reorganized (or restructured) in ways that I have suggested are associated with both effectiveness and equity (i.e., schools that are effective for all students). High schools should be smaller. There should be more intimate social relations among students and faculty in them. They should have an academic orientation that is directed toward all students. They should offer a type of instruction that encourages students to be actively involved in their own learning and focuses on higher-order thinking. They should be places where teachers take responsibility for all of their students' learning. High schools should function as communities. Schools like this are better places for all their students. Our evidence is that girls' schools are more likely to look this way, and I suggest that these organizational differences explain their effectiveness.

Sound easy? I don't mean to imply that it is. Moving schools in these directions is an enormous job. The large majority of U.S. secondary schools have a long way to go to look this way. Although reform efforts to reorganize or restructure schools in this direction are underway, their success in "bucking the bureaucracy" is uncharted at present. Moreover, reorganizing schools in the directions I've suggested is largely not a policy issue subject to top-down implementation (except, perhaps, school size). Rather than being decreed from on high, to succeed these reforms must be instituted school by school, usually by building coalitions of faculty who share these ideas and instigated by individual principals who are committed to these goals. Our evidence is that schools that look this way are better places for all their students, boys and girls, blacks and whites, rich and poor.[8] But changing teachers' attitudes, changing the nature of teaching, changing educational goals to focus on high-level courses and instruction for all students (and not just the most able or seeming most "deserving") are not easy things to do. One way to begin, surely, is to move more women into educational administration and not to assume that women make good principals only at the elementary level (assuming that "nurturance" is the major issue). I have spelled out a theory of school change that I believe has good empirical support and makes sense to me. But I certainly have not spelled out a program for school change.

NOTES

1. Throughout this chapter, when I use the plural personal pronoun ("we"), I am referring to my coauthor(s) in the particular study I describe. All of these studies have been conducted with the participation of other faculty and graduate student colleagues.

2. This finding seems to surprise many people. To me, this suggests just how far the assumption of female deficit in mathematics has "penetrated" the social conscience. The research on gender differences in mathematics suggests that girls actually outperform boys in the early grades, are equal in the middle grades, and the male advantage grows over the high-school years. In general, gender differences in academic outcomes seem to develop around the time of puberty.

3. We define gender reinforcement as "the perpetuation of gender-differentiated social definitions (conventional behaviors or studies typically associated with being male or female)". Embedded discrimination is defined as the residual sexism of a gender-stratified society that persists in such forms as linguistic usages, historical records, literary texts, or visual displays" (Lee, Marks, and Byrd 1994:102). In that article, we describe six different forms of sexism (of which gender reinforcement and embedded discrimination are the mildest forms), and we provide several examples of each form. Interested readers are referred to the article for more detail on the forms of sexism observed in a large number of single-sex and coed secondary school classrooms.

4. Two reasonable explanations for this come to mind. It could be because such attitudes are measured with notoriously low reliability. It could also be that this type of psychological state is simply not a function of school interventions (at least of the type I am interested in evaluating). It is not possible to untangle these two explanations with existing survey data.

5. This means that data were collected on the same students as they progressed through the educational system. For HS&B, these "waves" of data collection occurred every two years.

6. This series of studies was sponsored by the Center on Organization and Restructuring of Schools, a U.S. Department of Education-sponsored research center located at the University of Wisconsin-Madison and directed by Dr. Fred M. Newmann. The purpose of the studies was to investigate the effects of school restructuring on student outcomes.

7. Riordan (1990) has suggested that single-sex schools for African American boys may be advantageous. We have no particular evidence on this topic, and Riordan's evidence rests on a very small sample. Nevertheless, a gender-by-single-sex-by-race interaction is not impossible. I would conclude that there is very little support for either favoring or disfavoring this contention.

8. This evidence comes from a series of studies that have been conducted under the auspices of the U.S. Department of Education's Center on Organization and Restructuring of Schools, located at the University of Wisconsin-Madison and directed by Fred M. Newmann. See Lee and Smith (1993, 1995, 1996) and Lee, Smith, and Croninger (1995).

REFERENCES

American Association of University Women [AAUW]. 1992. *How Schools Shortchange Girls.* Washington, DC: Author.

Bryk, Anthony S., Valerie E. Lee, and Peter B. Holland. 1993. *Catholic Schools and the Common Good.* Cambridge, MA: Harvard University Press.

Lee, Valerie E., and Anthony S. Bryk. 1986. "Effects of Single-sex Secondary Schools on Student Achievement and Attitudes." *Journal of Educational Psychology* 78(5):381-395.

Lee, Valerie E., and David T. Burkam. 1996. "Gender Differences in Middle-grade Science Achievement: Subject Domain, Ability Level, and Course Emphasis." *Science Education* 80.

Lee, Valerie E., Xianglei Chen, and Becky A. Smerdon. 1995. *The Influence of School Climate on Gender Differences in the Achievement and Engagement of Young Adolescents*. Ann Arbor, MI: University of Michigan, School of Education (and AAUW, Washington, DC).

Lee, Valerie E., Susanna Loeb, and Helen M. Marks. 1995. "Gender Differences in Secondary School Teachers' Control Over Classrooms and School Policy." *American Journal of Education* 103:259-301.

Lee, Valerie E., and Helen M. Marks. 1990. "Sustained Effects of the Single-sex Secondary School Experience on Student Achievement and Attitudes." *Journal of Educational Psychology* 82(3):378-392.

Lee, Valerie E., and Helen M. Marks. 1992. "Who Goes Where? Choice of Single-sex and Coeducational Independent Secondary Schools." *Sociology of Education* 65(3):226-253.

Lee, Valerie E., Helen M. Marks, and Tina Byrd. 1994. "Sexism in Single-sex and Coeducational Independent Secondary School Classrooms." *Sociology of Education* 67(2):92-120.

Lee, Valerie E., and Julia B. Smith. 1993. "Effects of School Restructuring on the Achievement and Engagement of Middle-grade Students." *Sociology of Education* 66(3):164-187.

Lee, Valerie E., and Julia B. Smith. 1995. "Effects of High School Restructuring and Size on Gains in Achievement and Engagement for Early Secondary School Students." *Sociology of Education* 68(4):241-270.

Lee, Valerie E., and Julia B. Smith. 1996. "Collective Responsibility for Learning and Its Effects on Gains in Achievement for Early Secondary School Students." *American Journal of Education* 104(2):103-147.

Lee, Valerie E., Julia B. Smith, and Madalyn Cioci. 1993. Teachers and principals: Gender-related perceptions of leadership and power in secondary schools. *Educational Evaluation and Policy Analysis* 15(2):153-180.

Lee, Valerie E., Julia B. Smith, and Robert G. Croninger. 1995. Understanding High School Restructuring on the Equitable Distribution of Learning in Mathematics and Science. Paper presented at the annual meeting of the American Sociological Association, Washington, DC.

Marks, Helen M. 1994. The Effect of Participation in School-Sponsored Community Service Programs on Student Attitudes Toward Social Responsibility. Unpublished doctoral dissertation, University of Michigan.

Orenstein, Peggy. 1994. *School Girls: Young Women, Self-Esteem, and the Confidence Gap* (in association with the American Association of University Women). New York: Doubleday.

Riordan, Cornelius. 1990. *Girls and Boys in School: Together or Separate?* New York: Teachers College Press.

Sadker, Myra, and David Sadker. 1994. *Failing at Fairness: How America's Schools Cheat Girls*. New York: Scribners.

Tyack, David, and Elisabeth Hansot. 1990. *Learning Together: A History of Coeducation in American Public Schools*. New Haven, CT: Yale University Press.

CHAPTER 7

Race, Gender, and Ethnicity: How They Structure Teachers' Perceptions of and Participation in the Profession and School Reform Efforts

Michele Foster

Who are today's teachers? What are teachers' attitudes toward the profession? What are some of the policy issues that affect the professional lives of teachers as they enter the twenty-first century? How have teachers responded to these changes? Employing qualitative as well as quantitative data, this chapter addresses these issues. After a brief description of today's teaching force, it discusses some of the reasons for the declining numbers of teachers of color. Next, the chapter highlights some key points about teachers and teaching that were contained in the major reform documents of the 1980s. The chapter then explores teachers' experiences with various school reforms and the reactions of teachers to these experiences. Where available, data on differences and similarities in experiences and reactions among gender, racial, and ethnic groups are presented. Finally, the chapter suggests ways in which programs to restructure schools might take account of teachers' opinions, especially the opinions of women teachers of color who are so often ignored.

TODAY'S TEACHERS

There are more than two million public school teachers in the United States. The profile of the typical American teacher is a 42-year-old white woman who has taught for an average of 15 years, is a member of a teachers' organization, and holds a tenured position.

Students who enter teacher-training programs are predominantly white, female, and middle class. Some estimates are that 76 percent are female; 91 percent are white, and most come from suburban or rural backgrounds. Although 75 percent of the entire U.S. teaching force, except college and university, was composed of women in 1994, they were unevenly represented at the different levels of schooling. At the prekindergarten and kindergarten level, 98.1 percent were female. At the elementary level, the proportion of female teachers was 85.6 percent. At the high school level, however, the proportion of teachers who were female dropped considerably to 55.6 percent (U.S. Bureau of the Census 1995:411).

Since the late 1800s the teaching profession has been primarily a woman's profession, and both the pay and the status accorded teachers has been commensurate with occupations staffed primarily by women. In 1993 beginning teachers earned an average salary of $22, 505, but their average wages were between $5, 000 and $12,000 less than accountants, chemists, mathematicians, and engineers. Despite substantial increases over the decade, teachers are still paid comparatively less than employees who work in male-dominated professions. Whereas the 1994 average salary of teachers was $35,800 the average salaries of electricians, plumbers, and prison guards—male-dominated occupations with lower educational requirements—were $36,120, $40,080, and $25,938, respectively (U.S. Bureau of the Census 1995:165, 428; U.S. Department of Labor 1996:207).

Initially a male profession, teaching has been dominated by women since the turn of the century. The primary reasons for this change were economic, managerial, and philosophical. As more remunerative careers became available to men and not to women, women could be hired for less money. Women also were considered to be more pliant workers than men. Lastly, as conceptions of teaching changed to emphasize nurturing and patience, women were considered more appropriate for the role especially as elementary school teachers, where these qualities were deemed to be most important.

The low status ascribed to teachers was confirmed in a study conducted in the mid-eighties (National Education Association 1985). Although teaching was perceived to be a very demanding profession that contributed to society, teachers ranked much lower in occupational prestige than many other professionals such as physicians, college professors, judges, clergy, and lawyers.

Declining Numbers of Teachers of Color
Although teaching has historically been one of the primary occupations for blacks, the number of black teachers has steadily decreased since the seventies. In the mid-1950s, half of all black professionals in the United States were teachers (Cole 1986). By 1977, 22 percent of the 58,515 bachelor's degrees earned by African Americans were in education. Six years later, however, only 9 percent (or 5,456) of the bachelor's degrees earned by African Americans were education degrees (Stern 1988). Between 1970 and 1980 the percentage of black teachers dropped from 8.1 to 6.9 percent, while the percentage of other minorities in the teaching profession dropped from 3.6 to 3.4 percent. During the same period, the percentage of white teachers grew from 88.3 to 89.6 percent (National Education Association 1987). In 1981, the total percentage of ethnic minority teachers was only 9 percent. Six years later, although African Americans constituted 16.2 percent of the children in public schools, they comprised only 6.9 percent of the teachers. Latinos represented 9.1 percent of the children in public schools but only 1.9 percent of the teachers. Asian/Pacific Islanders comprised 2.5 percent of the children in public school, but less than 1 percent of the teachers. And Native Americans and Alaskan Natives represented 0.9 percent of the children in public schools but only 0.6 percent of the teachers (National Education Association 1987; Office of Educational Research and Improvement 1987). The precipitous decline in the number of African American teachers prompted some to note they were an endangered species (Cole 1986). Despite this decline, the percentage of ethnic minority teachers increased to 13 percent by 1991, the result of a growth in percentage of teachers of Latino origin, whose numbers had risen from 1.9 percent to 4 percent of public-school teachers (National Education Association 1991).

Reasons for the Decline
Three factors—desegregation, wider career opportunities, and the increase of testing at all levels—have combined to seriously constrain the number of individuals of color who choose teaching. Although not widely acknowledged in discussions about the current shortages

of African American teachers, desegregation had a profound effect on their numbers. Between the 1954 *Brown vs. Board of Education* decision and the early 1970s, approximately 31,584 African American teachers lost their jobs in 17 southern and border states (Ethridge 1979). African American teachers in Kentucky declined by 41 during the ten years between 1955-65, even though an additional 401 needed to be hired merely to keep pace with the increasing numbers of African American pupils. Moreover, a study of 467 school districts revealed that 127 of them had dismissed 462 African American teachers. As a result, by 1970, the student-teacher ratio among African Americans in the south was over twice that of the student-teacher ratio among whites (Stewart, Meier, LaFollette, and England 1989).

In addition to producing loss of jobs, desegregation also changed the relationships of African American teachers and their pupils in ways that made teaching less attractive to the teachers. This increased alienation of African American teachers is illustrated in the following statement from my life history research (Foster 1990, 1991a, 1991b) by an African American teacher who spent 43 years teaching first in segregated and later in desegregated schools:

It wasn't until after I began working I became disillusioned with what I saw in desegregated schools. The biggest difference is that we were able to do more with the black students in all-black schools. In other words, if I wanted to come in this morning and have my children put their books under the desk or on top of the desk and I'd get up on top of my desk and sit down. "Why are you here? Are you here just to make out another day? Are you here because the law says you must go to school? Are you here to try to better yourself?" This kind of thing I could talk to them about, well now that you're here, what must you do, what are the requirements? Do you know where your competition is? Your competition is not your little cousin sitting over there. Your competition is that little white kid sitting over in the other school. He's the one you have got to compete with for a job. And the only way that you're going to get that job is that you are going to have to be better than he is. And I could drill that into their heads. Once we integrated, I don't feel comfortable in a mixed racial class to really get into the things the whites did to us as black people. I don't really feel too comfortable talking about that because I know how I felt when they talked about me. But that kind of thing I couldn't do. I didn't want to pull them aside because they would feel that they were being pulled out of the mainstream. But this is the big difference. Another thing I got disillusioned with integration because I could not get to my people and tell them all the things that they needed to know. I couldn't beat into their minds that to compete with a white kid on an equal basis was not enough. I couldn't stop my class. I also saw a lot of black brothers get into the classes of white instructors who went into the class saying, not saying very loudly, but very clearly, this kid can't make it. And this really bothered me.

Beginning in the 1960s greater career opportunities in professions such as law, medicine, business, and engineering—largely the result of the civil rights' movement—have attracted large numbers of African Americans to these careers. The result is that African Americans, whose previous career options were limited, no longer choose careers in teaching. Expanding career choices have also affected the number of women who choose a career in teaching.

Like African Americans, women have enjoyed a greater range of occupational choices since the women's movement. Although more women are employed outside of the home than in the past, they have a larger choice of occupations, many of which have higher status and larger salaries. For example, between 1970 and 1994, the percentage of women engineers rose from 2 to 8.3 percent, the number of women lawyers from 5 to 24.6 percent, and the number of women physicians from 9 to 22.3 percent (U.S. Bureau of Labor Statistics 1977; U.S. Bureau of the Census 1995). Whereas the previous occupational structure limited the occupational choices of African Americans and women, the broadened occupational choices for these groups seem to have contributed to an increasingly negative image of teachers because of the assumption that the best qualified ethnic minorities and women no longer go into teaching.

One of the biggest barriers facing individuals of color seeking to become teachers has been the increase in testing. A required score of 835 on the SAT reduced Florida's entire candidate pool by 25 percent and reduced by 90 percent the number of black candidates who were eligible to matriculate into teaching training programs. Eighty-five percent of all candidates who took the Florida Teacher Exam in 1980, the first year the exam was given, passed. For African American candidates, however, the pass rate was only 35-40 percent (Dupre 1986). The failure rate for blacks in North Carolina was 87 percent compared to a rate of only 17 percent for whites, prompting one researcher to predict that, should the rate remain constant, North Carolina would be left with a teaching force that is 96 percent white (Hilliard 1980).

The statistics in California for the same period were not much better. There, of 6,644 minority candidates who sat for exams given to prospective teacher candidates in 1983, 3,854 (58 percent) failed. And although African Americans had the highest failure rate with only 530 (26 percent) of 2,040 candidates passing, other candidates of color also failed at substantially higher rates than whites. Only 39 percent—834 of 2,133—of Mexican Americans, and 50 percent—637 of 1,259—of Asian Americans taking the test qualified for entry into teacher education programs. Anglos passed at a rate of 76 percent, with 18,856 of 24,540 candidates qualifying for admission into teacher education programs (Gifford 1986). Comparable statistics are available for a number of other states, including Alabama, Texas, Pennsylvania, Georgia, Oklahoma, and Louisiana (Irvine 1988; Gifford 1986).

Despite criticisms of the way tests have been developed and used over the years, some researchers have used differences in test scores to support the racist notion that ethnic minorities are inherently inferior to whites in mental ability (Jensen 1980; Hernstein and Murray 1994). According to Gould (1981), standardized tests hinge on two fallacies, reification and ranking. The fallacy of reification has enabled test makers to develop and market abstract concepts of ability and intelligence as if they were hereditary, unitary, measurable commodities. Having reified the concepts of ability and intelligence in this manner, those who construct scales then raise the question of which individuals and groups have more or less of these commodities. This reasoning represents the fallacy of ranking which assumes that people and groups—such as those that differ in national origin, race, and ethnicity—can be rank-ordered in terms of how much of the supposed commodity they "possess" (Gould 1981).

There are other problems inherent in standardized tests. First, they do not predict how well individuals will do in later life and may merely measure how skilled people are at taking paper-and-pencil tests. Second, such tests are biased against people who are unable to solve problems at the rate of one minute or less per problem. Third, the tests are biased in favor of white middle-class experiences because many of the questions allude to information with which this group is more likely to be familiar. In addition, many people agree that the tests currently in use do not tap the energy, adaptability, perseverance, sense of humor, or other qualities that are indispensable to teaching.

Reasonable people do disagree, however, about what should be done. The low numbers of minorities who passed eligibility tests for teaching prompted the creation of a number of programs, pre-baccalaureate and baccalaureate, designed to recruit more teachers of color into the profession. College programs, community college transfer programs, loan forgiveness programs, and magnet or theme schools to encourage careers in teaching are examples of the kind of programs that were undertaken. The flaws that exist in standardized tests notwithstanding, a number of institutions have turned their attention to what they believe is the more critical task of helping students pass the tests.

The University of Florida in Gainesville, Grambling State University, The University of Arkansas at Pine Bluff, and Norfolk State University have instituted programs that insure that graduates of their teacher education programs are able to pass teacher examinations. Of the 200 candidates, including 50 ethnic minority students, who were enrolled in Florida's teacher education program between 1990-92, the overall pass-rate on the Florida Teacher Examination of candidates was 91 percent and for ethnic minority candidates it was 86 percent. The University of Arkansas at Pine Bluff and Norfolk State University have successfully raised the percentages of students passing the National Teachers Examination—Pine Bluff from 42 to 67 percent between 1983 and 1985 and Norfolk State from 28 to 71 percent between 1982 and 1985 (Whitehurst and Witty 1986; Antonelli 1985).

In 1980, Grambling, in danger of losing its accreditation because of its students' poor showing on the National Teachers Examination, undertook a comprehensive plan to insure that its students could pass the certification requirements. By 1985, Grambling had raised its students' pass rate on the National Teachers Examination from 5 to 85 percent. It accomplished this by adopting a three-pronged approach to helping students prepare for standardized tests. Grambling's program sought to improve students' basic skills; equip students with test-taking skills and strategies; and assist faculty in aligning their courses more closely with the professional competencies required by the National Teachers Examination.

Diagnosing and remediating students' basic skills were made priorities. Using content-related materials developed according to test specifications along with instruction on test-taking skills, students receive 10-12 hours of preparation for these tests. By requiring students to meet state requirements before graduating, Grambling has insured that its teacher education graduates will be eligible for state certification. One positive result of Grambling's new program is the increased numbers of students seeking admission to the College of Education. After averaging 1,200 students between 1972 and 1975, enrollment in the College of Education dropped to 200. By the spring of 1986, enrollment had reached 850 and was reported to be growing faster than any other program in the University (Spencer 1986). For its efforts, Grambling received the 1995 Showcase of Excellence Award presented by the American Association of State Colleges and Universities to institutions that had significantly improved the quality of their undergraduate teacher education programs. Grambling's success suggests that African American students will enroll in teacher education programs when they can be reasonably sure they will be given the support needed to meet the certification requirements upon graduation.

Policy makers have assumed that increasing the number of teachers of color is a goal worth pursuing not merely for the positive effect it may have on students of color but for the larger message it sends to children from the majority group about power and authority in America (Joint Center for Political Studies 1989). Yet, not all teachers agree that increasing the number of teachers of color is a goal worth pursuing. Although most teachers of color, 67 percent, feel that a greater minority presence is important, only 25 percent of teachers from non-ethnic minorities believe so (Metropolitan Life Insurance Company 1988). Ethnic minority teachers, moreover, agree with many of the program initiatives designed to recruit more teachers of color into the profession (Metropolitan Life Insurance Company 1988). Research supporting the idea that teachers of color will lead to improved academic achievement measured by standardized tests of students of color is limited. At least one research study, however, has found that black teachers are more positively disposed to teaching disadvantaged, low-achieving students with emotional needs than either Cuban or white teachers (Cohn and Kottkamp 1993).

REFORM DOCUMENTS AND THE TEACHING PROFESSION
As noted earlier, American teachers lack both the status and the pay characteristic of other professions. While this low status reflects the general devaluation of woman's occupations and professions, some scholars (Etzioni 1969; Lortie 1969, 1975) have argued that the low status is also related to the fact that the training received by teachers is not as intellectually complex as that of other professions and, unlike other professionals, teachers have not developed a shared technical knowledge base.

During the decade of the 1980s, a dozen policy documents calling for major reforms in American education were issued. Many of the reports spoke directly about restructuring and professionalizing teaching, which were linked to improving the preparation of teachers. In 1983 the National Commission on Excellence in Education published *A Nation at Risk: The Imperatives for Educational Reform*. This report noted that those entering the teaching profession were more likely to come from the least academically talented student populations and that teacher preparation programs emphasized methods courses at the expense of subject-matter courses. *A Nation at Risk* made several recommendations intended to improve both the preparation and the professionalization of teachers. Included among these recommendations were increasing salaries and tying salary increases, retention, and tenure to performance-based evaluations; adopting an eleven-month contract for teachers to allow for their continuing professional development; creating salary ladders that differentiate the novice teacher from the expert or master teachers; and involving master teachers in the creation of teacher education programs and the supervision of neophyte teachers.

Several other reports—including *A Nation Prepared: Teachers for the 21st Century*, released by the Carnegie Forum in 1986; *Tomorrow's Teachers*, authored by a group of deans of education (Holmes Group 1986); *First Lessons: A Report on Elementary Education in America* (Bennett 1986); and *Time for Results: The 1991 Governors' Report on Education* (National Governors'

Association 1986)—echoed the call for improving the knowledge and skills of the nation's teachers. These recommendations included increasing teachers' salaries to make them competitive with those of other professions; requiring a bachelor's degree in a discipline in the arts and sciences as a prerequisite to entering a teaching program; creating a new category of lead or master teachers; and developing career ladders with salaries appropriate to various levels.

One of the recommendations of *A Nation Prepared* (Carnegie Forum 1986) called for the creation of the National Board of Professional Teaching Standards, a certification board similar to national boards for lawyers and physicians. Not intended to supplant the minimum standards for beginning teachers, instead the National Board would establish advanced standards for experienced teachers and determine who meets them. The National Board was charged with creating a new method of assessment that would bear more fidelity to what teachers are required to do in day-to-day practice.

Based on demonstrated knowledge and skills, not on paper credentials, this new assessment would be developed around five core propositions. These are, first, that teachers are committed to students and their learning. Second, teachers must know the subjects they teach and how to teach them. Third, teachers are responsible for managing and monitoring student learning. Fourth, teachers must think systematically about their practice and learn from experience. Last, teachers are members of learning communities. A series of exercises developed around these core principles have been developed for a few specialty areas, and activities are being devised for several others. To date, the creation of activities that bear directly on the teaching and learning process have proceeded more effortlessly than others, such as, for example, those intended to gauge how well teachers are able to work collaboratively with parents.

It is too early to tell what effect these tests will have on the number of teachers of color. Initial certification tests administered from 1993 through 1995 suggest that, like other tests, these also have some adverse impact on teachers of color. In the 1993-94 field test of its certification system, 38.6 percent of all candidates who elected to participate in the Test on Early Adolescence/English Language Arts Certification Assessment were certified. However, whereas 41.6 percent of the white non-Hispanic candidates who elected to participate in the assessment were certified, only 16.6 percent of

African American candidates who elected to participate in the same assessment were certified.

In comparison to this gap of 25 percentage points between successful white and African American candidates, the gap produced by gender was much smaller. The percentages of women and men certified in the 1993-94 field tests were 39.8 and 29.1, respectively, a difference less than half as large as the one found for race. As these figures for gender indicate, women do not appear to be disadvantaged by the National Board of Professional Teaching Standards assessments, but men and African Americans may be. This conclusion needs to be accepted with extreme caution, however, because participation in the National Board certification tests is voluntary, and there is no way to know whether the participants are representative of the total population of teachers.

Non-representativeness seems particularly likely given the small numbers of African Americans who participated in the field tests described above. In 1993-94 only thirty-eight African American candidates participated in the National Board tests, and only one of these was male. By the following year, the number of African Americans participating had dropped below ten, and none of these passed the examination. In contrast, 45.1 percent of whites who took the tests in 1994-95 were certified, making the racial gap substantially larger than it had been the year before. (The gender gap in 1994-95 narrowed slightly from the previous year, with 41.6 percent of women and 33.3 percent of men achieving certification.)

Mindful of the need to create assessment instruments that are fair to ethnic minority candidates, researchers are currently undertaking a more rigorous, thorough, and careful program of research to insure that the National Board's content standards and associated assessments are not biased against ethnic minorities. Relevant to this effort is the question of whether the attitudes, behaviors, and skills required to teach in the classrooms populated by middle-class white students are the same as those needed to teach in the classrooms composed primarily of students of color or those composed primarily of urban pupils who live in poverty. Several researchers have addressed this issue. Irvine (1990) argues that lack of cultural synchronization—the tendency of teachers to misunderstand and fail to appreciate the cultural backgrounds, language, values, home environments, or learning styles of African American students—is one cause of their failure.

Other scholars who have examined teachers who are effective with particular groups of pupils have identified characteristics of their practice. Based on a review of the literature, Foster (1993, 1994) has specified five factors that characterize the practice of effective black teachers. These factors include expressing cultural solidarity with students, linking classroom content to students' experiences, using familiar cultural patterns, incorporating culturally compatible communication patterns, and focusing on the whole child. From an empirical study of effective teachers of African American students, Ladson-Billings (1994) has developed sets of postulates that mark culturally relevant, as opposed to assimilationist, teaching. These postulates are concerned with teachers' conceptions of self and others, of knowledge, and of social relations. Finally, in a longitudinal study Haberman (1995) has identified attributes of "star" teachers, individuals who are successful with poor urban students. Comprised of attitudes as well as behaviors, these attributes include persistence, protecting learners and learning, the ability to generalize principles from practice, a professional not a personal orientation toward students, developing mechanisms to protect themselves from stress, the capacity to admit mistakes, and the belief that even in the most difficult circumstances, teachers can make a difference and should be held accountable.

While none of these attributes is necessarily in conflict with those proposed by the National Board of Professional Teaching Standards, there is the danger that these newer tests may end up replacing a set of correct answers with a set of preferred teaching styles, styles that may be unrelated to the academic growth of students least well served by the schools. Perhaps the most important lessons to be drawn from these studies are Haberman's (1995) observations that functional behaviors of effective teachers of poor, urban children can be taught but the ideology undergirding them cannot and must be selected for, that the most successful teachers of poor urban children are over thirty, which is ten years older than the traditional teacher education candidates, and, finally, that the training of teachers for poor urban students is best accomplished in the most difficult urban schools, not in most advantaged suburban ones, which is the current practice. The current practice of preparing teachers under ideal conditions and then awarding them a certificate that enables them to work in any school is wrong headed. According to Haberman, best practice ought to be thought of as teaching that occurs under the worst, not the best, conditions.

Alternative Certification

In order to alleviate shortages of teachers in certain locations or in certain subject-matter specialties, many states have developed alternative certification routes. According to Pipho (1986), by the late 1980s, at least twenty-seven states had introduced some approach to alternative certification of new teachers. Those favoring alternative certification argue that such programs are a way to attract academically talented individuals into teaching who are unlikely to enter the profession through traditional routes. Such is the case with the program called Teach for America, whose participants are largely drawn from Ivy League and other elite colleges.

Not all observers are enthusiastic about emergency and alternative route certification programs. In a harsh and stinging critique of Teach for America and other alternative certification routes, Darling-Hammond (1994) argues that in too many instances teachers recruited under such programs are not exposed to a systematic curriculum, to ongoing interactions with faculty, to adequate mentoring, or to any kind of assessment. Lacking courses in curriculum theory, models of teaching, child development, and educational foundations, participants in Teach for America (TFA) often retreated to rote learning, worksheets, and punitive disciplinary measures. Moreover, TFA teachers had a much higher attrition rate than other new teachers. In 1990 only 42 percent were still teaching, which is half the retention rate for teachers trained in teacher education programs.

Citing a study that compared Dallas teachers certified through alternative routes with those certified via traditional routes, Darling-Hammond (1994) notes that teachers with alternative certification were found to be deficient in every category of teaching and that their students achieved less well in reading and language arts than teachers who had participated in teacher education programs. Even worse, teachers with alternative certificates are more likely to be placed in the classrooms of impoverished urban and rural students, those most likely to benefit most from experienced, competent, and well-trained teachers.

TEACHERS' ATTITUDES TOWARD SCHOOL REFORMS

As the major focus of the reform documents has directly concerned teachers, it is instructive to consider how teachers have responded to these initiatives, what they think are the key issues facing American education, and what their general attitudes are toward the profession.

A series of yearly surveys of teachers conducted between 1984 and 1988 (Metropolitan Life 1984, 1985, 1986, 1987, 1988) provides information about teachers' attitudes. One assumption of these reforms was that they would lead to improved teaching and consequently better student achievement. When questioned in 1984 and 1985, teachers had mixed views about the effect of various proposed reforms on the quality of teaching. In the 1984 survey, teachers overwhelmingly supported the idea of career ladders—giving teachers the opportunity to take on more responsibility for higher pay, of making it easier to fire incompetent teachers, and of requiring teachers to pass competency exams before becoming certified. Teachers were less enthusiastic about periodic retesting in subject matter, higher salaries for teachers who work in areas of shortage, and hiring people who were not certified to teach. New teachers tended to be more enthusiastic than older ones, and high school teachers were more likely to support these proposals than teachers at other levels. Seventy-one percent of teachers believed that merit pay could work if an objective standard could be found on which to base decisions.

When questioned a year later, only 36 percent of teachers believed that the reforms had a positive effect on teachers. The impact of the reforms on students was perceived to be larger, with 42 percent reporting that they felt the reforms had a positive effect on students and 44 percent reporting no effect. Queried about specific reforms, teachers were most likely to endorse mentor teacher programs (82 percent in favor) and least likely to endorse merit pay schemes (71 percent opposed). Teachers were almost evenly split on the idea of career ladders, with 49 percent favoring the concept and 46 percent opposed to it. In this survey, as in the one conducted in 1984, younger teachers reported more favorable attitudes toward all three reforms. Only 17 percent of the teachers surveyed in 1986 worked in school systems that had one of these reforms in place. Half of the teachers endorsed the idea of specialty certification boards such as the National Board of Professional Teaching Standards.

Although these surveys measure teachers' attitudes, they do not capture teachers' experiences with the innovations, nor do they plumb the depth of teachers' experiences. A 1986 study by the National Education Association questioned teachers about how the various reform efforts in their school districts had affected them. The range of answers, some of which are quoted below, support and expand the data from the surveys.

> We pay better teachers more is easy to say but difficult to carry out. Tennessee's career ladder plan, enacted in 1984, has led to an enormous bureaucracy and a high degree of teacher mistrust in the system. Secrecy and manipulation of data in order to maintain a quota make the evaluations unworkable and unfair. Merit pay brought success to some politicians, but the $14,000 starting salary won't attract the best and brightest into the teaching profession. It's driving them away.

> I got a $3,000 bonus under the master teacher program implemented last year. The test I took to qualify for the bonus had very little to do with what I do in the classroom. The money for bonuses would be better spent for increased salaries and classroom improvements. For any politician to feel that a business person knows more about education than an educator is absurd. If I could talk to the governor of Florida and his cabinet, I would tell them to drop merit pay. Absolutely.

> We have a lot of disgruntled teachers here in Texas. Before March all we heard about was the teacher and administrator competency test. Newspapers predicted that 10 percent would fail. How's that for building morale? The career ladder plan has cause a lot of disagreement within school districts. I've taught for 29 years, and I know what we really need to improve schools: more work on classroom discipline, school attendance, and parental cooperation.

California's education reform package, passed in 1983, includes a mentor teacher program that allows teachers to share skills, methods, and curriculum ideas with other teachers. The program is working well in my district. We're looking at curriculum development, standardized tests, and gifted and talented programs, among other things. I serve on a curriculum committee that includes both mentors and other key people from the schools. We get valuable feedback from our colleagues at school. I'm planning activities for the extended day program that will help kids enjoy school and encourage them to stay in school.

A study of teachers in Dade County, Florida (Cohn and Kottkamp 1993), questioned them about their attitudes toward merit pay before such a program was actually implemented and immediately following its implementation. These teachers endorsed the principle of merit pay—rewarding meritorious teachers—but, like other teachers, they doubted whether the implementation could be unbiased. They also worried that merit pay schemes would create cleavages among teachers. Follow-up interviews conducted after merit decisions were disclosed illuminate some of the dilemmas underlying teachers' attitudes. When actually implemented, merit pay proved problematic for the teachers judged meritorious as well as those judged not worthy. The most pervasive dilemmas were the lack of correspondence between teachers' scores and their performance, the reliance on limited observations, and the schism it created between meritorious and non-meritorious teachers.

Regarding increasing teacher participation in school management, 90 percent of the teachers thought increased participation in managing school affairs was desirable. Teachers were more favorably inclined toward participation in those activities of school management that were directly linked to students' learning such as discipline, textbook selection, and in-service programs. Teachers showed less enthusiasm for hiring new teachers and evaluating colleagues and even less interest in tasks typically under the purview of administrators such as budgeting and scheduling and handling students' non-education problems (Metropolitan Life 1986).

Research conducted over three years in 12 school districts on shared decision-making confirms many of these attitudes. The study (Weiss 1995) found that many teachers were skeptical about whether their decisions would be respected. In some schools, teachers' decisions were overturned or ignored and even when they were upheld many teachers who had witnessed cycles of aborted reform efforts had misgivings about the newest reforms. Similar to what was discovered in the surveys, the researchers found that teachers were more interested in matters of student discipline or in curricular and pedagogical changes. Because teachers sought to avoid conflict with colleagues, they were reluctant to serve as peer evaluators. Moreover, when reform-minded or younger teachers took leadership roles in implementing change, they were often meet with resistance and disapproval.

A study of a small number of urban African American teachers (Foster 1993) reached similar conclusions. This study classified teachers into three groups—the cynical resisters, the coincidental cooperators, and the reform minded—according to their attitudes toward and their degree of participation in school reforms. Both the cynical resisters and the coincidental cooperators were teachers with long tenure in their respective school systems who had witnessed repeated cycles of aborted reforms and who were consequently reluctant to participate in the newest reforms. The main difference between these two groups was that the kinds of school reforms that were introduced into the schools at which the coincidental cooperators taught were consistent with their values, which involved working directly with students.

As in the surveys, the younger teachers in Foster's (1993) study were most enthusiastic, most likely to embrace school reforms and become involved in them. Even younger teachers, however, would terminate their participation in reform efforts unless certain condition such as a shared vision for positive student outcomes could be achieved. Two of the three cynical resisters in this study were men, whereas the teachers in the other two categories were women, which may point to gender differences in teacher attitudes toward restructuring. But the qualitative nature of the study and its non-random sample suggests that this point needs to be interpreted cautiously.

Another study of restructuring schools found that despite their success with African American students and their enthusiasm for participating in school reform programs, the input of African American teachers who worked in schools dominated by a majority of white teachers was disregarded (Lipman 1996). The study also found that tacit taboos against raising racial issues and the wish to keep white middle-class families enrolled in the school system were the primary reasons that conversations about race were suppressed. The result was the marginalization of the African American teachers who gradually disassociated themselves from the reform efforts.

There are a few lessons that emerge from these studies. One is that teachers are more inclined to buy into those aspects of educational reform that are closest to what goes on in their classrooms. A second is that various configurations of status and power relations in the schools and the communities they serve can either foster or stifle the participation of certain groups of teachers.

Teacher Satisfaction

Despite the controversies about teacher training and teacher quality, reported levels of job satisfaction among teachers have increased over the last decade. A survey that questioned teachers about job satisfaction each year between 1984 and 1988 (Metropolitan Life 1984, 1985, 1986, 1987, 1988) found that in 1984, 40 percent reported that they were very satisfied. The percentage of teachers reporting the same level of satisfaction rose to 44 percent in 1985 and fell to 33 percent in 1986. However, by 1987 the satisfaction level had equaled that reported in 1984, and by 1988, 50 percent of teachers reported being very satisfied. Women and teachers with more than five years experience reported the greatest increase in levels of satisfaction.

Between 1987 and 1988, the number of women reporting that they were "very satisfied with" teaching rose from 41 to 55 percent, whereas the percentage of men reporting the same level of satisfaction rose only one percent from 39 to 40 percent. Teachers who report higher levels of satisfaction with their careers are more likely than others to judge their relationships with students as positive, and women and teachers in elementary schools, the majority of whom are women, are more like to report that their relationships with students are positive. Women teachers are also more likely to report that they have greater informal levels of interaction with their students.

Between 1981 and 1991, the percentages of teachers who said they certainly would or probably would choose to teach again had risen from 46 to 59 percent. Despite increasing levels of satisfaction, the number of teachers who said they are likely to leave the profession remained stable at 26 percent, but teachers with less than five years experience were more likely to say they will leave. Although levels of satisfaction are positively correlated with teachers' likelihood of leaving the profession, minority teachers at all levels of satisfaction were more likely to report that they were likely to leave teaching. Forty percent of ethnic minority teachers compared to 25 percent of non-minority teachers said that they were possibly or very likely to leave the profession. Minority teachers with fewer years' experience were most likely to indicate that they planned to leave teaching, with 55 percent of those with less than five years' experience and 43 percent of those with five to nine years' experience stating that they were very or possibly likely to leave teaching. The corresponding figures for non-minority teachers were 31 percent for those with less than five years' experience and 27 percent for those with five to nine years' experience.

One explanation for this disparity is differences in work conditions: ethnic minority teachers surveyed were three times more likely than the non-minorities to work in the inner city, to work with students from low socioeconomic backgrounds, and to report that their schools had to contend with serious social problems (Metropolitan Life 1988). In addition, ethnic minority teachers expressed harsher criticism of their colleagues, a greater percentage claiming that their fellow teachers had minimal expectations for student learning, only went through the motions when teaching, and demonstrated little command of subject matter. The feeling that one's own views are not being heard or respected may also be greater among minority teachers. All of these themes emerge in the following statement by a Chicago teacher who has taught in Philips High School in Chicago, one of the high schools that serves students from the public housing project known as the Robert Taylor Homes:

> There are some successful schools, but ours is not. There are successful teachers. There are all kinds of success stories around there, but they're so isolated. Too many teachers are jealous of each other. We see one succeed and rather than trying to help, we try to tear down, we don't understand the basis of their success or that one has to work hard for what one gets. Teachers may glean ideas from here and there, from yourself, your students and colleagues and then build from that but there is no panacea out there. The solutions comes

from within. An idea might not work for me, but it might work for you.

The unhappy moments take place outside the classroom. Mostly I'm just disappointed in the lack of concern and care. Over the years the administration has refused to entertain ideas, some of the ideas that you put forth. Yet five or six or two or three years later, when everything else has failed, you hear your ideas being bandied about. No one will ever admit it of course. It is as if they feel you are trying to take something away from them or trying to show them up. Rather than stifling, a school can urge, motivate, and make an effort to bring out teachers' talents. Teachers have many talents. Even the worst teachers that you can think of have some kind of talent. But teachers have to get away from petty jealousies and work together for a common good. You don't see too much of that at the high school level. And teachers have to stop trying to get away with doing nothing. Convincing ourselves that what we are doing is for the kids when it really is not for them. Talkers don't do that much anyway. I like doers. The life of a teacher successful to teach in a mediocre school is a difficult and lonely one. If you are teaching at a school where kids are learning, there is the possibility of some collegiality. But if there are only a few kind of islands or safe havens, you're an island. You're a loner. It's frustrating because you're alienated from the school and from your colleagues. It's frustrating because you can't communicate and there is no one with whom you can discuss things. Sometimes it makes you feel as though you are some kind of idiot. It's upsetting, but I have too much pride to let it get me down. All of that can be very painful.

In my study of African American teachers from which this quotation is taken (Foster 1990), teachers referred to a "golden age" (Louis and Miles 1990). They highlighted a period when relationships between school and community were closer, when there was much greater correspondence among the views of the teachers, and when the political climate of the 60s and 70s in the black community served as a galvanizing force for academic excellence among African American students. This period disappeared, it was felt, once the struggle for formal educational opportunity had been achieved (Comer 1988; Foster 1990). These feelings were strongest in teachers who had worked in schools with all-black faculties and student bodies and among teachers who had attended such schools as children.

Some researchers maintain that recalling a "golden age" is conservative and retards innovation because it stresses a return to the past and typically blames students and communities for the declining educational climate at the local school (Lowe and Kantor 1989; Kantor and Lowe 1989). For these teachers the notion of a golden age is cast in a different light. To them it is reminiscent of a period when the schools took greater responsibility for establishing and maintaining working relationships with students and community and when the charged political climate in the black community facilitated these efforts. The myth of the golden age can be a conservative call for a return to ineffective ways. But as Comer's (1988) research has amply demonstrated, particular aspects of the past, especially those that attempt to create closer relationships between community and school, can be successfully incorporated into school reform efforts of the present (Siddle-Walker 1993). Such reforms seem likely to increase the satisfaction and retention rates of African American teachers.

Another study by Moore (1987) confirms many of these findings. This study found that teachers from upper socioeconomic backgrounds were more satisfied with their careers than teachers from lower socioeconomic backgrounds, that white teachers reported higher levels of satisfaction than either African American or Latino teachers, with Latino teachers expressing the least satisfaction with their careers, that older teachers—those in their forties—were more satisfied than teachers in their twenties, and that women were more satisfied than men. According to this study the typical profile of a teacher expressing the highest levels of satisfaction is a white woman in her forties who belongs to a higher socioeconomic background. In contrast, the typical profile of a teacher expressing the most dissatisfaction with the profession is a younger Latino or African American male teacher from a low socioeconomic background. These men cited the low status, pay, and power and the lack of respect for their work as the primary reasons for their dissatisfaction.

One male equated his struggle for acceptance as an African American with that required of teachers to gain recognition:

I see my own struggle as a Black man coinciding with teachers struggles to receive acceptance as professionals . . . . We have to be just as militant about gaining recognition as the civil rights and women's movements were (Moore 1987:22).

TEACHER VOICES AND SCHOOL RESTRUCTURING

A large-scale five-year study of 44 schools in sixteen states (Newmann and Wehlage 1995) has found that, although there is no one best model of school restructuring, it is more likely to be successful in raising student achievement when four interrelated factors are present. First, the focus of school restructuring must be on student learning. The primary activities of successful schools were constructed around the goal of student learning. Second, the pedagogy and accompanying assessment measures must be authentic. Successful schools employed authentic pedagogy—instructional techniques that require students to think, acquire in-depth understanding, and apply these understandings to real-world situations—and students from all socioeconomic backgrounds benefited from this pedagogy. Third, the organizational changes should develop the capacity for the creation of professional communities. Although the creation of new organizational structures was a critical element in the most successful schools, introducing new structures and practices sometimes backfired and distracted faculty efforts from student achievement. Without high levels of trust, leadership, and the development of professional skills, structural changes were unlikely to produce the necessary changes. Fourth, external organizations and groups must institute policies that enable schools to enhance students learning. The external influences on schools—local, state and federal regulations, parent and citizens groups, and unaffiliated, autonomous projects—could pull schools into so many directions that they made successful school reform impossible. In schools where school reform efforts were successful, teachers tended to have developed a shared consensus that encompassed academic work of high intellectual quality, and they were able to articulate their expectations to parents and students.

Educational research is increasingly acknowledging diversity among students resulting from cultural, ethnic, and social class background, but too many researchers continue to treat teachers as members of an undifferentiated group (Foster 1990, 1991a, 1991b; King 1991). They have failed to consider how different backgrounds of teachers and divergent experiences and understandings shape their response to school reform or to ponder how diversity can be used to produce the twin goals of improving the achievement of students currently least well served by existing schooling arrangements and providing the means for teachers from diverse backgrounds to develop shared consensus, mutual respect, and the capacity to achieve more equitable outcomes for students from diverse backgrounds.

Consequently, while large-scale studies such as this may be useful for understanding the community and institutional factors that facilitate school restructuring, they provide no guidance or insight into the processual factors that might enable the voices of women, ethnic minorities, and other marginalized teachers to become active participants in the discourse of school change even when they appear discordant. Some critics have argued that the perspectives of ethnic minority teachers, researchers, teacher educators, and parents are often excluded from ongoing discussions about what curricula, pedagogy, and teaching styles are appropriate for children from their communities (Joint Center for Political Studies 1989; Delpit 1988, 1986; Grant and Gillette 1987).

By way of illustration, although ethnic minority and non-minority teachers agreed that minimum standards for students, greater school funding for troubled schools, before and after-school activities, and counseling, health services, and other support structures could help students overcome educational problems, much larger percentages of ethnic minority than non-minority teachers believed that other changes would help disadvantaged students overcome their educational disadvantages. These changes include establishing magnet or theme schools, creating specialized schools for ten-to fourteen-year-olds, assigning students the same teachers for several years, having specified standards students must meet before being promoted, allowing students to choose the school they want to attend, and holding principals and teachers more accountable for failing students. (Metropolitan Life 1988).

Writing about recent research that has made it a point to include the teachers' voice, Hargreaves (1996) warns us not to dismiss "the voices of marginalized and disaffected teachers whose perspective may threaten our views." Indeed, two studies have examined how even well-intended reform efforts marginalize teachers who may hesitate to embrace or even resist change. A study of several schools that were participants in the Coalition of Essential Schools found that some teachers were part of a "vanguard," teachers actively committed to school reform, while other teachers remained unconvinced that changes were necessary (Muncey and McQuillan 1992). Another study of a site-based management program in Dade County found that teachers had coalesced into two groups based on their enthusiasm or lack thereof for the proposed reforms (Collins and Hanson 1991) . In both cases teachers who were supporters of school change formed cliques that effectively shut out the voices of the teachers who were reluctant to embrace the proposed changes. In turn, teachers who were excluded from conversations perceived that those committed to change were being favored and were behaving as if they were administrators.

The process of change required to achieve permanent, equitable school reforms will be incremental and slow, will involve risk, and will produce conflict. Teachers will need to confront their different philosophies of education, plumb their personal and cultural perspectives, and probe how their prejudices consciously and unconsciously affect their beliefs about the inability of poor children to learn. As with past reforms there is no guarantee that current restructuring efforts will automatically enfranchise students from non-mainstream backgrounds. Without serious, on-going discussions about the ways race and gender structure schooling, influence the way schools operate, and shape the perceptions of those who work in them, contemporary school restructuring efforts will not radically transform schools.

REFERENCES

Antonelli, George A. 1985. "Revitalization of Teacher Education in Arkansas." *Action in Teacher Education* 7(3):63-64.

Bennett, William J. 1986. *First Lessons: A Report on Elementary Education in America*. Washington, DC: U.S. Government Printing Office.

Carnegie Forum on Education and the Economy. 1986. *A Nation Prepared: Teachers for the 21st Century*. New York: Carnegie Forum.

Cohn, Marilyn M., and Robert B. Kottkamp. 1993. *Teachers: The Missing Voice in Education*. Albany: State University of New York.

Cole, Beverly. 1986. "The Black Educator: An Endangered Species." *Journal of Negro Education* 55(3):326-334.

Collins, Robert A., and Marjorie K. Hanson. 1991. " School-Based Management/ Shared Decision Making Project, 1987-1988 through 1989-90: Summative Evaluation Report" ERIC Document ED 331922.

Comer, James P. 1988. "Is 'Parenting' Essential to Good Teaching?" *NEA Today* 6(January):34-40.

Darling-Hammond, Linda. 1994. "Who Will Speak for the Children? How 'Teach for America' Hurts Urban Schools and Students." *Phi Delta Kappan* 76(1):21-34.

Delpit, Lisa. 1986. "Skills and Other Dilemmas of a Progressive Black Educator." *Harvard Educational Review* 56(4):389-385.

Delpit, Lisa D. 1988. "The Silenced Dialogue: Power and Pedagogy in Educating Other Peoples Children." *Harvard Educational Review* 58(3): 280-298.

Dupre, Beverly B. 1986. "Problems Regarding the Survival of Future Black Teachers." *Journal of Negro Education* 55(2):55-66.

Ethridge, Samuel B. 1979. "Impact of the 1954 Brown v. Topeka Board of Education Decision on Black Educators." *Negro Educational Review* 30(4):217-232.

Etzioni, Amitai. (Ed.). 1969. *The Semi-Professions and Their Organization: Teachers, Nurses, Social Workers.* New York: The Free Press.

Foster, Michele. 1990. "The Politics of Race: Through African-American Teachers' Eyes." *Journal of Education* 172(3):123-141.

Foster, Michele. 1991a. "Constancy, Connectedness, and Constraints in the Lives of African-American Teachers." *NWSA Journal* 3(2):233-261.

Foster, Michele. 1991b. "'Just Got to Find a Way': Case Studies of the Lives and Practice of Exemplary Black High School Teachers." Pp. 273-309 in *Readings on Equal Education*, Volume 11: Qualitative Investigations in Schools and Schooling, edited by M. Foster. New York: AMS Press.

Foster, Michele. 1993. "Urban African-American Teachers' Views of Organizational Change: Speculations on the Experiences of Exemplary Teachers." *Equity and Excellence in Teaching* 26(3):16-24.

Foster, Michele. 1994. "Effective Black Teachers: A Literature Review." Pp. 225-241 in *Teaching Diverse Populations: Formulating a Knowledge Base*, edited by E. R. Hollins, J. E. King, and W. C. Hayman. Albany: State University of New York.

Gifford, Bernard R. 1986. "Excellence and Equity in Teacher Competency Testing: A Policy Perspective." *Journal of Negro Education* 55(3):251-271.

Gould, Stephen J. 1981. *The Mismeasure of Man.* New York: W. W. Norton.

Grant, Carl, and Maureen D. Gillette. 1987. "The Holmes Report and Minorities in Education." *Social Education* Nov/Dec. :517-521.

Haberman, Martin. 1995. "Selecting 'Star' Teachers for Children and Youth in Urban Poverty." *Phi Delta Kappan* 76(10):777-781.

Hargreaves, Andy. 1996. "Revisiting Voice." *Educational Researcher* 25(1):12-19.

Hernstein, Richard J., and Charles Murray. 1994. *The Bell Curve: Intelligence and Class Structure in American Life.* New York: The Free Press.

Hilliard, Asa. 1980. "The Changing Black Teacher and Diminishing Opportunities for Black Teachers." Paper presented at the National Invitational Conference on Problems, Issues, Plans and Strategies Related to the Preparation and Survival of Black Teachers. (From ERIC, Abstract NO. ED 212 565.)

Holmes Group. 1986. *Tomorrow's Teachers. A Report of the Holmes Group.* East Lansing, MI: The Holmes Group.

Irvine, Jacqueline Jordon. 1988. "An Analysis of the Problem of the Disappearing Black Educator." *The Elementary School Journal* 88(5):503-513.

Irvine, Jacqueline Jordan. 1990. *Black Students and School Failure: Policies, Practices and Prescriptions.* Westport, CT: Greenwood Press.

Jensen, Arthur R. 1980. *Bias in Mental Testing.* New York: The Free Press.

Joint Center for Political Studies. 1989. *Visions of a Better Way. A Black Appraisal of Public Schooling*. Washington, DC: Author.

Kantor, Harvey A., and Robert Lowe. 1989. "Reform or Reaction?" *Harvard Educational Review* 59(1):127-138.

King, Joyce. 1991. "Unfinished Business: Black Students' Alienation and Black Teachers' Pedagogy." Pp. 245-271 in *Readings on Equal Education*, Volume 11: Qualitative Investigations in Schools and Schooling, edited by M. Foster, New York: AMS Press.

Ladson-Billings, Gloria. 1994. *The Dreamkeepers: Successful Teachers of African Children*. San Francisco: Jossey Bass.

Lipman, Pauline. 1996. "The Missing Voice of Culturally Relevant Teachers in School Restructuring." *The Urban Review* 28(1):41-62.

Lortie, Dan C. 1969. "The Balance of Control and Autonomy in Elementary School Teaching." Pp. 1-53 in *The Semi-Professions and Their Organization: Teachers Nurses, Social Workers*, edited by A. Etzioni. New York: The Free Press.

Lortie, Dan C. 1975. *Schoolteacher: A Sociological Study*. Chicago: University of Chicago Press.

Louis, Karen Seashore, and Matthew B. Miles. 1990. *Improving the Urban High School: What Works and Why*. New York: Teachers College Press.

Lowe, Robert, and Harvey Kantor. 1989. "Considerations on Writing the History of Educational Reform in the 1960's." *Educational Theory* 39(1):1-9.

Metropolitan Life Insurance Company. 1984. *The Metropolitan Life Survey of the American Teacher*. New York: Author.

Metropolitan Life Insurance Company. 1985. *The Metropolitan Life Survey of the American Teacher of Former Teachers in America*. New York: Author.

Metropolitan Life Insurance Company. 1986. *The Metropolitan Life Survey of Teachers: Restructuring the Teaching Profession*. New York: Author.

Metropolitan Life Insurance Company. 1987. *Survey of the American Teacher, 1987: Strengthening Links Between Home and School*. New York: Author.

Metropolitan Life Insurance Company. 1988. *The Metropolitan Life Survey of the American Teacher, 1988: Strengthening the Relationship Between Teachers and Students*. New York: Author.

Moore, Barbara M. 1987. Individual Differences and Satisfaction with Teaching. ERIC Document (ED 282 851).

Muncey, Donna E., and Patrick J. McQuillan. 1992. "The Dangers of Assuming a Consensus for Change: Some Examples from the Coalition of Essential Schools." Pp. 47-69 in *Empowering Teachers and Parents: School Structuring Through the Eyes of Anthropologists*, edited by G. S. Hess, Jr. Westport, CT: Bergin & Garvey.

National Board of Professional Teaching Standards. n.d. *What Teachers Should Know and Be Able to Do*. Detroit: Author.

National Commission on Excellence in Education. 1983. *A Nation at Risk: The Imperatives for Educational Reform*. Washington, DC: U.S. Department of Education.

National Education Association. 1985. *Survey of NEA K-12 Teacher Members*. Washington, DC: Author.

National Education Association. April 1986. *NEA Today*. Washington, DC: Author.

National Education Association. 1987. *Status of the American Public School Teacher 1985-86*. Washington, DC: Author.

National Education Association. 1991. *Status of the American Public School Teacher. 1990-1991*. Washington, DC: Author.

National Governors' Association. 1986. *Time for Results: The Governors' 1991 Report on Education*. Washington, DC: National Governors' Association.

Newmann, Fred M., and Gary C. Wehlage. 1995. *Successful School Restructuring: A Report to the Public and Educators*. Madison, WI: Wisconsin Center for Education Research.

Office of Educational Research and Improvement. 1987. *Digest of Educational Statistics, 1987*. Washington, DC: U.S. Government Printing Office.

Pipho, Chris. 1986. "Kappan Special Report: States Move Reform Closer to Reality." *Phi Delta Kappan* 68(4):K1-K8.

Siddle-Walker, Emilie V. 1993. "Interpersonal Caring in the 'Good' Segregated Schooling of African-American Children: Evidence From the Case of Caswell County Training School." *Urban Review* 25(1):63-77.

Spencer, Thelma. 1986. "Teacher Education at Grambling State University: A Move Toward Excellence." *Journal of Negro Education* 55(3): 293-303.

Stern, Joyce D. 1988. *The Condition of Education in Postsecondary Education*. Washington, DC.: U.S. Department of Education Office of Educational Research and Improvement.

Stewart, Joseph, Jr., Kenneth J. Meier, Robert M. LaFollette, and Robert E. England. 1989. "In Quest of Role Models: Change in Black Teacher Representation in Urban School Districts 1968-86." *Journal of Negro Education*. 58(2):140-152.

United States Bureau of the Census. 1995. *Statistical Abstract of the United States: 1995* (115th edition). Washington, DC: U.S. Government Printing Office.

United States Bureau of Labor Statistics. 1977. *Working Women: A Data Book*. Washington, DC: U.S. Government Printing Office.

United States Department of Labor, Bureau of Labor Statistics. January 1996. *Employment and Earnings*. Washington, DC: U.S. Government Printing Office.

Weiss, Carol H. 1995. "The Four 'I's' of School Reform: How Interests, Ideology Information and Institution Affect Teachers and Principals." *Harvard Educational Review* 65(4):571-592.

Whitehurst, Winston, and Elaine Witty. 1986. "Racial Equity: Teaching Excellence." *Action in Teacher Education* 3(1):51-59.

CHAPTER 8

Gender and School Administration

Marilyn Tallerico

The purpose of this chapter is to examine what is known about gender in school administration, to suggest ways in which gender equity can be fostered through school leadership, and to consider implications of this scholarship for educational policy. I draw on my own and others' work to analyze existing empirical data and discuss relevant theory. My emphasis is on school administrative practice and how it might be improved. I conclude by situating my arguments within the tradition of liberal social policy, contrasting the theoretical and political pragmatism of that tradition with other more critical perspectives.

ADMINISTRATIVE WORKFORCE ANALYSIS

There have been a number of comprehensive, recent reviews of gender in school administration (Bell and Chase 1993; Montenegro 1993; Ortiz and Marshall 1988; Sadker, Sadker, and Klein 1991; Shakeshaft 1995). All reach quite similar conclusions: that inequities in school administration persist and that women continue to be underrepresented in positions of educational leadership. Research to support those conclusions includes consideration of historical trends in hiring and placing men and women administrators as well as investigation of "availability" data such as evidence of certification and graduate degree completions in educational administration.

We know, for example, that approximately 7 percent of all superintendencies, 24 percent of all assistant superintendencies, and 34 percent of all principalships in the United States are held by women (Montenegro 1993). When principalship data are desegregated, we find the proportion of women decreases as the grade-level of schooling increases. That is, approximately 37 percent of elementary, 23 percent of middle school, and 8 percent of secondary school principals are women (Bell and Chase 1993). Although each of these percentages represent increases from five and ten years ago, Shakeshaft (1989) points out that, in 1928, over half of all principals were women, therefore recent trend data should be interpreted with caution.

In general, women administrators are found in greater proportions in "staff" rather than "line" leadership roles. The former include positions such as program coordinators, directors, districtwide supervisors, and administrative assistants of various sorts. In contrast, line positions are typically defined as those with direct authority over others, often with formal evaluative responsibilities for subordinates (e.g., principals and superintendents). For example, I recently collected administrative workforce data from two states, New York and Missouri, in order to answer the question more specifically, "Where *are* the women administrators in public education?" Results are displayed in Tables 1 and 2, and they reflect the well-documented trend that as the formal authority of the administrative position increases, the percentage of women occupying that role declines (Ortiz and Marshall 1988; Shakeshaft 1989).

These tables also reflect a significant challenge that researchers face when attempting to document and analyze school administrative workforce information: job titles and data collection differ from state to state. Bell and Chase (1993) remind us of the difficulty of aggregating data when job definitions are not consistent across studies, and they urge great care in interpreting summary data. Shakeshaft (1995:xii) underscores the fundamental problem as follows:

> After nearly two decades of attention to the underrepresentation of women in school administration, it is still difficult to systematically and accurately track the number of women in school administration. Some states have partial data, a few have none, and some have complete information. Additionally, state-by-state data are often not comparable, due to overlapping categories and job titles. This is not sloppy scholarship by researchers, but rather the lack of a reliable, uniform nationwide data base that lets us know just

how many women are school administrators and at what levels.

Table 1

Percent of School Administration Positions Occupied by Women State of Missouri, 1994

Assistant Elementary Principals	68 %
Supervisors	68 %
Elementary Principals	53 %
Assistant Middle School Principals	40 %
Administrative Assistants	35 %
Directors of Elementary Education	33 %
Assistant High School Principals	26 %
Middle School Principals	22 %
Assistant Superintendents	17 %
High School Principals	10 %
Superintendents	6 %

Source: School Data Department 1995.

Table 2

Percent of School Administration Positions Occupied by Women New York State, 1990

Assistant Directors/Coordinators	55 %
Directors/Coordinators	45 %
Assistant Elementary School Principals	45 %
Elementary School Principals	32 %
Assistant Secondary School Principals	25 %
Assistant/Deputy/Associate Superintendents	23 %
Business Managers	20 %
Secondary School Principals	15 %
Superintendents	6 %

Source: Information Center on Education 1992.

While acknowledging these important caveats, it is important to mention at least briefly two additional groups: school board members and professors of educational administration. Both of these groups are known to be influential in the hiring and placement of school administrators, and both have historically been characterized by high proportions of white men. The most recent national data available indicate that approximately 11 percent of educational administration professors (McCarthy, Newell, Kuh, and Iacona 1988) and 42 percent of school board members ("Demographics" 1995) are women. Each of these figures represents increases over previous decades. Ortiz and Marshall (1988:130) report that just 2 percent of professors of educational administration were women in 1975, and 8 percent in 1983. Of U.S. school board members, 12 percent were women in 1972 (Campbell, Cunningham, Nystrand, and Usdan 1985), 37.1 percent in 1983 ("Seventh" 1985).

In my own research on school boards and superintendents, I have found that the lack of a critical mass of women in these roles contributes considerably to the complexities of their work (Tallerico 1992a; Tallerico and Burstyn forthcoming; Tallerico, Burstyn, and Poole 1993). That is, they are often tokens and "outsiders" in the key leadership and governance relationships they are expected to negotiate. For example, the isolation and "lonely at the top" feelings which affect all superintendents are compounded by the scarcity of women in superintendent cohort groups. Many of the women interviewees in our superintendent studies reported being among the "pioneers" in their region: "I was the first woman superintendent in that county"; "There were only four of us in the state when I was hired"; "I was the first black woman ever appointed there." School board membership often reflects similar patterns, as the following excerpt from an interview with a woman board member illustrates:

> It's tough being a new member on the [school] board. And it's *very* tough being the only woman in 17 years in a male-dominated district. And I'm not feeling sorry for myself; it's just the reality.

In sum, although in some areas of the country and in some roles, progress has been made in integrating women into school leadership positions, most researchers in this field agree that the disproportionate representation of men and women continues to merit concern. To further strengthen claims of disproportionality and underrepresentation of women in administration, scholars often point to a second body of information to be discussed in the ensuing section.

Availability Data

The basic premise here is that progress in hiring and placing women school administrators has never caught up with their availability (Klein and Ortman 1994; Sadker et al. 1991; Snyder 1992). There are at least three kinds of data which can be considered valid proxies of women's availability for school administrative roles: the teacher pool, academic degrees earned, and certification/licensure attainment.

Most public school administrators begin their careers in education as teachers, and virtually all state certification/licensing systems for administrators require some prior teaching experience. Thus, K-12 teachers can be considered the essential "pool" from which prospective school administrators are drawn. What do we know about that pool? It is largely female. The National Center for Education Statistics (1994) reports that, in 1990-91, 72.1 percent of public school teachers were women, and in 1981, 66.9 percent. Bell and Chase (1993) report data desegregated by grade level from 1987 indicating that 87 percent of elementary teachers, 57 percent of middle school teachers, and 53 percent of high school teachers were women. Hence, it is clear that there are ample numbers of women in the teaching workforce pool from which administrators emerge.

Graduate degrees earned in educational administration provide another approximation of the available pool of prospective school administrators. Over the past 25 years, there have been significant increases in the proportions of women earning both master's and doctoral degrees in educational administration. From Table 3 (below) it can be seen that, since the mid-1980s, the majority of these degree recipients have been women. While it is impossible to assess how many of those master's and doctoral students earned their degrees with the specific intent of pursuing school administration positions, it can reasonably be inferred that the current underrepresentation of women in this field cannot be explained away by lack of formal academic preparation.

Table 3
*Percent of Graduate Degrees in Educational Administration
Earned by Women*

	1970	1981	1988	1992
Master's	20 %	43 %	57 %	60 %
Doctorates	9 %	32 %	48 %	51 %

Source: National Center for Education Statistics 1984, 1990, 1994.

Nor can it likely be explained by inadequate supplies of state certified/licensed women. Although there is no national data base on recipients of administrative licenses by sex, anecdotal evidence from U.S. professors of educational administration indicates a radical shift in the demographics of students pursuing administrative certification coursework and programs: from predominantly male some 15-20 years ago to predominantly female during the past decade. In 1985, Pavan reported certification data from the state of Pennsylvania showing that "the percentage of women certified each year was much greater than the percentage employed in administrative positions" (cited in Sadker et al. 1991:281). The trend data I have examined from the State of New York demonstrate that more women than men have been earning administrative certificates since the mid-1980s. Comparing the earliest and most recent data available, shown in Table 4, it is interesting to note that, over the 17-year period, the total number of administrative certificates has increased by about 1,400 (from 2,695 in 1972 to 4,092 in 1989). However the number of men has declined by about 22 percent (from 2,112 to 1,648), while the number of women has quadrupled (from 583 to 2,444). Yet, still, hiring and placement rates do not match the significant gains that women have made in attaining the necessary credentials required by state policy to practice school administration.

Table 4
Administrative Certificates Awarded by Sex
New York State

	1972	1976	1980	1984	1989
Females	583	1,198	804	1,463	2,444
Males	2,112	2,237	1,232	1,279	1,648
Total #	2,695	3,435	2,036	2,742	4,092

Source: Information Center on Education 1992.

Taken together, existing information on the gender demographics of the K-12 teaching pool, recipients of master's and doctoral degrees in educational administration, and state licensing awards point to a supply of prospective women administrators much greater than their rates of attainment of school administration positions would suggest. Although incomplete, such data tend to strengthen the argument that women continue to be underrepresented in the ranks of public school leadership, and that this imbalance warrants the attention of policymakers.

Attrition

These three proxies of prospective administrator availability are those most commonly cited in the educational leadership literature. I would argue, however, that *attrition* may be an equally important factor to explore in order to better understand the under-representation of women in school administration. With such longstanding, disproportionate participation of white males in school leadership, the loss of even a few women can be significant (Tallerico et al. 1993). The attrition and retention of women have received surprisingly little empirical attention, despite the obvious potential connections between those factors and improving the numerical representation of women in school administrative roles.

Instead, much of the scholarship relevant to female school leaders has focused on improved means of preparing, recruiting, sponsoring, and selecting women for work in educational administration. These foci, coupled with the availability data summarized above, place the emphasis on access and entry-level considerations. Yet studies of college student attrition have taught us that exclusive focus on "minority recruitment" without equal attention to issues of retention, does little more than create a revolving door for members of historically underrepresented groups.

Joan Burstyn, Wendy Poole, and I have begun to examine issues related to the attrition and retention of school superintendents by focusing on the question: Why are some women exiting the superintendency? I will incorporate excerpts from our interviews with women superintendents to illustrate several points in the ensuing section. The question I turn to now is, if extant workforce, availability, and attrition data cannot explain the under-representation of women in school administration, what can?

RELEVANT THEORY

There is little agreement as to why the gender imbalance in school administration exists, but three distinct theoretical possibilities have characterized the educational leadership literature (Bell and Chase 1993; Estler 1975; Hansot and Tyack 1981; Ortiz and Marshall 1988; Schmuck 1980; Shakeshaft 1989). Some look to women themselves for explanations, focusing on psychological traits, inherent qualities, and personal characteristics. These are essentially person-centered theories, which tend to underscore individual agency and so-called "internal barriers" to advancement into school administration. Personal attributes such as self-image and confidence, motivation, and aspirations fall into this category. In the field vernacular, this focus is manifested in belief statements about women such as: They're just not assertive enough; they don't want the power; they lack self-confidence; they don't aspire to line positions; they're unwilling to play the game or work the system. Schmuck (1987:9) illuminates this conceptual framework by pointing out that, when the focus is on person-centered explanations, individuals (in this case, women) are "held responsible for their own problems," with solutions to those problems then framed in terms of changing "the defect or weakness in the individual." Shakeshaft describes it as a "blame the victim" perspective (1989:82).

In contrast, others look to the educational system itself and argue that there are structural and systemic barriers that work against the advancement of all candidates who are not white males. These barriers may be overt (e.g., discrimination in employment and promotions; inappropriate or illegal application and interview questions) but are probably more often subtle (e.g., selective informal sponsorship, networking, and mentorship of prospective administrators; conscious or unconscious gatekeeping by those who influence hiring decisions). Thus, systemic gender bias is accompanied by limited opportunities for women. This "organizational perspective" (Schmuck 1980:244) or "discrimination model" (Estler 1975:369) turns our attention away from the individual to the education system itself, with its complex of institutional structures, policies, and practices.

Yet others look for theoretical explanations not in women as individuals nor in educational institutions, per se, but in society as a whole. This perspective underscores the folkways and norms of American culture, the different ways that boys and girls are socialized, the lack of female role models in positions of authority in general, endemic differences in gender expectations, and society-wide stereotypical thinking about "what's ladylike" and who "looks like" a leader. The schools, then, are viewed as just one small piece of a larger culture generally hostile to gender equity (Sadker et al. 1991). Bell and Chase (1993:151) point out that this perspective is "supported by the broader sociological literature on women in male-dominated positions." Estler (1975) underscores the interrelatedness of cultural and structural theoretical explanations.

An Illustration

In our own research on women who exited superintendencies, we found structural and cultural models more useful than psychological ones (Tallerico and Burstyn forthcoming). The structural barrier apparent in our investigations was systemic gender stratification which relegated women superintendents to extraordinarily challenging work contexts. Specifically, we found higher proportions of women superintendents than men superintendents in two types of school districts: large, urban districts (for women of color) and small, rural districts (for whites). Such districts are less promising work contexts than medium-sized, suburban districts because, among other factors, they are more likely to suffer from declining student enrollments and financial difficulties. We argued that placements in such unpromising settings impede leadership success and retention, perpetuating what Bell (1988:38) has referred to as "a hierarchy of school districts, arranged according to their desirability," with women and persons of color occupying the superintendency in those settings lowest in the hierarchy.

We concluded that this gender stratification could best be understood as a function of fundamental structures of sponsorship and gatekeeping characteristic of the field of school administration (Ortiz and Marshall 1988). An experience of a woman interviewee from our research illustrates how differential sponsorship and gatekeeping can work behind the scenes:

> There had been 150 applicants and the [search] consultant, I think this is interesting, picked 10 for [the school board's] review. I was not among the 10. And one of the school board members asked the consultant, "Wasn't there anyone who applied who had a good background in curriculum and instruction?" And he said, "Yes, but I don't think you people are ready for a woman."

However, institutional practices and structures could only partially explain these patterns of gender stratification in the superintendency. We also needed to consider broader sociopolitical frameworks for understanding culturally defined roles in American society. The women participants in our research provided numerous illustrations of sex-typed expectations which worked to their disadvantage in the superintendency. One stated, for example, "People still look at it as being a man's job. You have entry level that is female, then you have the higher administrative level that is male." Another observed the wider community of which her school district was a part and commented, "A woman in a power position [here] has always had a hard time getting people to trust them and accept them."

Others told us stories which vividly illustrated socially accepted images of leadership based on aggressiveness, physical strength, or authoritarianism. Such narrow, sex-typed mental models make it appear that women superintendents do not "fit the bill" and create obstacles to trust, acceptance, and credibility. The following excerpt from our interview data illustrates this point.

> I think it is more difficult for a woman. Because they always ask you questions like, "Can you be strong enough?" One of my board members here asked me, and I didn't even quite know what he meant, "Can you shine your boots on

someone?" What he meant was, Could I kick ass?! And after he explained that, I said, "That's not my style. I get people to do what they need to do, but I use different tactics."

SO WHAT?

An assumption underlying the theoretical perspectives and illustrations summarized above is that the continued underrepresentation of women in school administrative positions must be more thoroughly understood in order to be remedied. Why be concerned about "remedying" the disproportionately low numbers of women in leadership and administrative roles in schools? Three related rationale are most typically mentioned in the literature.

One argument is that boys and girls benefit from having women role models in positions of authority in schools. Students' career aspirations may be raised, or their appreciation for the leadership potential of women may be broadened. While additional studies are needed in schools to confirm such hypotheses, many of the women respondents in my own research expressed strong beliefs in such "role modeling." To illustrate, I quote an African American woman who had exited an urban superintendency. She underscores the value of role modeling along two dimensions, gender and race:

I think that our kids are too important not to have a diverse group of women and minorities serving the population. One of the reasons I did not close the door completely [to ever pursuing another superintendency] is just that. That there are just so very few people who are even qualified to go in and run urban school systems. I still think there's a chance for the kids there. And we need to have people who look like those kids.

A second rationale emphasizes optimal utilization of the existing talent pool in education. The argument here is that schools are too important to let *any* potential source of excellence in leadership and management go underutilized. Again, availability and placement data are often cited to support the claim that women educators are not being adequately or equitably tapped for school administration.

A third argument, supported by research in schools, is that women bring special, needed attributes to the practice of educational leadership (Dunlap and Schmuck 1995; Ortiz and Marshall 1988; Sadker 1985; Shakeshaft 1989). These contributions reflect "the positive stereotypes of female leadership," such as democratic and participative management styles, focus on the human side of organizations, emphasis on teaching and learning, and sharing power and authority through collaboration (Schmuck 1995:213). In the organizational literature outside of education, these characteristics have been described as the "female advantage" that women often bring to leadership roles (Helgesen 1990).

Much less widely cited is a moral argument for attending to gender imbalances in the school administrative workforce. Put quite simply, it's the "right thing" to do. That is, it is morally objectionable to ignore gender or other inequities. Ortiz and Marshall (1988:136) allude to the general neglect and undervaluing of this potentially powerful rationale as follows:

> Analyses of sex-equity policy suggest that it has not yet achieved the status of morally legitimate policy; instead it continues to be viewed as a vehicle for providing a compensatory benefit to a special interest group.

WHAT CAN BE DONE

Taken individually or together, these four arguments (above) have been the impetus for repeated calls over the past 25 years to strengthen the recruitment and support of women and members of other underrepresented groups for leadership positions in schools. There is a large body of action-oriented, advocacy literature which suggests and illustrates multiple approaches to increasing women's representation in school administration. Although that work is too extensive to review here, for recent examples, see National LEADership Network (1992), Tallerico (1992b), Angione, Brown, Haneke, and Repa (1990), and Tallerico, Burstyn, and Poole (1993). The kinds of solutions advocated typically reflect one or more of the three theoretical frameworks summarized earlier. In other words, they run the gamut from actions focusing on the individual (e.g., assertiveness training and political skill-building for women), to the organizational (e.g., implementing nonsexist hiring guidelines and developing networking, mentorship, and support systems for women), to the cultural (e.g., broad public policy initiatives and radical restructuring of all social institutions). Scholars who have led the way in initiating and sustaining the salience of these issues in the field of educational administration and policy leadership include Charol Shakeshaft, Patricia Schmuck, Susan Klein, Catherine Marshall, and Colleen Bell. (See any of their publications for additional readings.)

As reflected so far in this chapter, however, and as underscored by Sadker, Sadker, and Klein (1991), most of the research related to gender and educational leadership has focused on inequities *in* school administration rather than on how gender equity can be promoted *through* school administration. I believe it is important to keep sight of the dual goals of increasing the representation of women school administrators *and* changing educational leadership practice. To address the latter, let us turn now to a question which more directly links school administration to the experience of children. That is, What can be done to foster gender equity *through* school leadership?

One way of approaching this question is to consider both the "everyday acts" of school administration as well as the development and enactment of gender-equity policy. Perhaps not surprisingly, neither pro-equity activism on the part of school administrators nor the implementation of gender equity policies have been studied extensively. Moreover, most gender policy analysis has "focused on descriptions of federal and state legislation and regulations rather than on the implementation of these policies at the district and school level" (Sadker et al. 1991:280). We rely, therefore, on literatures that are largely normative and prescriptive (American Association of School Administrators 1975; Aquila 1981; Carelli 1988; Freeman 1990; Klein 1985; National LEADership Network 1992).

The Practice of Gender-Responsible Leadership

What are the everyday acts of K-12 administrators thought to promote gender equity in schooling? I will consider five important categories of administrative practice to selectively illustrate responses to this question: (a) organization of the curriculum; (b) curriculum content; (c) instructional supervision; (d) community relations; and (d) shared decision making. (For additional treatment, see Birmingham, Carelli, Giacobbe, and Tallerico 1995.)

Curriculum Organization. Pro-equity administrators monitor both enrollment and achievement outcomes by sex for the various curricular tracks known to exist in schools (e.g., college preparatory, gifted and talented, special education, advanced placement, vocational). They conduct similar analyses of elective courses, particularly in content areas traditionally dominated by one sex, such as boys in advanced mathematics, the physical sciences, and technology, or girls in the humanities and foreign languages. They question any disproportions revealed by such analyses, share data with the entire staff, and mobilize school resources to support greater parity in participation and achievement rates of boys and girls. They problematize patterns of sex segregation and articulate a vision of other, gender-balanced ways of organizing the school curriculum to ensure equal opportunities for all children. In addition, they ensure that criteria and procedures for the assignment or selection of students for programs, courses, or classes are developed and applied with equity goals in mind. They pay attention to the symbolic details that communicate the school curriculum, including gender-free course titles and descriptions in program catalogues (such as substituting "parenting" for "motherhood" in publications about family life skills classes).

Curriculum Content. Beyond attention to how the curriculum is organized and communicated, gender-responsible leaders also focus on its substance. They include gender equity as a criterion for assessing or revising any grade-level or content-area curriculum. These criteria raise questions such as, Are women's experiences and contributions included? Are gender issues a part of multicultural or diversity curricula? Are all programs, courses, and classes conducted without differentiation by gender in assignments, materials, services, or other treatment?

When one department, school, or subject area revises curricular content to be more inclusive and less sexist, pro-equity administrators ensure that vehicles are in place to disseminate those successes. They try to ensure that curriculum improvement teams do not work in isolation of one another, so that ideas promoting gender fair curricula are easily shared. They allocate funds for, acquire, and bring to teachers' attention the availability of special resources such as those produced by the National Women's History Project and the Women's Educational Equity Act Publication Center.

Supervision of Instruction. When conducting observations of teachers' classrooms, gender-responsible leaders "notice" differential patterns of interactions by sex. They note possible biases in teacher-student communication, attention, and classroom activities (Klein and Ortman 1994). And, more importantly, they provide constructive feedback to both male and female teachers to assist in eliminating such biases. They recognize and support instructors who attempt to promote gender equity in their classrooms. They share publications with their staff, related particularly to the differential treatment of boys and girls documented in the research. And they see that staff development initiatives are designed to raise awareness and to problem solve around gender-equity concerns. Topics such as the following could be included: gender differences in communication and learning styles; sex biases that commonly occur in classroom interactions; the impact and incidence of gender bias in texts and tests; how to overcome discriminatory practices in evaluation; prevention and response to sexual harassment; and self-examination of assumptions about sex-role identification and stereotyping.

Community Relations. School-community relations involve multiple levels of interaction, communication, involvement, and service. Pro-equity school administrators pay careful attention to the smallest details of public communications, such as nonsexist language in all newsletters and other written correspondence for parents and community members. They ensure equitable representation of females and males in photographs and graphics used in news releases, television spots, program brochures, and the like. On another level, they include gender equity issues in adult or community education programming in the school district, including information about what parents can do to minimize sex-role stereotyping at home. They include in their public relations programs information about the schools' gender equity policies and pertinent legislation.

Gender-responsible school leaders also utilize the services of community groups supportive of gender equity efforts, for example, the American Association of University Women and the National Organization for Women. They nurture relationships with local public opinion leaders of both sexes and try to achieve gender balance in parent-teacher organization membership and leadership.

They ensure that student involvement in the community affords opportunities to work with both women and men, including non-traditional placements in service experiences. And they involve parents and community members in evaluating the schools for gender equity, recognizing that third-party perspectives can be useful in gaining fresh insights about the taken-for-granteds in schooling.

Shared Decision Making. The current emphasis on more democratic governance and participative management also has implications for the practice of gender-responsible leadership. For example, pro-equity school administrators recruit and retain representatives of both sexes on school-site, advisory, or other team-leadership groups. Moreover, they unobtrusively monitor those teams' small-group dynamics in order to identify and eliminate sex-stereotyped behaviors and gender biases (for example, by noticing patterns of turn-taking, tone, deference to the perspectives of a few, verbal participation rates, who interrupts whom, who speaks the longest or most frequently, etc.). Of course, they avoid the assignment of sex-stereotyped tasks to committee/group members (e.g., women assuming note-taking functions or men with exclusive responsibility for financial analyses). Gender-responsible school leaders model nonsexist behaviors and ensure that biased language, assumptions, interactions, and outcomes are not tolerated in shared decision-making groups.

Summary. There are innumerable other technical, political, interpersonal, cultural, and symbolic aspects of school administration in which pro-equity activism could be exhibited. The five areas described above are intended to demonstrate selected ways in which educational leaders could begin. These particular categories were chosen for both their currency in the educational administration literature and their emphasis on core features of schooling: curriculum and instruction. However, as argued earlier, the everyday practice of educational administrators provides just one means of addressing the question, "What can be done to promote gender equity through school administration?" A second means, school policy, is considered in the ensuing section.

Implications for Policy

There are a number of specific areas within which educational administrators would be able to exercise leadership, both in terms of advocacy for policy *development* and oversight of policy implementation *in* schools. I will briefly discuss seven such examples, in an effort to move from consideration of individual administrator's everyday acts towards *systems'* change of U.S. school practice. (For broader discussion of comparative and international policy perspectives, see Stromquist in this volume.)

Administrative Licensure. The certification and licensing of school administrators are state policy functions. States vary widely in the degree of prescriptiveness of their criteria for earning such licenses. However, it would be possible to impact the expected knowledge-base and competencies desired of school administrators by including licensing standards reflecting gender-affirmative leadership. For example, are certification applicants familiar with recent research demonstrating that girls and boys receive different amounts of teachers' attention in classroom instruction? Are they equipped with skills to provide feedback to instructors about possible gender biases in the school's extracurricular activities? Are they knowledgeable about what were described earlier as the gender-responsible everyday acts of school leaders? If these or similar standards were prominent in state certification systems, it is likely that related pro-equity changes would occur in both the university training programs aimed at preparing prospective school administrators for state licensure, as well as the formal "assessment centers" for new administrator evaluation prevalent in some states (e.g., Arizona, Missouri).

Personnel Performance Appraisal. As change in state licensing structures at the preservice level could serve to promote gender equity, so too could local school district policy for assessing faculty, staff, and administrators' on-the-job performance. With regard to the latter, it would be important to emphasize gender equity standards not solely in terms of personnel *accountability*, but with equal attention to pro-equity *incentives*. For example, are systems in place to recognize and reward school principals who examine testing data by sex, or for teachers who actively recruit girls for school leadership positions traditionally occupied by boys? What kinds of institutional supports exist for personnel who foster gender equity in the schools? Are there organized structures for supporting, mentoring, and retaining staff employed in fields historically dominated by the opposite sex (for example, for male teachers in primary grades or home careers; for female teachers of technology, advanced-level mathematics, or physical sciences)? Are all performance appraisal policies free from provisions which treat personnel differently on the basis of sex?

Professional Development. Systems for continuous staff development are increasingly seen as logical extensions to the preservice preparation, licensure, and inservice performance appraisal of school personnel. The rapidly changing demographics of the student population and explosion of information technologies are directly related to the continuous professional growth needs of staff. As such, many federal and state educational mandates are currently accompanied by requirements for ongoing staff development in schools. Many local districts have initiated practices and guidelines in support of the continuous professional development of teachers and administrators.

Consistent with the thrust of this volume, it is critical that gender equity in schooling become an integral substantive component of local staff development policy and goals. Strategies to promote equity for girls and boys in classrooms and schools should be incorporated with other instructional improvement or skill-building programs for educational practitioners. (See a prior sub-section titled "Supervision of Instruction" for listing of suggested foci for pro-equity staff development.)

Textbook and Curriculum Approval. In most states, local school district governing boards are responsible for the adoption of specific textbooks and curricula that frame children's schooling experiences. These approval and adoption systems provide another policy arena in which gender equity goals may be either fostered or thwarted. Local policy could include standards of approval based on "gender fairness" or, ideally, on "gender affirmation." Scott and Schau (1985) provide useful distinguishing definitions for these terms. Essentially, sex fairness involves the elimination of overtly sex stereotyped or gender-biased content, illustrations, and characters. In contrast, gender-affirmative educational materials focus on the important place and contributions of women (or other underrepresented groups) in the various knowledge bases shared through schooling.

Gender-affirmative textbooks and materials can move the system from program improvement based on an "add women and stir" approach towards transformative curricula which integrate multiple levels of diversity and include critique of extant social systems. The guidelines and standards provided by local textbook and curriculum adoption policies could increase the salience of sex affirmative goals. They could also serve as important "checks and balances" for more mundane applications of gender equity goals, such as attending to gender-balanced authorship of instructional materials or consideration of non-traditional publishers, such as the Women's Educational Equity Act Center or Advocacy Press.

Sexual Harassment. In contrast to the more general policy initiatives recommended above, sexual harassment is a particular policy arena warranting action in today's schools. Both prevention and response should be addressed in such policy. Moreover, it should be multi-faceted, attending to the various verbal, nonverbal, and physical forms harassment may take and the various student-to-student, adult-to-adult, and child-adult relationships in schools. Procedures need to be in place systemwide to allow the prompt and thorough investigation of all allegations and the confidentiality of both victims and accused. Among the questions school leaders and policy makers should ask themselves are: Are there clear procedures for voicing complaints, filing grievances, appealing, and resolving issues related to sexual harassment? Do policies provide for speedy internal resolution of grievances and multiple levels of assistance and appeal? Are there steps to protect the complainant from reprisal and retaliation? Are there identifiable consequences and consistent enforcement of sexual harassment policy? And, perhaps most importantly, how is leadership being exercised to promote school environments free of harassment?

Title IX. Compliance with federal Title IX law is another area with quite specific policy implications for local districts and school administrators. This legislation was enacted in 1972 and intended to prohibit discrimination on the basis of sex in all educational programs and activities receiving federal financial assistance. Brief policy statements ensuring compliance with Title IX and nondiscrimination on the basis of sex have become standard parts of most official documents, reports, and program or employment notices emanating from today's schools. Yet, in many cases, compliance is more lip service than real. "Equal opportunity employer" and "we do not discriminate" have become commonplace catch-phrases used in the schools, at the same time that inequities between boys and girls in achievement outcomes, sports, and other extracurricular activities persist. The underrepresentation of women in school leadership positions may also be indicative of minimalist approaches to the enactment of Title IX in educational employment practices. It seems clear that the implementation of local policies to monitor and enforce both the spirit and letter of Title IX legislation could do much to promote gender equity in schooling.

Resource Allocation. Some of the policy recommendations discussed above will require additional funding. All of them require the allocation of human resources. The distribution of scarce funds and contested values is at the heart of contemporary school politics and policymaking. For these reasons, progress has been slow in achieving gender equity in education, despite decades of pro-equity advocacy and scholarship. The development and implementation of policy, even with concomitant resource allocation, may not be enough. Continued progress requires a mustering of skill *and* will; strategies, vision, and long-term commitment. These remain daunting, but much needed, tasks of school leadership and administration.

LIBERAL SOCIAL POLICY
The policy suggestions proffered above illustrate a personal standpoint of liberal optimism. How I have framed the issues of gender and school administration and approached their resolution reflect strong underlying assumptions that the existing educational system can be improved, though with considerable additional or redirected effort. A kind of theoretical and political pragmatism is inherent in these policy recommendations. They reflect faith in organizational development. They demonstrate belief that working within extant governance and institutional structures to formulate and implement policy will effect change throughout the system to

promote gender equity. They are clearly, to use Marshall's terms, "domesticated, controlled policy options" (see Chapter 3).

In all analyses, it is important to acknowledge the limitations of underlying assumptions. As other authors in this volume point out, the fundamental weakness of traditional liberal and compensatory approaches is that the basic system remains intact. In contrast, more radical critiques assume that the "systems that created and perpetuated inequities cannot be relied upon to implement equity policy" (Marshall 1993:3). As Rizvi (1993:211) explains, what may be required instead is "a radical appraisal of our society's materialist, racist, and sexist culture, which continues to be transmitted in schools." "It has to be acknowledged," continues Rizvi (1993:216), "that most administrative work takes place in a context of schooling that does not permit radical reform. School administrators, no matter how well-intentioned, work in a context that is inherently conservative."

Awareness of the conservative context of school organizations is important. It is equally important to be aware that multiple perspectives must be brought to bear in order to understand and resolve issues as complex as those associated with gender, equity, schooling, and school leadership. At the same time, there is a need to work towards gender equity on as many levels as possible, including the individual, interpersonal, organizational, and societal. A strength of the liberal perspective driving this chapter is that it underscores concrete actions which individuals can take to foster organizational improvement in today's schools. Other perspectives which emphasize cultural change complement this level of gender-responsible leadership by creating more broadly favorable contexts for reform across institutions and societies. It is clear that the perennial struggle to promote social justice for women and girls demands openness to varied interpretive lenses and multi-faceted personal and policy interventions.

REFERENCES

American Association of School Administrators [AASA]. 1975. *Sex Equity in School: Executive Handbook Series.* Arlington, VA: Author.

Angione, Christine M., Martha D. Brown, Diane Haneke, and J. Theodore Repa, with Richard Bamberger and Maxine Giacobbe. 1990. *A View from the Inside: An Action Plan for Gender Equity in New York State Educational Administration.* Albany, NY: CASDA-LEAD Center.

Aquila, Frank. 1981. *Title IX: Implications for Education of Women.* Bloomington, IN: Phi Delta Kappa Educational Foundation.

Bell, Colleen. 1988. "Organizational Influences on Women's Experience in the Superintendency." *Peabody Journal of Education* 65(4):31-59.

Bell, Colleen, and Susan Chase. 1993. "The Underrepresentation of Women in School Leadership." Pp. 140-154 in *The New Politics of Race and Gender: The 1992 Yearbook of the Politics of Education Association*, edited by C. Marshall. Washington, DC: Falmer.

Birmingham, Gloria Q., Anne O'Brien Carelli, Maxine Giacobbe, and Marilyn Tallerico. 1995. *Take a Good Look: A Gender Equity Handbook for Administrators*. Albany, NY: New York State Association of Women in Administration.

Campbell, Roald F., Luvern Cunningham, Raphael O. Nystrand, and Michael D. Usdan. 1985. *The Organization and Control of American Schools* (5th ed.). Columbus, OH: Merrill.

Carelli, Anne O'Brien (Ed.). 1988. *Sex Equity in Education: Readings and Strategies*. Springfield, IL: Charles Thomas, Publisher.

"The Demographics of School Board Service." 1995. *American School Board Journal* 182(1):37.

Dunlap, Diane, and Patricia A. Schmuck (Eds.). 1995. *Women Leading in Education*. Albany, NY: State University of New York Press.

Estler, Susan E. 1975. Women as Leaders in Public Education. *Signs: Journal of Women in Culture and Society* 1(2):363-386.

Freeman, Sue Wooten. 1990. "What About the Teachers?" Pp. 14-20 in *Dolls and Dungarees: Gender Issues in the Primary School Curriculum*, edited by E. Tutchell. Philadelphia: Open University Press.

Hansot, Elisabeth, and David Tyack. 1981. *The Dream Deferred: A Golden Age for Women School Administrators* (Policy Paper No. 81-C2). Stanford, CA: Stanford University School of Education, Institute for Research on Educational Finance and Governance.

Helgesen, Sally. 1990. *The Female Advantage: Women's Ways of Leading*. NY: Doubleday.

Information Center on Education. 1992. *Women Administrators in New York State Public Schools 1968 to 1991*. Albany, NY: The State Education Department.

Klein, Susan S. 1985. *Handbook for Achieving Sex Equity Through Education*. Baltimore: Johns Hopkins University Press.

Klein, Susan S., and Patricia E. Ortman. 1994. "Continuing the Journey Toward Gender Equity." *Educational Researcher* 23(8):13-21.

Marshall, Catherine (Ed.). 1993. *The New Politics of Race and Gender: The 1992 Yearbook of the Politics of Education Association*. Washington, DC: Falmer.

McCarthy, Martha M., L. Jackson Newell, George D. Kuh, and Carla M. Iacona. 1988. *Under Scrutiny: The Educational Administration Professoriate*. Tempe, AZ: University Council for Educational Administration.

Montenegro, Xenia P. 1993. *Women and Racial Minority Representation in School Administration*. Arlington, VA: American Association of School Administrators.

National Center for Education Statistics. 1984. *Digest of Education Statistics*. Washington, DC: U.S. Department of Education, Office of Educational Research and Improvement.

National Center for Education Statistics. 1990. *Digest of Education Statistics*. Washington, DC: U.S. Department of Education, Office of Educational Research and Improvement.

National Center for Education Statistics. 1994. *Digest of Education Statistics*. Washington, DC: U.S. Department of Education, Office of Educational Research and Improvement.

National LEADership Network. 1992. *Strengthening Support and Recruitment of Women and Minorities to Positions in Educational Administration: A Resource Manual*. Washington, DC: U.S. Department of Education, Office of Educational Research and Improvement.

Ortiz, Flora I., and Catherine Marshall. 1988. "Women in Educational Administration." Pp. 123-141 in *Handbook of Research on Educational Administration*, edited by N. Boyan. New York: Longman.

Rizvi, Fazal. 1993. "Race, Gender, and the Cultural Assumptions of Schooling. Pp. 203-217 in *The New Politics of Race and Gender: The 1992 Yearbook of the Politics of Education Association*, edited by C. Marshall. Washington, DC: Falmer.

Sadker, Myra. 1985. *Women in Educational Administration: The Report Card #4*. Washington, DC: Mid-Atlantic Center for Sex Equity, The Network, Inc.

Sadker, Myra, David Sadker, and Susan Klein. 1991. "The Issue of Gender in Elementary and Secondary Education. Pp. 269-334 in *Review of Research in Education*, Vol. 17, edited by G. Grant. Washington, DC: American Educational Research Association.

Schmuck, Patricia A. 1980. "Changing Women's Representation in School Management: A Systems Perspective." Pp. 239-259 in *Women and Educational Leadership*, edited by S. K. Biklen and M. Brannigan. Lexington, MA: Lexington Books.

Schmuck, Patricia A. 1987. "Introduction." Pp. 1-17 in *Women Educators*, edited by P.A. Schmuck. Albany, NY: State University of New York Press.

Schmuck, Patricia A. 1995. "Advocacy Organizations for Women Administrators. Pp. 199-224 in *Women Leading in Education*, edited by D. Dunlap and P. Schmuck. Albany, NY: State University of New York Press.

School Data Department. 1995. *FTE Counts and Salary Data 1994-1995*. Jefferson City, MO: Missouri Department of Elementary and Secondary Education.

Scott, Kathryn P., and Candace G. Schau. 1985. "Sex Equity and Sex Bias in Instructional Materials. Chapter 12 in *Handbook for Achieving Sex Equity Through Education*, edited by S. S. Klein. Baltimore: Johns Hopkins University Press.

"Seventh Annual Survey of Board Members." January 1985. *American School Board Journal* 172(1):29-31.

Shakeshaft, Charol. 1989. *Women in Educational Administration*. Newbury Park, CA: Sage.

Shakeshaft, Charol. 1995. "Foreword." Pp. xi-xiv in *Women Leading in Education*, edited by D. Dunlap and P.A. Schmuck. Albany, NY: State University of New York Press.

Snyder, Thomas D. 1992. *Digest of Education Statistics, 1992*. Washington, DC: National Center for Education Statistics, Office of Educational Research and Improvement, U.S. Department of Education.

Tallerico, Marilyn. 1992a. "Promoting Gender Equity in Educational Administration, *The Council Journal of New York State School Superintendents* 9(1):50-66.

Tallerico, Marilyn. 1992b. "School Board Membership: Gender Issues and Women's Perspectives." *Urban Education* 26(4):371-389.

Tallerico, Marilyn, and Joan N. Burstyn. Forthcoming. "Retaining Women in the Superintendency: The Location Matters." *Educational Administration Quarterly*.

Tallerico, Marilyn, Joan Burstyn, and Wendy Poole. 1993. *Gender and Politics at Work: Why Women Exit the Superintendency*. Fairfax, VA: National Policy Board for Educational Administration.

CHAPTER 9

Epilogue: Schooling, Gender, Equity, and Policy

Peter M. Hall

INTRODUCTION

The preceding chapters have explored in numerous ways how gender and schooling are related. Nelly Stromquist ends her comparative analysis of state policies by emphasizing the limits of reform due to the patriarchal state but still encourages initiatives by feminists. Catherine Marshall's analysis of American gender policy, her own experiences, and the contributions of different feminists lead her to suggest not only conventional ("safe and domesticated") reforms such as pre- and in-service teacher training but more radical and outrageous ones that challenge deepseated cultural assumptions and attract attention. Donna Eder's vivid and chilling depiction of young adolescent male rhetoric and action in the context of student cultures and school extracurricular programs culminates in provocative questioning of the role of competitive athletics, the suggestion of action strategies for young women, and the recommendation of conflict-resolution programs. Cynthia Hudley's evaluation of her research on a program for African American males suggests caution about such segregated programs and encourages consideration of equity efforts for all in the context of broad school reform efforts and the overall requirement of macrosocial change. Valerie Lee reviews research that found positive achievements by young women in single-sex schools and argues that this is due to the organizational character of those schools. She recommends school restructuring as a means of producing equity, not only for women but for all students. Michele Foster clarifies how diversity in the teaching force affects responses to the same school reforms advocated by Lee and argues the consequent necessity to give voice to silenced or ignored minorities and their concerns for their students if those reforms are to be successful. Marilyn Tallerico documents the failure of male-dominated school systems to recruit and promote women administrators and offers a number of gender-responsible leadership practices and state and local district policies that could promote gender equity.

In this chapter I discuss and extend some implications of the previous chapters and their policy recommendations. I concur with Lee, Foster, and Hudley that gender equity as well as race and class must be considered within the context of school restructuring. Toward that end I elaborate upon Lee and Foster to present a more complete model of a restructured school. In addition I will reformulate a perspective on multicultural education to fit gender equity and then integrate Tallerico's suggestions for gender-responsible leadership practices into that formulation. I then pick up where Lee ends by reviewing some scholarship on the restructuring and systemic reform processes to suggest some approaches for programs of school change. Central to these approaches is the creation of a mobilizing vision around equity for all and how schools can hinder or facilitate that vision. The development of this vision points to the necessity of reculturing the school and demystifying ideas about class, gender, and race.

Eder's description of young adolescent student cultures and nonclassroom activities prompts attention to middle-grades schooling and the goals and accomplishment of middle-school reform programs. It also directs our attention to efforts, even at the elementary level to shape gender conceptions and relationships. In this context, I also want to address the broad purposes of schooling, the articulation/coordination of reform efforts, and the larger societal context. Moving to the larger context leads to discussing the issues raised by Stromquist, Marshall, and Bank about the limits of reforms due to structure, culture, and contradiction. In so doing, it is necessary to clarify the meaning of gender, the gendered nature of schools as organizations, and the role of social movements in constructing gender. The chapter ends with a call for research to document interplay between structure/ culture and agency.

RESTRUCTURING AND EQUITY
Hudley says race- and gender-specific programs should be

explored within the current multiple models of school reform. On an academic level, Lee answers Hudley's question about the interactive effects of multiple reform efforts that occur simultaneously by showing how restructuring produces equity and effectiveness. On a practical level, it makes no sense to suggest gender- and race-specific reforms independent of these transformational models since they dominate the contemporary agenda. At the same time, Fullan (1996) has discussed the consequences of reform overload and fragmentation. Overload occurs because there are constant numerous planned and unplanned changes to which educators must simultaneously respond. Fragmentation results because policies and programs often are contradictory or disjointed, and thus practitioners cannot determine how they all cohere and make sense. Strategic responses to these pressures are often to lie low and wait for the next wave or utilize some small portion of what makes sense and include it in conventional practice. Gender, race, or class inequity represent such large and interrelated issues that to regard programs for their eradication as add-ons or conventional school improvement does not suffice or make much impact. Rather they must be integrated within a systematic restructuring of schooling that is premised upon a philosophy, vision, and mission committed to equity and effectiveness.

Lee points out that schools with the following characteristics are more likely to be effective and equitable—smaller size, a core academic curriculum for all students, communal, nonbureaucratic social organization, emphasis on higher-order critical thinking, constructivist teaching that encourages and facilitates student engagement and active learning, leadership that is democratic, participatory, personal with a focus on student learning, a belief that all students can learn the material to which they are given access, and a staff that takes responsibility for student learning. Foster draws on the same literature and notes the emphasis on student learning, the connection of authentic assessment to authentic pedagogy (i.e., constructivist teaching), the creation of professional communities, and the provision of external support to schools to enhance student learning.

These are not simply lists but, in fact, interrelated, interdependent elements that together constitute a system which is sustained by interactive processes. The elements cannot simply be added one by one because changing one has consequences for others. This is why the process must be seen coherently and as a set of moving internal relationships. Thus to emphasize higher-order critical thinking and contructivist/active learning means changing pedagogy, curriculum, and assessment. Teachers' roles then change significantly as they move toward creating the conditions for and facilitating learning rather than lecturing and instructing. They must also do more diagnosing and planning student learning, structuring of grouping and activities, and evaluating their efforts. Curriculum will require more depth, coherence, and integration across fields/subjects. Thus there would be more interdisciplinary and team efforts. Teachers then need to have more time for reflective practice, collaborative planning, and in-school professional development. Time would also be restructured to be more flexible for student progress, larger problem-based projects, class sessions, and modular topics. Student groupings will be altered for cooperative learning, independent demonstration/projects, elimination of tracking and ability grouping, and personalization. To compensate for large size, smaller learning communities of students and teachers will be constructed.

Accomplishing these dramatic transformations depends upon establishment of a common culture, decentralized decision-making, and shared governance. These schools operate less on rules, regulations, and hierarchies than on a collective sense of ends and means based upon a mutually aware consensus. It also requires ability to collaborate, build teams, problem solve, and resolve conflict. The shared governance involves openness to community, family, students, and perhaps other public agencies. Above all, the school thinks and acts as a "learning organization/community" constantly checking its accomplishments, revisiting its mission, and altering or changing to be more reflective, effective, and equitable.

James Banks (1993) proposed a model of multicultural education designed to produce equity and understanding. The five elements of that model are *content integration, knowledge construction, prejudice reduction, equity pedagogy, and empowered school cultures and structures*. In the first volume of this series (Hall in press), I argued that this approach could be merged with the restructuring process to produce equity. In fact many of the suggestions made by those promoting racial and ethnic equity

(Jackson 1995) and multiculturalism (Banks 1993) are similar to the organizational and processual transformations advocated by proponents of restructuring. Here I assert that Banks' five elements can be reframed for gender and again utilized to support equity.

Content integration involves more than "add and stir" celebrations of holidays and heroines into the curriculum. Infusion of gender and racial-ethnic materials should be throughout the curriculum. While necessary, it is clearly insufficient. The *knowledge construction* process means not only active, engaged hands-on learning but also exploring the significance of perspective for understanding the relationships between authority/ power and truth, the changing consequence of historical and social conditions for knowledge, and different systems of creating, validating, and giving meaning to knowledge. It means explicit discussion of sexism, racism, and classism as belief systems. Knowledge construction shares with critical thinking affirmation and facilitation of problem finding, questioning, reflecting, analyzing, arguing, imagining, and synthesizing.

Prejudice reduction explores cultural and other similarities and differences, linking belief systems to attitudes and perceptions, and critiques stereotypes and practices that limit human development and interaction. It is premised upon learning to know one another as simultaneously unique individuals, similar human beings, and members of different social categories. Gender is clearly one of those categories. If content integration is said metaphorically to provide mirrors for some underrepresented students, it also—together with prejudice reduction and knowledge construction—provides a "window" for all students to see each other. Awareness and sensitivity to similarity and differences facilitate socially responsible and personally responsive interaction and the development of community.

Equity pedagogy means rejecting tracking and ability grouping, adopting high standards and expectations for all but also finding the teaching-learning strategies that maximize learning, e.g., ensuring that young women are fully involved in science laboratory classes. To the extent that we can verify individual learning styles, "ways of knowing," or cultural patterns, we need to foster equal opportunities, multiple interests, utilization of cultural resources, and varying strategies to maximize not only learning but demonstrations of learning. Finally *schools* need to be *empowered* to restructure their culture, organization, and practice to produce equity. This is made possible and strengthened by collaborative, democratic, and participatory leadership as noted by Tallerico and Lee. The gender-responsible leadership practices that Tallerico advocates—curricular organization and content, instructional supervision, and shared decision making—are similar to or subsumed under multicultural education and restructuring for equity. They entail leadership that values, enunciates, monitors, and revises to promote equity.

PROGRAMS FOR SCHOOL CHANGE

While we may know what schools should look like to produce equity, there is a great deal of ambiguity and uncertainty about how to produce them. Much of the research has demonstrated that it is a more complicated, difficult, longer, and nonlinear process than envisioned. There are quite a few failures along the way. Citing Muncey and McQuillan's (1992) study of early Coalition of Essential Schools members, Foster notes the polarization between the administration-favored "vanguard" of teachers and those less convinced of the need for change who were excluded from participation.

There is, however, some recent research that illustrates how schools can move from partial support for change to broad-based support and schoolwide change that transcend those political divisions. Based upon their active participation and qualitative research in five Coalition schools, Wasley, Hampel, and Clark (1995) have formulated six interrelated and mutually reinforcing propositions. The more all are present, the greater the degree of change and the extent of schoolwide support that occurs. The six are paraphrased as follows:

1) Schools whose members collectively develop a consensual vision of their intended future benefit most from continuing to revisit the vision to determine whether change efforts are working or will work and to re-establish consensus about the meaning of the vision.

2) Schools whose members see the interconnectedness of their efforts and have a coherent sense of the changes are better equipped to achieve their goals.

3) Schools whose members are able to deal with difficult and often controversial issues are more likely to continue to involve the whole school community.

4) Schools whose members are able to receive and act on good external critical feedback regularly make more progress than those that proceed autonomously.

5) Schools whose members develop skills in rigorous self-analysis focused on student gains have a critical tool that broadens and deepens their efforts.

6) Schools whose members are able to focus simultaneously on multiple aspects of restructuring, curriculum, pedagogy, assessment and school culture are more likely to make significant progress.

The authors thus make central the establishment of a vision that is continuously reflected on and about change efforts, the ability to see coherence and systematic connections and to focus simultaneously on what is closest to student learning in practice and approach—curriculum, pedagogy, assessment, and school culture (expectations, standards, climate), the interaction between rigorous self-analysis and external critical feedback, and the willingness to deal with difficult issues that can provoke conflict.

While I agree with Lee that restructuring should take place school by school with the development of coalitions of committed teachers and principals, unless this process is in some way supported, as Foster mentions, by external organizations, its effects will be limited and short lived. Certainly the schools need to reach out and involve their local communities. In addition they must be facilitated by their local school boards and central administrations, who must agree to the decentralization and also to provide necessary resources and capacity-building expertise to the schools. In addition, the state-level agencies and governmental branches must provide incentives, (de)regulations, that allow districts and schools to proceed—at the same time holding them accountable to both equity and effectiveness standards. Certainly many of the ideas suggested by Tallerico and Marshall in regard to equity can be part of such state policies—licensure, certification, provision of professional development, performance evaluation, and curriculum development.

At the national level through Goals 2000, President Clinton's Department of Education, spearheaded by Marshall Smith, has crafted a plan for systemic reform aimed at coordinating the decentralized federal system toward ensuring equitable opportunities and high levels of educational achievement for all students. The development of voluntary national standards, the provision of incentives to states to create centralized standards, congruent curriculum frameworks and assessment programs, and the encouragement and facilitation of decentralized local district implementation are supposed to produce broad school change and dramatic increases in student learning. There are, however, numerous reasons to be skeptical about this process.

Fullan (1996:421) believes educational change is "inherently, endemically, and ineluctably nonlinear." Even the most systematically sophisticated plan imaginable will unfold in a nonlinear, broken-front, back-and-forth manner. Given the complexity, places for problematic coordination, and possibilities for contingencies, disjunctures are inevitable. Thus Fullan believes the example of systemic reform is flawed. Rather, he argues, than attempting to structure systemic coherence, success is more likely if clarity and coherence can be achieved in the minds of the majority of teachers. However, rather than leaving this development to chance or to its creation school by school, Fullan argues for purposeful and structured networking of schools that support change, organized around a powerful vision or themes for improvement. Networking strategies include ongoing systemic multilevel staff development, multiple avenues for sharing ideas, integration with schoolwide and district priorities and mechanisms, and a commitment to inquiry, progress assessment, and continuous improvement. Examples of such existing networks might include the Coalition of Essential Schools and Accelerated Schools.

In addition to networking, Fullan supports two efforts, at the building site, school restructuring and reculturing. He suggests that success at these three efforts can produce coherence and relieve overload and fragmentation. In addition, the three can provide "a move to scale" by creating a critical mass of teachers and schools committed to "new norms necessary to sustain a culture of systemic reform" (1996:422).

Foster observes that minority teachers' opinions were often not valued. In addition, she cites evidence that they believed their non-minority colleagues had minimal expectations for minority youth. In a study of a restructuring school (Lipman 1996), Foster says the author found tacit taboos against raising racial issues so that they were suppressed and the minority teachers distanced themselves from the restructuring process.

Eubanks, Parish, and Smith (in press) develop the idea that the first step in transforming schools is to dramatically change the discourse in schools. The limits to school improvement, they argue, are grounded in the conventional wisdom and everyday talk among educators that justifies existing practices due to the alleged limits and failings of poor minority children and their families. They argue that those ideas and beliefs must be made visible and discussable so that a new awareness can develop about the potentialities of all children and the ability of schools to further those ends. The Coalition of Essential Schools in its recent Futures Committee report (1995) acknowledges, in essence, that it has a similar problem. The report recommends as one of its organizational principles that "CES, its centers, and member schools should model democratic practices and should deliberately and explicitly address challenges of equity in relationship to race, class, and gender" (1995:8). This issue will be, for many schools, one of the difficult and often controversial issues that must be dealt with in order to move to schoolwide change. It also represents a way of resolving the problem of the exclusion of minority voices from the change effort that Foster underlines. The issue of gender, class, and racial equity could, in fact, be the powerful theme referred to by Fullan (1996) around which the vision and mission of the restructuring process might find consensus, coherence, and commitment. Unless school communities recognize the necessity to talk about, do talk about, and work through issues of gender, race, and class in relation to equity and make that a part of their mobilizing philosophy, they will not empower themselves to produce authentic equity and effectiveness.

SCHOOLS, PEER CULTURES, AND REFORM
Eder has displayed the prevalence of sexual aggression within the culture of a Midwestern middle school. She and her colleagues observed and recorded its pervasiveness in extracurricular activities and around the cafeteria tables. While the focus was on students, it was clear that coaches instructed young men in aggressive practices and other adults reinforced them through their

legitimation of supporting activities (e.g., cheerleading). This research strongly resonates with Marshall's call for creating safe places in schools for females. Eder offers a number of suggestions based upon her research. She believes that the emphasis on athletic competition, aggression, violence, and success leads to a devaluation of others—losers, subordinates, women. Thus these types of sports need to be replaced by others based upon self-challenge and activities that can serve as alternatives. Appropriately, she argues that young women can benefit from learning to challenge rather than to avoid their aggressors, that young men can learn how others interpret their actions, and that all can benefit from learning how to resolve conflict. Finally Eder calls adults into account to become active in handling and preventing sexual harassment. In addition, in the larger work on which this paper is based, the authors state that "attempts need to be made to reduce the extent of social ranking within middle schools" (Eder, Evans, and Parker 1995). Given that this was primarily a study of students, one wonders whether adults were aware of what Eder and her colleagues heard and observed and, if so, how they explained it.

There is a powerful irony that Eder's research was conducted in a middle school. Middle schools were designed, in part, to slow down young adolescents' entry into the world of competition, popularity, and sexuality and to give them time to experience their growth and development in more personal, communal, experimental, and reflective ways. Interscholastic athletic competition is supposed to be limited in favor of intramurals and exploratory activities. All-school dances are expected to be eliminated or occur infrequently. Students are organized into communities with small group advisors where they can openly and mutually discuss personal and social problems they experience. Staffs of middle schools should be knowledgeable about and responsive to the developmental needs of young adolescents. Middle schools emerged to provide a student-centered contrast to the impersonal junior high and to rectify the decline in self-esteem that some students, particularly young adolescent women, experience in the transition from elementary school (Simmons and Blyth 1987). In fact, the middle school model entails many of the characteristics, described by Lee, of good effective schools—no tracking, cooperative learning, team teaching, integrated interdisciplinary curriculum, small learning communities. Oakes and her colleagues (1993) indicate that middle schools should be driven by cooperative, communitarian, and democratic values.

There has been an emerging powerful consensus in favor of the middle school model for the middle grades (Mergendoller 1993; Carnegie Council on Adolescent Development 1989). Despite the strong impetus for such a program, MacIver and Epstein (1993) have demonstrated that few middle grade schools have implemented the recommended practices and that the few that have done so have not done them well. For example, they indicate that advisory groups most often do mechanical tasks—distributing notices, making announcements, rather than discussing problems. Mergendoller (1993) observed that reform effort has been characterized more by rhetoric than by planning and that structural changes have often been made in ways that do not affect central experiences of students or everyday practice. He attributes some of this to a lack of support and training. It is noteworthy that gender roles and relationships and student cultures are not explicitly mentioned or discussed in much of the middle school reform literature (Ames and Miller 1994; Carnegie Council on Adolescent Development 1989; Mergendoller 1993). Given that this is a central part of the psychosocial development of young adolescents, one would expect some attention to these matters.

One of the Nine Common Principles of the Coalition of Essential Schools contains the belief that a school should *explicitly* and self-*consciously* have a tone of decency that includes fairness, generosity, and tolerance (emphasis added). The values and language that Eder describes do not show this tone. In a school model that is supposed to promote community, cooperation, and service to others, that description is disturbing. It is important that the middle school model be supported and implemented because it is the most appropriate form for young adolescents and it can with good practice provide equity in process and outcome. But it is also clear that gender, human development, and interpersonal relationships must become a focus of attention and discussion.

There is, at least, one good example of what a good on-going discussion might produce. Best (1983) describes how her interest in the reading problems of boys led to an exploration of children's gendered cultures in elementary school. The aggressive masculinity Eder describes is shown by Best to emerge in the early grades, be fostered by parents, and be institutionalized by third or fourth grade. It is premised not only by identification with "maleness" but by differentiation, opposition, and devaluing of "femaleness." Best became concerned with the stereotypes, objectification, and consequent constraints on both genders' roles and interactions. She developed a long-term dialogue that broke down those perceptions and facilitated the development of genuine cross-gender relationships that lasted through the high school years.

While this might be the result of an exceptional teacher, it is also a model to emulate. In addition, Thorne's (1993:163-166) suggestions for promoting cooperative relationships among students seem worthy of presenting:

> 1. In grouping students, use criteria other than gender or race. . . .
> 2. Affirm and reinforce the values of cooperation among all kids regardless of social categories. . . .
> 3. Whenever possible, organize students into small, heterogeneous, and cooperative work groups. . . .
> 4. Facilitate kids' access to all activities. . . .
> 5. Actively intervene to challenge the dynamics of stereotyping and power.

Certainly the above underscore the fact that concerns about those issues require attention as early as the elementary years.

Issues of gender and other forms of equity and effectiveness are present from students' first days at school. It follows that it is important that schools and school districts make efforts to ensure articulation between school levels. What begins in elementary schools needs to continue at middle and secondary levels. The expectations for secondary levels require foundations at the elementary level. It is also the case that numerous state and national restructuring or reform programs focus on different areas or different levels. While they have many similarities, they tend to operate independently, pursue sometimes different emphases, and follow their own course. Some states, such as Missouri, have begun to systematically link various reform initiatives in order to increase program coordination and expansion of the state capacity for change. In addition at the national level, the Atlas Communities represent the integration of several major restructuring programs to pool ideas, share efforts, and increase synergy. Some programs, such as Comer schools and Caring Communities, work to involve local communities and families as well as public and social service agencies in their programs and in their buildings. These efforts at coordination, integration, and extension are not without serious problems, but they do offer the possibility of attending to various forms of inequity on a more systematic and conscious basis.

Eder's chapter provides an entry into a very different area. Much of the concern in the educational literature and even in this volume equates equity with educational achievement and attainment. Much of the national educational reform agenda is premised upon development of human capital, international competition, and economic productivity. Increasingly, the purpose of education has been defined in instrumental and economic terms—education leads to occupation. One implication of Eder's chapter is that we excessively stress competition and domination. We lose something of ourselves and others in this process. Even the corporate community's desire for production of workers who can cooperate is for purposes of competition and productivity. Thus it poses potential problems and contradictions in its implementation.

Clearly some feminist writings emphasize other ethics such as "caring" (Noddings 1992). While I do not want to suggest an essentialist maternal or nurturing gendered character or less rigorous education, I do want to suggest that, in its elaboration, caring potentially resonates with conservation, democracy, and an expanding quality of life. There are alternative ethics suggested by others for using education to promote public service, participation in civil life, and the search for knowledge. Berliner and Biddle (1995) believe meaningful use of leisure is a goal toward which schooling should attend. We ought, at least, to use concerns about gender and equity to explore alternative visions and philosophies of schooling and education.

LINKING SCHOOLING TO LARGER CONTEXTS
There are numerous reminders in this volume that the educational institution cannot adequately be analyzed and understood if it is decontextualized, treated as if abstracted, and isolated from the larger society. Hudley reminds us of the limits of (short-term) school-based solutions to macro-social problems. Inner-city decay,

residential segregation, economic instability, governmental retrenchment, and public cynicism do not bode well for concerted efforts to redress inequities in the short run. They certainly do not suggest the provision of additional resources to public schools. Stromquist argues that schools are part of the patriarchal state and not civil society. This structuring limits the possibility for gender equity through political reform. Marshall's accentuating response to that perspective is to advocate individual and collective radical and outrageous actions. Both would argue that state institutions require dismantling and reconstruction in more democratic and egalitarian directions.

Eder calls into question not only our schools but implicitly our professional sports, mass media, economic system, other institutions, and our culture. The sexual aggression expressed by boys in schools is one manifestation of what is reinforced by adult males in locker rooms, gymnasia, and the playing fields. It is easy to connect this socialized aggressiveness with the increasing emphasis on winning, intimidating, and the dramatic evidence of violence in the arena and stadia of the NHL, NBA, NFL, and major league baseball. One can also make a quick correlation with increasing awareness of violence in the society and its relationships to social contexts of community and family. The American Sociological Association (1996) has recently issued a call for the implementation of a national research agenda because of the magnitude of the problem. One significant factor they cite is the presence of violence in the media. There is also the fact that the media and professional sports are economic enterprises and that the prevailing ethos of profit-making, materialism, competition, and the definition of success may overwhelm the more civil, cooperative, human elements of social life. While none of the authors in this volume advocate acceptance of the status quo or passivity as a response and they do all offer options for change, none would, I believe, reject the idea that significant changes in lessening inequality and insensitivity in the economic, political, legal, higher educational, communication, and familial institutions would greatly facilitate progress in elementary and secondary schools.

Many writers have commented on the changing nature of what has been called post-industrial or post-modern society. They note the transition from production-based, class, economic issues and interests to those grounded in gender, race, ethnicity, generation-age, religion, and quality of life. These "new social movements" and their parallel identity priorities have definitively fragmented the old politics and problematized social theory as well as political coherence. These divisions lead to statements about priorities and assertions of "my cause is more just than your cause." In response, politicians seeking (re)election strive to construct a centrist majority instead of principled and substantial solutions to social problems. So it is important to remember that the patriarchal state is also a racial state (Omi and Winant 1994) as well as a classed state. As social scientists have begun to focus on the intersections of gender, class, and race, perhaps a politics that somehow is constituted around these intersections and others is appropriate. As Lee observes, one form of inequity remains an inequity and the aim is equity for all.

Friedland and Alford (1991) in response to these emerging identities and movements in a post-industrial period suggest a view of society as an interinstitutional order that is simultaneously interdependent and contradictory. The central institutions of contemporary Western capitalist society are, they state, economic market, bureaucratic state, democracy, nuclear family, and Christian religion (but with science as competition). These institutions shape individual preferences and organizational interests as well as behaviors to attain them. However, each institution has a separate cultural logic that is potentially contradictory with the others and that is simultaneously available to all individuals and organizations. The cultural logics are, respectively, accumulation and commodification, rationalization and regulation of behavior, participation, community and loyalty, and truth and the construction of reality.

Individuals and organizations transform the institutional relations of society by exploiting the contradictions. The structural contradictions and the competing logics offer problems, opportunities and alternatives to individuals and organizations to alter society. Thus while it would be folly to suggest an easy answer to the dilemma posed by the Stromquist and Marshall position on the power of the conservative patriarchal state in contrast to the reform suggestions of Tallerico and others, the state is not monolithic nor omniscient. The perspective presented by Friedland and Alford (1991) does provide a rationale for understanding why and how actors may find means to create better schools and societies.

THE NEED FOR RESEARCH

Most social scientists share with Barbara Bank the belief that gender, i.e., distinctions between male and female, masculine and feminine, is not a natural, objective or constant object but rather varies over time, within societies, and among cultures. There is a general understanding that these distinctions are socially defined, constructed, and produced through social processes, practices, and actions. The meaning of gender, particularly in contemporary times, is also socially and politically contested. Within the gendered patriarchal state are lodged ostensibly formal and legitimated societal definitions of gender, but the state is also the target, the venue, and an "actor" in efforts to change or sustain these definitions (as expressed by law, decisions, and policies) by organized collectivities. Simultaneously in other institutions, organizations, and everyday life, actors play out their potentially divergent perspectives on gender. While there are clearly inequalities in society that tend to produce themselves, there are also contradictions and contingencies that present opportunities for action. Because changing social and historical conditions change consciousness, behavior, and social forms, and actors, in turn, change social and historical conditions, there is a continuing need to study the relationships between gender, its meanings, and other social processes including schooling. What we know or observe now may not be assumed to be lasting and universal.

Additionally, Acker (1992) has suggested that organizations in our society are gendered—that is patterned by gender and then reproductive of it through organizational structures, processes, and practices. She argues that four basic gendered processes in organizations reproduce male dominance—structural divisions of labor and power, symbol systems and forms of consciousness, interaction orders between and within genders, and internal interpretive sense-making by individuals. To this point, there have been few systematic examinations of this perspective and the interrelated processes. Since schools are organizations, the perspective is quite applicable to them (see Acker 1995). Schools are not only workplaces but learning places so there is a unique opportunity to explore how the two are related: how do students "learn" gender from their "teachers" and how does teaching children and youth affect the gendering of the workplace?

It is not uncommon for educational organizations and institutions to develop policies that lack strong research bases and implement them without research to study that process and its consequences. Educational research is not now receiving, nor has it in the past been given, sufficient priority and resources (Berliner and Biddle 1995). There are some critical problems noted in this volume that demand research attention. Hudley points to the need for "careful, longitudinal, and comparative study" of race-specific and gender-specific programs in the context of other school reforms. There is also an absence of studies on the effects of these specific programs on cross-gender and cross-race relationships. Bank also stresses the need to examine how official school cultures emphasizing academic values are related to student cultures. Since these values are at the core of the current reform agenda, advocates would be presumed to actively influence student values about learning. However, as Bank observes, there are numerous countervailing influences to limit this influence. It is therefore important to study the conditions that facilitate or hinder this process. In general, we also lack sufficient research on the whole process of school restructuring. Given the extent and complexity of change called for in restructuring, traditional school improvement studies do not suffice. There do exist some case studies and a few comparative studies of multiple cases (Prestine and Bowen 1993; Newmann and Wehlage 1995), but a sufficiently systematic longitudinal comparative analysis of a critical mass of schools is lacking.

A major research agenda is suggested by the increasing interest of social scientists in the intersections of gender, race, and class. Past research has documented how schools respond inequitably to each separately. Foster, Hudley, Lee, and Bank all raise issues related to the overlap or relationship between at least two of the categories. Grant (1992) offered a striking foundation for this agenda in showing the differential roles teachers constructed or reinforced for young African American and white girls in classrooms in the Midwest and the South. In addition, there is research that illustrates how youth may differentially respond to and resist external attributions about who they are and how they should behave and how they negotiate their multiple worlds. (Heath and McLaughlin 1993; Fordham 1991; Phelan and Davidson 1993). It would seem appropriate that an interdisciplinary congress be convened to create a (inter)national research program around these intersections.

In conclusion, it is crucial to continue to theorize gender, other constructed social categories, and inequality. It is vital to stimulate varied scholarship of sufficient scope and depth focused on the relationships among these categories, schooling, institutions, and the larger socio-historical context. At the same time it is imperative that efforts to alter the contexts, structures, cultures, processes, and practices of schooling for the benefit of all children be promoted. Research, policy, and practice should and must mutually inform each other if we are to create a more equitable society.

REFERENCES

Acker, Joan. 1992. "Gendering Organizational Theory." Pp. 248-260 in *Gendering Organizational Analysis*, edited by A. J. Mills and P. Tancred. Newbury Park, CA: Sage Publications.

Acker, Sandra. 1995. "Gender and Teachers' Work." *Review of Research in Education* 21:99-162.

American Sociological Association. 1996. *Social Causes of Violence: Crafting a Science Agenda*. Washington, DC: ASA.

Ames, Nancy, and Edward Miller. 1994. *Changing Middle Schools: How to Make Schools Work for Young Adolescents*. San Francisco: Jossey-Bass Publishers.

Banks, James. 1993. "Multicultural Education: Historical Development, Dimensions, and Practice." *Review of Research in Education* 19:3-49.

Berliner, David C., and Bruce J. Biddle. 1995. *The Manufactured Crisis: Myths, Fraud, and the Attack on America's Public Schools*. Reading, MA: Addison-Wesley Publishing Co.

Best, Raphaela. 1983. *We've All Got Scars: What Boys and Girls Learn in Elementary School*. Bloomington, IN: Indiana University Press.

Carnegie Council on Adolescent Development. 1989. *Turning Points: Preparing American Youth for the 21st Century*. Washington, DC: CCAD.

Coalition of Essential Schools. 1995. *Looking to the Future: From Conversation to Demonstration*. Report of the Futures Committee. Providence, RI: CES.

Eder, Donna, with Catherine Colleen Evans, and Stephen Parker. 1995. *School Talk: Gender and Adolescent Culture*. New Brunswick, NJ: Rutgers University Press.

Eubanks, Eugene, Ralph Parish, and Dianne Smith. In press. "Changing the Discourse in Schools." In *Race, Ethnicity, and Multiculturalism*, edited by P. M. Hall. New York: Garland Publishing.

Fordham, Signithia. 1991. "Peer-Proofing Academic Competition Among Black Adolescents: 'Acting White' Black American Style." Pp. 69-93 in *Empowerment Through Multicultural Education*, edited by C. Sleeter. Albany, NY: State University of New York Press.

Friedland, William, and Robert Alford. 1991. "Bringing Society Back In: Symbols, Practices, and Institutional Contradictions." Pp. 232-263 in *The New Institutionalism in Organizational Analysis*, edited by W. Powell and P. DiMaggio. Chicago: University of Chicago Press.

Fullan, Michael. 1996. "Turning Systemic Thinking on its Head." *Phi Delta Kappan* 77:420-423.

Grant, Linda. 1992. "Race and the Schooling of Young Girls." Pp. 91-113 in *Education and Gender Equality*, edited by J. Wrigley. London: The Falmer Press.

Hall, Peter M. In press. "The Integration of Restructuring and Multicultural Education as a Policy for Equity and Diversity." In *Race, Ethnicity, and Multiculturalism*, edited by P. M. Hall. New York: Garland Publishing.

Heath, Shirley, and Milbrey McLaughlin (Eds.). 1993. *Identity and Inner City Youth: Beyond Ethnicity and Gender*. New York: Teachers College Press.

Jackson, Anthony. 1995. "Toward a Common Destiny: An Agenda for Further Research." Pp. 435-453 in *Toward a Common Destiny*, edited by W. Hawley and A. Jackson. San Francisco: Jossey-Bass Publishers.

Lipman, Pauline. 1996. "The Missing Voice of Culturally Relevant Teachers in School Restructuring." *The Urban Review* 28:41-62.

MacIver, Douglas, and Joyce Epstein. 1993. "Middle Grades Research: Not Yet Mature but No Longer a Child." *Elementary School Journal* 93:519-533.

Mergendoller, John. 1993. "Introduction: The Roles of Research in the Reform of Middle Grades Education." *Elementary School Journal* 93:443-446.

Muncey, Donna, and Patrick McQuillan. 1992. "Preliminary Findings from a Five-Year Study of the Coalition of Essential Schools." *Phi Delta Kappan* 74:486-489.

Newmann, Fred, and Gary Wehlage. 1995. *Successful School Restructuring*. Madison, WI: Center on Organization and Restructuring of Schools, University of Wisconsin-Madison.

Noddings, Nel. 1992. *The Challenge to Care in Schools: An Alternative Approach to Education*. New York: Teachers College Press.

Oakes, Jeannie, Karen Quartz, Jennifer Gong, Gretchen Guiton, and Martin Lipton. 1993. "Creating Middle Schools: Technical, Normative, and Political Considerations." *Elementary School Journal* 93:461-480.

Omi, Michael, and Howard Winant. 1994. *Racial Formation in the United States: From the 1960s to the 1990s*, 2nd edition. New York: Routledge.

Phelan, Patricia, and Ann Davidson (Eds.). 1993. *Renegotiating Cultural Diversity in American Schools*. New York: Teachers College Press.

Prestine, Nona, and Chuck Bowen. 1993. "Benchmarks of Change: Assessing Essential School Restructuring Efforts." *Educational Evaluation and Policy Analysis* 15:298-319.

Simmons, Roberta, and Dale Blyth. 1987. *Moving into Adolescence: The Impact of Pubertal Change and School Context*. Hawthorne, NY: Aldine de Gruyter.

Thorne, Barrie. 1993. *Gender Play: Girls and Boys in School*. New Brunswick, NJ: Rutgers University Press.

Wasley, Patricia, Robert Hampel, and Richard Clark. 1995. "Stepping Up to Whole School Change." Presented at Coalition of Essential Schools Fall Forum, November 5, New York.

Name Index

Subject Index

racial inequity.
Institute for Retraining the Professorate, 83
instruction, *see* teaching.

Kids Against Cruel Treatment in Schools (KACTIS), 109, 110

language routines, 95, 108, 109, 221
  gossip, 95, 106
  insult exchanges, 95, 98, 99, 100, 103, 104, 105, 106, 107, 108, 109
leadership, 22, 25, 26, 63, 74, 75, 78, 79-80, 82, 83, 84, 86, 88, 117, 126, 175, 180, 187, 188, 193, 197, 198, 199, 213, 216
  gender-responsible, 81, 199-207, 212, 216
  men's style of, 77
  theory of, 80, 194-197
  women's style of, 26, 153, 197-198
League of Women Voters, 67

male hegemony, *see* power, male.
masculinity, 14, 36, 39, 55, 59, 94, 98-99, 101, 106, 107, 126, 221
merit pay, 172, 173, 174. *See also* teacher salaries.
Minister Responsible for the Status of Women, 49
misogyny, 25

multicultural education, 18, 129, 200, 212, 214, 215, 216

National Association for the Advancement of Colored People (NAACP), 18-19, 117
National Association of Secondary School Principals (NASSP), 72
National Board for Professional Teaching Standards, 168, 169, 170, 173, 184
National Coalition for Women and Girls in Education (NCWGE), 70, 91
National Commission on Excellence in Education, 68, 91, 167
National Educational Longitudinal Study (NELS), 138
National Organization for Women, 19, 82, 201
National Policy for Gender Equity in Australia, 80-81
National Program for the Promotion of Equal Opportunity for Women in the Educational Area (PRIOM), 44
National Teachers Examination, 165, 166
nongovernmental organizations (NGOs), 33, 40, 44, 46, 51-53, 55, 59
  Forum for African Women Educationalists (FAWE), 52

Contributors

Barbara J. Bank received her Ph.D. from the University of Iowa and is an associate professor of sociology and women studies at the University of Missouri in Columbia. Her scholarly interests lie in the areas of social psychology, gender studies, and the sociology of youth and education. Recent and forthcoming publications focus on peer cultures and their challenge for teaching; friendships in Australia and the U.S.; and the gendered accounts undergraduates give about personal relationships and academic achievements. Her current research is a longitudinal study of identities, values, and community among undergraduates at a women's college.

Donna Eder, Professor of Sociology at Indiana University in Bloomington, received her Ph.D. from the University of Wisconsin at Madison. She is an expert on the peer cultures of school children and adolescents and has written insightfully about many aspects of these cultures including gossip, humor, teasing, extracurricular activities, popularity, and girls' talk about romance and sexuality. Her recent publications include an examination of the cultural aspects of the women's movement and a book for Rutgers University Press called *School Talk: Gender and Adolescent Culture*.

Michele Foster is a professor in the Center for Educational Studies at the Claremont Graduate School in California. She received her doctorate from the Graduate School of Education at Harvard University. Her many scholarly papers and publications are focused on African American teachers, the ethnography of speaking, sociolinguistics, urban education, ethnic and gender identity. She is the recipient of several fellowships including a National Academy of Education Spencer Postdoctoral Fellowship, a University of North Carolina Minority Postdoctoral Fellowship, and a Smithsonian Fellowship. In 1992, she received an early career achievement award from the American Educational Research Association.

Peter M. Hall, Professor of Sociology and Education at the University of Missouri, received his Ph.D. from the University of

Minnesota. His scholarly interests include social and educational policy, school restructuring, complex organizations, political sociology, and symbolic interactionism. He is the editor of *Race, Ethnicity, and Multiculturalism,* the book that resulted from the first Missouri Symposium on Research and Educational Policy. His current projects include an ethnographic study of a restructuring high school and a monograph on the social organization of the policy process. Recent scholarship has focused on school district multicultural policy formation, production of a state educational program from legislated statute, and integration of pragmatic and critical policy perspectives. In 1994, Hall received the George Herbert Mead award for career contributions from the Society for the Study of Symbolic Interaction.

Cynthia A. Hudley is an associate professor in the Graduate School of Education at the University of California, Santa Barbara. She joined the faculty there in 1991, the same year in which she received her Ph.D. in educational psychology from U.C.L.A. and was chosen the outstanding doctoral graduate by the U.C.L.A. School of Education Alumni Association. She brought to her doctoral studies considerable experience as a special education teacher and resource specialist, and these experiences have shaped her productive re-search agenda focused on the social development of at-risk youth, school-based interventions to reduce aggression, and the effects of alternative educational programming on the motivation and achieve-ment of ethnic minority adolescents.

Valerie E. Lee, Associate Professor of Education at the University of Michigan, received her Ed.D. from the Harvard Graduate School of Education. Her numerous book chapters and articles have examined high school organization and its effects on teachers and students, and her co-authored book on Catholic schools was selected as the best book in the sociology of education, 1991-1994, by the American Sociological Association. Her past and present research has been supported by grants from the National Science Founda-tion, the AAUW Educational Foundation, the Spencer Foundation, the Klingenstein Foundation, and the U.S. National Assessment of Educational Programs. From 1990-95, she served as a principal investigator for the OERI-sponsored Center on

Reorganization and Restructuring of Schools, and she is currently investigating the ways in which gender, schools, and classrooms affect science learning, mathematics learning, and adolescents' academic development.

Catherine Marshall is a professor of educational leadership at the University of North Carolina, Chapel Hill. Since receiving her Ph.D. from the University of California, Santa Barbara, she has produced numerous publications on educational administration, gender issues, policy research, and the micropolitics of education including four books: *The Assistant Principal, Culture and Education Policy in the American States, Designing Qualitative Research,* and *The New Politics of Race and Gender.* From 1985-90 she was editor of the *Peabody Journal of Education,* and she was president of the Politics of Education Association from 1990-92. Her current writing projects include *Reframing Policy Analysis* (Falmer forthcoming), a two-volume collection demonstrating ways in which educational policy analysis can incorporate a focus on gender.

Nelly P. Stromquist is a professor of international development education in the School of Education and a faculty affiliate with the Center for Feminist Research at the University of Southern California. A former president of the Comparative and International Education Society, she received her Ph.D. in education from Stanford University. Her research addresses questions of educational change and gender equity. Her most recent books include *Literacy for Citizenship: Gender and Grassroots Dynamics in Brazil* (SUNY forthcoming) and two edited works: *Gender Dimensions in Education in Latin America* (Organization of American States 1996), and the *Encyclopedia of Third World Women* (Garland forthcoming).

Marilyn Tallerico, Associate Professor of Teaching and Leadership, earned her Ph.D. from Arizona State University and joined the Syracuse University Faculty in 1988. Her research centers on relations between school boards and school superintendents, politics of education, and gender issues in educational administration. Her current work focuses on retaining women in the superintendency, with an article forthcoming in *Educational Administration Quarterly.* Other recent publications have appeared in *The Journal of Staff Development, Qualitative Sociology,* and the *Journal of School Leadership.*